The World According to

GARRY BUSHELL

The World According to
GARRY BUSHELL

Garry Bushell

metro

Published by Metro,
an imprint of John Blake Publishing Ltd,
3 Bramber Court, 2 Bramber Road,
London W14 9PB, England

www.johnblakepublishing.co.uk

First published in hardback in 2008

ISBN 978 1 84454 617 6

British Library Cataloguing-in-Publication Data:

A catalogue record for this book is available from the British
Library.

Design by www.envydesign.co.uk

Printed in the UK by CPI William Clowes Beccles NR34 7TL

1 3 5 7 9 10 8 6 4 2

Papers used by John Blake Publishing are natural, recyclable
products made from wood grown in sustainable forests.
The manufacturing processes conform to the environmental
regulations of the country of origin.

For Tania, Julie, Danny, Robert, Jenna and Ciara

By the same author

The Face
Two-Faced
Cockney Reject (with Jeff Turner)
Running Free
Dance Craze – The 2-Tone Story

Contents

Introduction

'England is a memory now,' says Morrissey, and he's right. England, my England, is slowly dying; curling up at the edges like the last cheese sandwich in the works canteen.

Everything that made the country special is being flushed away. Third-rate politicians have conned us into becoming a subservient province of the European Union. Their open-door immigration policy, coupled with the demented self-loathing of multi-culturalism, is making us strangers in our own land. Even celebrating Christmas has become a moral minefield.

They've led us into disastrous foreign wars in the name of 'democracy', while at the same time stripping the word of meaning at home. Free speech, habeas corpus, the presumption of innocence... all are gone or going.

Blair and his weasels treated the House of Commons with contempt, by-passing it regularly while packing the Lords with brown-nosing cronies. Incompetent, control-freak Brown shows no sign of being any different. Political debate has become a joke. When I was a kid, Labour was a socialist party. A significant number of Labour MPs wanted to nationalise the commanding heights of the economy and improve the lot of the working man. The Tories were for free enterprise, low taxes and self-improvement. We had Left v Right, Red v Blue, and never the twain shall meet. Not any more. Now, all three major parties believe in pretty much the same things.

There are still a Them and Us in politics, of course. 'Them' are the political élite and 'Us' is everyone else, Joe Public, the poor mugs whose only role in life is to pay taxes through the nose to subsidise Their follies.

We're here to be ruled, and generally ignored – except when our lords and masters feel like lecturing us on how to live our lives. Don't smoke in pubs... don't use too much salt... don't eat the wrong kind of food... don't tell the wrong kind of jokes... don't protest within shouting distance of Westminster without permission... don't hunt... don't smack your kids... don't take long-haul flights... don't binge drink... DON'T THINK... *Jawohl, mein Commandant*!

We become more regulated and less free with every passing month. And woe betide anyone who steps out of line. The élite have ways of controlling every argument – question multi-culturalism and you're a racist; oppose European integration and you're a Little Englander. Our borders are more violated than Belle de Jour on a good night, but if you point that out you'll be denounced as a hysterical fascist.

In fact, they will call you an extremist simply for expounding common-sense beliefs that have been held by fair-minded British people for generations. The latest glib insult is 'denier' for anyone who dares to pick apart the Green hysteria gripping our rulers, the implication being that to argue that human activity may not be the main cause of climate change is as wicked as denying the Nazi Holocaust. Our job is simply to stump up new 'green' tax revenue, to pay, for example, the £80 billion that it will cost to pepper our coast-line with giant wind turbines – hideous, 400ft-high eyesores that ruin the landscape, don't work efficiently and will have to be subsidised by around £32 billion a year by you and me paying higher electricity bills.

Yeah... but, no... but yeah... comes the reply, but we're saving the planet! (Wanted: one small boy to assess the existence of the Emperor's green clobber. Must have 20/20 eyesight and no fear of demonisation.)

I admit that, at the grand old age of 52, some of my opinions will be written off as a mix of nostalgia and the grumpiness of middle-age. I don't expect anyone in their thirties to understand how irritating it is to be told temperatures in Centigrade and distances in kilometres. And I know everything changes... but not always for the better.

The steady decline in popular culture is beyond dispute. The mass media is top-heavy with actors who can't act, singers who can't sing and comedians who aren't funny. The world's most famous magician is David Blaine, and he can't do tricks. Across the board, the crap is rising.

In the 1960s, English footballers came home with a World Cup in their hands, inventive English rock bands conquered the globe and we set the pace in youth cults. Even English art had something to say. Now it's in the hands of charlatans. Damien Hirst will slice up a Friesian, stick the bits in a glass case and give it some pretentious title. The *Guardian* will pronounce him a genius and some nitwit with more money than sense will shell out millions for his 'art'. He's the greatest operator since Arthur Daley.

We were English back then, but we were British, too. It was a United Kingdom, and it remained so until New Labour pushed through devolution and made the English second-class citizens.

I grew up in streets called Indus, Grenada, Kashmir, Nigeria and Canberra... the old Empire was all around us. We weren't ashamed of it; it was a source of pride. We were poor but we knew who we were. 'Patriotism' wasn't a dirty word, and neither was 'proletarian'. Workers were organised, they had muscle, solidarity and self-belief. There was a sense of togetherness; we were in the same boat, we looked out for each other.

What did we have to apologise for? Our forefathers had been exploited, too.

Being working class then meant something; it was synonymous with loyalty, hard graft and standing up for yourself, common sense and decency.

If we'd been told that within our lifetimes the white working-class male would become the only acceptable hate figure in polite society, no one would have believed it.

My dad was a fireman (not a 'firefighter'); the whole family voted Labour, and believed in 'inevitable' progress towards the coming socialist Utopia. The NHS, created by the post-war Labour Government, was the envy of the world, but this was before Labour deserted the working class to suck up to millionaires and minorities; this was when hospitals were places where you went to be cured of illnesses, not to play medical Russian roulette with deadly infections.

Being Labour didn't mean being liberal. Our morality was conservative – something that was scorned and then thoroughly undermined by middle-class, hippy ideas, free love and anything-goes permissiveness. It's bequeathed a nation of single mums on State hand-outs, fathers persecuted by the divorce courts, the Child Support Agency and soaring abortion rates. Liberation! Hurrah! Still, it's made the lawyers rich, and I understand dogging is very fashionable in certain areas.

Back then, most people believed that crime should be punished, that women should be treated with respect, and that the death penalty for murder was justifiable. Men were expected to be men. If something needed to be done, you got on with it. If something went wrong, you kept a stiff upper lip about it. Self-pity was like Pete Doherty – it didn't wash.

I often wonder, watching today's TV, how disgusted my uncles would have been by the emotionally incontinent, half-male specimens on display. Two of them had been prisoners-of-war. In the face of adversity, they kept smiling through – they had the bulldog spirit that middle-class, bleeding-heart *EastEnders* writers will never understand.

But, you may say, thank God we don't have to live through the upbringing or experiences that they had, that we're not caught up on a global war for our survival as a people and as a nation. And it's true – there are no doodlebugs overhead, and no bombs dropping on London like the one that blew off my nan's roof.

But that doesn't mean we're safe. There's a new Battle of Britain brewing and most of us don't seem the least bit bothered about it. One enemy is in power; another is living among us, full of hate for our world, our values and our way of life.

Many thousands of our people, despairing of the way the country is going, are voting with their feet and colonising the Med. For the rest of us, the choice is simple – we either agree that recovery from this decline is impossible, and so we follow suit, pack our bags and scarper for the sun.

Or we stay and fight.

The Clash sang about the English Civil War. We should set our sights higher – what we need is an English revolution. As George Orwell wrote, 'Nothing ever stands still, we must add to our heritage or lose it, we must grow greater or grow less, we must go forward or backward.'

Like Orwell, I believe in England and I believe that we shall go forward.

It's time to draw a line in the sand.

Garry Bushell

Immigration – The Lie of the Land

'Civilisations die from suicide, not by murder.'
Arnold Toynbee

Panic on the streets of London? Not really. Panic on the streets of Birmingham? Not yet. But there has been panic aplenty in the offices of the *NME* after Morrissey broke ranks with received opinion and apparently made a few brief but accurate comments about mass immigration.

In an interview with the right-on rag, rock star Morrissey said that Britain's identity was being lost due to an 'immigration explosion'. The former Smiths singer is reported to have said, 'The gates of England are flooded. The country has been thrown away.' He went on, 'Although I don't have anything against people from other countries, the higher the influx into England, the more the British identity disappears, so the price is enormous. If you travel to Germany, it's still absolutely German. If you travel to Sweden, it still has a Swedish identity. But travel to England and you have no idea where you are, so the price is enormous.

'It matters because the British identity is very attractive. I grew up into it and I find it very quaint and amusing. Other countries have held on to their basic identity, yet it seems to me that England was thrown away. You can't say, "Everybody, come into my house, sit on the bed, have what you like, do what you like." It wouldn't work... If you walk through Knightsbridge on any bland day of the week you won't hear an English accent.'

A reasonable observation you might think, and a common-place one outside of liberal circles. The Government's own poll, published in December 2007, showed that nearly eight out of ten British people (77 per cent) want a cap on immigration. But that didn't prevent Morrissey's words from triggering an inevitable 'racism row'. The *NME* disassociated itself from the rock star, declaring his views 'inflammatory' and claiming his words had 'dangerous echoes' of the British National Party.

Anti-racism activists immediately waded in – Denis Fernando, of Unite Against Fascism, raged that Morrissey had 'shown a complete insensitivity to people and misunderstanding of what Britain is about'. Mr Fernando, by the way, is not just against fascism, he is also a member of the secretive far-Left Socialist Action; and who better than an obscure, revolutionary Marxist sect to lecture us on misunderstanding Britain?

The reaction was so irrational and extreme that Morrissey – himself the son of Irish immigrants, and a man comprehensively untainted by racial prejudice – was forced to take legal action against the music paper, saying his quotes had been 'butchered, redesigned, re-ordered, chopped, snipped and split'.

This is an explosive area, so take my hand and hold tight, because we are about to take a stroll through a minefield. Immigration has been a taboo subject in this country for more than a decade. The Far Left and their allies – human rights lawyers, the Refugee Council and other members of the *Guardian*-reading classes – have managed to stifle the immigration debate for years simply by screaming 'racist' or 'fascist' at anyone who brings it up. This is a suppression of debate, incidentally, that has played neatly into the hands of the Far Right. But were the words Morrissey is said to have used insensitive or, worse, racist? Or are they actually a brief but accurate reflection of the way things are?

I'm not too up on the intricacies of life on the street in Knightsbridge, but it's certainly true that large parts of London no longer look or sound English. Travel on a bus in Newham, close your eyes, and you'll be forgiven for thinking that Babel Enterprises were laying on guided tours of the Tower, without a guide. I recently went to a gym in Canning Town where every voice you heard was speaking in an Eastern European language. I found it disorientating and disturbing. I'm used to Woolwich where everyone speaks Punjabi.

Morrissey is wrong, though, when he says the gates of England are 'flooded' because, as far as I can see, New Labour tore down the gates entirely in 1997. When they swept to power, Labour gave up our border controls without a thought to the consequences. This resulted in the biggest wave of immigration to these islands in history. Five million immigrants have arrived in the UK since 2000 alone; that's workers and their dependents. Five million! Think about that number – that's more than the population of Wales and Northern Ireland combined, all pouring in, wanting somewhere to live, something to do, somewhere to educate their kids, somewhere to go when they're poorly...

That's not a rational immigration policy, it's a human tsunami, which has put an unprecedented strain on the country's infrastructure of healthcare, schools and transport and our limited housing stock. The pressures of accommodating all these extra people has inevitably begun to wear down Britain's fine traditions of tolerance and understanding.

Labour's come-as-you-are immigration policy has caused the biggest social changes in British history, and yet I don't recall that particular pledge in their 1997 election manifesto. There was no section proudly proclaiming: 'Vote for us and we'll give your job to an Albanian'. In fact, they barely mentioned immigration at all. Even now, not one single mainstream political party is prepared to talk openly about the problems that have arisen from the opening up of our borders, let alone discuss how to tackle them.

So let's do it now, calmly and rationally. Let's ask who continued mass immigration benefits and who it doesn't, and see where we go from there.

First, though, for the benefit of Mr Fernando and his comrades, let me set out my stall on the big issue. When it comes to people, I'm colour-blind. I haven't got a racist bone in my body, and never have had. I've had black girlfriends and, according to Channel 4, I may even be one-sixteenth African myself. The London I grew up in had a substantial West Indian population who contributed plenty to our popular culture, not least to Mod and Skinhead subculture. Black music invigorated our charts, Chrissie Powell should be knighted and I dearly wish Lenny Henry was still funny. If Pluto Shervington's 'Dat' isn't played at my funeral, I'll want to know why. This discussion is not about race, it's about numbers, identity, culture and social cohesion. It's also about lies, liberal wish fulfilment and the evil good men do.

Lie One is that Britain needs an open-door immigration policy because there aren't enough workers in Britain to do the work that needs doing. But, of course, there are plenty of domestic workers around – they just aren't working. We've got 1.7 million on the dole and another 2.7 million claiming long-term incapacity benefit. And why have we got so many unemployed? Because a labour force from Eastern Europe is happy to come here and under-cut wages throughout the building industry and beyond. Our old friend Capitalism needs immigration to keep labour costs down.

Lie Two is that we need the immigrants to top up our depleted pension pots. Home birth rates are falling, the argument goes, and without Johnny Foreigner riding to the rescue the country will be up the proverbial creek without a paddle. Except, hold on a mo, won't the immigrants get old, too? Won't they need pensions themselves?

Immigration doesn't solve our pension crisis, it just

postpones it. And if the only solution we can think of is to invite in another 10 million, then maybe even the *NME* might notice that the country is changing a bit.

Lie Three is that all of us benefit from this influx of eager beavers grateful to work for a pittance. Not so. It's great if you're a well-off, professional couple in Hampstead. You can get your gardeners, home-helps, window-cleaners and au pairs much cheaper. But how does it help you if your previous job was doing Mr and Mrs Hampstead's ironing or catering or walking their dog for a few bob an hour more? Suddenly, you're out of a job, or working for less, waiting longer for social housing and watching the neighbourhood change beyond recognition. Researchers at Harvard University have shown that, in the long run, immigration just transfers wealth from the poor to the rich.

Lie Four is the Home Office claim that immigrants contribute £6 billion a year to the economy. This was reported as fact by the BBC, the *Guardian* and other well-meaning people who dearly wish that it was true. The Government report says immigration boosts economic growth by 0.5 per cent a year (which is where they get the £6 billion figure from). But it also admits that immigration is increasing the population by 0.5 per cent a year. In other words, the Gross Domestic Product is unaffected by immigration. The Home Office could find no evidence that immigration makes the country richer.

Lie Five is that all immigrants are bright-eyed, bushy-tailed and dead keen to work. Certainly, the 750,000 industrious Poles working here have been a boon to

Britain's service industries. But what about the half-a-million Somalis? More Somalis live here than in any other country in the world, except Somalia; eight out of ten of them are out of work. The Poles pull the weight, while the Somalis pull strokes. It might make sense for the UK to import skilled labour (although it'd make more sense to train up our own sparks, plumbers and plasterers rather than bus them in from Gdansk); but why import unemployed layabouts? We've got enough home-grown ones, ta very much.

The only people who benefit from mass immigration are the wealthy, and the immigrants themselves. It's a triumph of market forces over all other considerations, including those of common sense. So why did a Labour Government encourage it?

Partly from well-intentioned naïveté – the old-fashioned, liberal belief that the country would be a better place if it was a great big melting pot (big enough to take the world and all it's got). Partly from self-interest – they assumed, probably rightly, that first-generation immigrants would naturally vote Labour. And partly – perhaps even largely – from an inbuilt hatred of the south of England. More than half of England's population is now crammed into the south-east, making us the most densely peopled country in the world. Labour despises the south-east for its green belt, its countryside, its village life, and its robust Conservative majority.

As late as the 2005 General Election campaign, Home Secretary Charles Clarke was insisting, 'We want more immigration.' And more immigration they got. The party only woke up to the problems it caused in 2006 when working-class voters in their safe seats, feeling alienated and disenfranchised, began defecting to the BNP. And, even then, Labour persisted with the lie that without mass immigration this country would fall apart.

So can anything be done? Absolutely. A strong British Government would clamp down on immigration immediately, reclaim our borders, admit no more migrants for at least five years and round up and deport those here illegally. A strong Government would control future immigration strictly, as it is done in Australia and New Zealand, and insist that no one can enter who can't speak the language or provide for their dependents. A strong government would put a rocket up the arse of the wilfully unemployed, and encourage our citizens to breed for Britain.

Only we haven't got a strong Government. Privately, MPs acknowledge that there's sod all Gordon Brown can do to limit immigration because everyone in the European Union has the automatic right to move here should they so desire. Under EU law, there is little we can do to restrict the right of residence of anyone from the other 26 member states. And article 62 of the new EU treaty will abolish all remaining controls. In other words, once some chancer has slipped into the EU from anywhere else in the world, there will be nothing to stop them coming here. We can't restrict the number of asylum-seekers we admit either, because that, too, is controlled by the EU. The obvious answer – for us to leave the EU and reclaim control of our borders – doesn't seem to have occurred to them.

*   *   *

IT IS often said by the pro-immigration lobby that Britain is a country of immigrants. This is deliberately misleading or, in plain English, another lie. The peoples they talk about – the Angles, Saxons, Celts, Vikings, Jutes, Franks, Frisians, Normans (who were also of Viking blood) and the rest were not so much immigrants as invaders. They didn't come to work. They came to raid, plunder, pillage and conquer. They were met by armed resistance, and they often destroyed the home culture, replacing it with their own. They were largely Germanic tribes, however, from pretty much the same northern European stock; assimilation was easy. Even the Norman conquerors were relatively few in number – no more than 10,000, and perhaps as few as 5,000.

Immigration as we know it began after 1066, with the arrival of Jewish money-lenders (who were later expelled by Edward I), Italian merchants, Hansa traders, Flemish weavers, gypsies and German Palatines. From the 16th century, small numbers of Africans ('blackamoors') arrived and, from the 19th century on, a smattering of Indians and Chinese. In 1871, the total Chinese population in Britain was 207. Until the 19th century, the Huguenots – French Protestants – constituted the largest immigrant wave, and only 50,000 of them stayed in the British Isles.

After 1882, Jewish refugees fleeing the Russian Empire began to arrive; the Census of 1911 puts their number at 120,000. A further 55,000 Jews arrived between 1933–39. After the Second World War, their numbers peaked at around 400,000, tailing off through emigration or assimilation to an estimated 285,000 by the mid-1990s.

Full-on immigration began in earnest from 1945, as successive Governments encouraged newcomers to settle from the Caribbean, Africa and South Asia. This was immigration on a scale never previously experienced.

In 1939, the Indian population of Birmingham was 100; in 1955, the total number of Indians and Pakistanis in Britain was 10,700. By 1991, the census put their number at 1,316,810, with a further 162,835 Bangladeshis. In 2007, the numbers are estimated at 2 million Indians, 1.6 million Pakistanis, 400,000 Bangladeshis and 350,000 other south Asians. Our Black African-Caribbean population is estimated at 566,000.

Britain's transformation into a multi-racial society was never put to a vote and it wasn't painless, but it was surprisingly peaceful given the extent of the changes. To counter bigotry, successive Governments built up a thriving race-relations industry. This – rightly, in my view – made discrimination on the grounds of skin colour illegal. The big mistake was the creed of multi-culturalism – a form of cultural self-loathing – which all the major parties bought in to. Rather than bring up the children of these new immigrants with a shared British culture, the multi-culturalists insisted on 'diversity'. 'All cultures are equal,' they said. To try and instil the values of the old British monoculture on the young was a form of cultural imperialism.

The first victim of the new creed was Ray Honeyford, the headmaster of a Bradford school who argued that, because the new immigrants were here to stay, they needed to be integrated into British society; English, therefore, should be their first language, and they should be well versed in Britain's history and culture. For sticking to this eminently reasonable point of view, Honeyford was branded a racist – the placards said 'Ray-cist'; be still my aching sides – and he was drummed out of his job. For the multi-culturalists, it seems, all cultures might be equal, but no opinions can be tolerated other than their own.

The result was that Britain became a society of religious and ethnic apartheid; our inner cities have been Balkanised, fragmented, full of no-go areas, hostility and street signs few native English people can begin to fathom out. At one time, this only happened after a people were invaded and subjugated; now we surrender our identity in a one-way-street of 'understanding'.

When I worked in East London a few years ago, there was a normal state primary school over the road from our plant where every sign was written in Urdu. Not Urdu and English, just Urdu. I pointed out to a colleague that this was crazy. 'Oh,' she said, 'you can't say that, it's racist.'

It isn't, of course. To suggest that the English-born children of Asian immigrants would be better off learning English than being confined to an inward-looking educational ghetto is the opposite of racism.

Multi-culturalism was well-intentioned; it was meant to make newcomers feel at home. 'Your culture is as important as ours,' it said but, in practice, multi-culturalism exacerbates the sense of otherness, it increases alienation, offends common sense and creates a society built on vastly conflicting loyalties.

The price tag of multi-culturalism is the death of the old British culture. Native English kids are taught about Diwali and Eid at schools that no longer stage nativity plays for fear of causing 'offence'.

To the hard-line multi-culturalists, Britain's customs, values and traditions are apparently worthless; they must be chucked away for the sake of the new order. But surely immigrants should adapt to our culture, not us to theirs? And if the cross of St George, the Union flag, the Christian God, female emancipation, tolerance, secular democracy and respect for law or the principle of freedom of speech offends you, the answer is simple – don't come here.

The Far Left have taken PC logic even further by getting into bed with people whose views on social issues make the old Monday Club look like Channel 4 trendies. The multi-cultural madness held sway in schools and colleges for 20 years, until 9/11 and the subsequent al-Qaeda attacks on British cities made even the doziest liberal think again. Many of the bombers were the products of the brave, new multi-cultural education system that had been imposed years before. Honeyford was right.

Two sets of people lose out – British-born Asians, denied a chance ever to feel fully British, and the indigenous working-class whose culture, history and communities are sacrificed on the altar of 'progress'.

Chief Rabbi Jonathan Sachs commented, 'In a debate where there are no shared standards, the loudest voice wins.' And those who should be on our side – teachers, vicars, social workers, politicians, the BBC and the rest – aren't shouting very hard.

Yet when I look at Britain's contribution to engineering, science, literature, drama, popular culture, liberty and the rights of man, I don't see anything to be ashamed of. If I wore a hat I'd gladly take it off to Isambard Kingdom Brunel, Sir Isaac Newton, Thomas Newcomen, James Watt, Edward Elgar, Shakespeare, Dickens, Orwell and all those other unfashionable Dead White Males. Not to mention Sir Timothy John Berners-Lee, the Londoner who invented the Internet. I'm not saying that our culture is superior to any other country's, just that it's ours and we need to cherish, preserve and build on it.

Back in the real world, a feeling of injustice swells the rising indignation about continued immigration. People see new arrivals getting preferential treatment, receiving benefits and jumping queues.

Vic, my late father-in-law, a life-long Labour voter, put it simply. 'It's like being in a Christmas club in a working man's club,' he said. 'Every week you put your quid in expecting a pay-out at the end of the year, and then, days before Christmas, a load of people who haven't put in a penny turn up and the club secretary starts handing them your cash.'

According to the *Economist*, the newcomers who attract the most approbation are those who strain the British sense of fair play, in particular bogus asylum-seekers – economic migrants using 'asylum' as a way in – and illegal immigrants.

This growing sense of grievance isn't helped by Government incompetence; barely a week goes by without a new immigration cock-up. In October 2007, the Government was forced to admit that it got its figures for migrant workers absurdly wrong. Ministers had been routinely claiming that the number of foreign nationals working in the UK had increased by 'only' 800,000 since Blair was elected. In October, they confessed that they had miscalculated. The real figure, they said, was 1.1 million, so they had effectively managed to lose 300,000 people, which is as many as the entire population of Nottingham. Added to that, the former Labour Minister Frank Field says the true figure is closer to 1.6 million, and even that doesn't include the 400,000 UK citizens who were born overseas, or the 300,000 foreign students they admit a year with no guarantee that any will ever go back.

In November 2007, the Government was forced to correct an assurance which they had glibly given three years previously that no more than 13,000 immigrants would settle in England per year following EU enlargement. The Office for National Statistics estimates that 13,000 is the number of babies born in UK hospitals in 2007 to Polish mothers alone. 240,000 kids with parents from Poland, the former Czechoslovakia and Lithuania have been registered at British schools since the enlargement.

In December 2007, internal Government papers revealed that immigration bosses have 'no interest in deporting foreign criminals'. Officials were told not to bother rooting out any overseas convict sentenced to less than a year behind bars. Later that same month, it emerged that the Government has taken to 'bribing' illegal immigrants to go home – not legal migrants who aren't happy here being helped out on a voluntary repatriation scheme, but *illegal* ones. So far, 23,000 of the scumbags have been paid a total of £36 million to return to their native lands when all they deserve is a boot on to the nearest tug-boat.

In January 2008, it was reported that 25,000 illegal aliens stay in Britain every year due to Government inaction, and dozens of private colleges were exposed as fronts for illegal immigration. So it goes on.

No wonder voters are disgruntled. No wonder they're holding their noses and voting for fringe parties that take them seriously. Meanwhile, idiot politicians in their ivory towers discuss amnesties for the 600,000 illegal immigrants we know about... that's a Liberal Democrat policy.

In London, my home town, one third of the population are now said to be immigrants, and half of all children are born to foreign mothers. No wonder so many Londoners are upping sticks. According to the Office for National Statistics, 400,000 British people emigrated last year for the more welcoming shores of Spain, Portugal, the USA and Australia. A further 1 million are expected to leave by 2011, a disproportionate number of them from the south-east of England.

Clearly, these emigrants – or, should we say, evacuees – aren't quite as sold as the Lib Dems on the joys and benefits of unfettered immigration.

But we can't all pack our bags and leave. Those of us who are left have a duty to our forefathers, the people who built Britain with their blood, sweat and sacrifice, to make a stand for it... and that means taking the immigration debate into the mainstream.

Random Immigration Gags

- Albanian goes into the off licence and says 'Can you recommend a good port?' 'Yeah,' says the shop-keeper. 'Southampton. There's a boat going at 9am, be on it.'

- Gordon Brown says immigrants who settle in this country must speak English. This sparked protests from several immigrant groups and one Loyd Grossman. An indignant immigrant spokesman said: 'Ok, we'll speak English as soon as Brown learns how to pronounce Bournemouth.'

- Asylum seekers arriving here from Sangatte say they are fleeing bent cops, bad Government and crap food. Fair enough, but why go to France in the first place?

- They say it's cruel to turn away hard-working people desperate to live the dream. Why? We do it every week on *The X-Factor*.

- The Queen received the President of Poland this week. Apparently he offered to do Gordon Brown's job for £2 an hour, cash in hand, no questions asked.

- Mass immigration is really just a way to depress wages and create a permanent under-class of exploited labour. To which Gordon Brown replied: 'And the problem is...?'

Graffiti: I applied for the job but there was already a Czech in the post.

2

There'll Always Be an England

'There is a forgotten, nay almost forbidden word, which means more to me than any other. That word is "England".'
Sir Winston Churchill

How would it play in Dublin if a senior Irish politician demanded that the country stopped celebrating St Patrick's Day because of the shame brought on Catholicism by paedophile priests and indiscriminate bombers?

What would they say in Paris if the boss of TV channel TF1 said that Bastille Day should be abolished because of the odium of Vichy or the crimes of French imperialism in Algeria and Indo-China?

Imagine how it'd go down in Holyrood if some stern-faced son of the Manse called for the abolition of Burns Night celebrations because of Scotland's long history of bigotry, obesity, lousy food, gloominess and heroin addiction.

The reactions would, you'd imagine, run the gauntlet from hilarity to apoplexy.

There isn't a country in the world without some kind of stain on its national character: the Spanish torture cattle, for God's sake; the Yanks blunder from one foreign-policy disaster to another; and let's not get started on Colombia, not without a razor blade and a large supply of straws.

All of these nations manage to set aside at least one day a year when they can make a song and dance about their cultural identity.

The one nation that doesn't is England.

The English, are the only people in the world who are repeatedly told that it is wrong to celebrate our history and heritage and whose major cultural institution, the BBC, thinks its achievements are shameful and its customs are somehow distasteful.

Tony Blair – who was born and privately educated in Scotland – gave the Sweaty Socks their own Parliament, stating rightly that they are a 'proud and historic nation'. But his Deputy, John Prescott, who was born in Wales, is on record as saying, 'There is no such nationality as English.'

No such nationality as English! Presumably, the English are merely dutiful citizens of north-west Europe, whose main purpose seems to be to subsidise 'proud and historic' Scotland. Prescott and Blair, you may recall, even tried to chop England up into nine regions, with expensive talking shop assemblies, regional flags and identities. They wanted to Balkanise us, to do away with England altogether in order to ram us more efficiently into the Euro-mincer.

In his ten years as Chancellor of the Exchequer, Gordon Brown handed £60 billion more public money to Scotland than to England – enough to build 238 hospitals. He couldn't have rubbed our noses in it more if he'd lined up every English MP in the House of Commons and poured congealed porridge oats down the front of their pants while a platoon of pipers wheezed out that rotten dirge 'O Flower of Scotland' in the background.

Our rulers are infected with a disdain for everything English that runs as deep as one of our many derelict coal mines. George Orwell, the great patriotic socialist, detected it back in the 1930s when he wrote that 'England is perhaps the only great country whose intellectuals are ashamed of their nationality.' This stemmed partly from the guilt of Empire, and partly from the influence among the Oxbridge élite of a powerful group of traitors who preferred Stalin's Russia to their own country. Now their descendents want to dissolve us into the EU after falling out of love with a succession of foreign tyrants from Castro to Mao to Osama Bin Laden via the Irish Republican Army. It's the *Guardian* mentality – England is always in the wrong, no matter what murderous rogue we are up against. But are they right?

In fact, the English have far less to be ashamed of than other European nations. We aren't as militaristic as the Germans or as xenophobic as the French. The Royal Navy sank the slave trade and the British Empire is remembered by many with a degree of affection wherever its influence was felt.

When it comes to patriotism, though, the standard response of the urban intellectual is the mocking sneer. This is true of many on the Right as well as the Left, but it's the self-loathing of the left-wing intellectuals that irritates me most. These sniggering fools don't even know the roots of their own radicalism. For every Francis Drake in English

19

history there was a Wat Tyler; for every Wellington there was a Captain Swing. Military achievement understandably shaped our self-image. The stout yeomen of England have been beating off invaders for centuries – we saw off Bonaparte and smashed the Spanish Armada – but England gave the world parliamentary democracy and the trade unions, too.

Every child should learn the story of the Tolpuddle Martyrs, six farm labourers from Dorset, who founded the Friendly Society of Agricultural Labourers to fight wage cuts after their nine-shillings-a-week wage (45p) was slashed to six shillings (30p). In February 1834, these good, hard-working men were arrested for unlawful assembly and charged with 'administering unlawful oaths' – forming a trade union, in other words. The six were found guilty as charged and sentenced to seven years' imprisonment in the penal colony in New South Wales, Australia, 'not,' said the judge, 'for anything they had done, but as an example to others.'

They were an example to others all right. The men became popular heroes and the inspiration for the new trade union movement.

Nearly two centuries later, our belief in democracy, liberty and social justice made English-speaking civilisation the rock that broke the tidal wave of continental fascism. Our openness, our belief in tolerance, free speech and the rights of man were the living proof that the totalitarian state with its secret police, censorship and slave labour was neither 'infallible' nor inevitable. But these qualities that made us different are now increasingly under threat.

The English are a strong-willed people, rightly proud of our traditions and freedoms. Keith Waterhouse wrote that our defining national characteristic is 'constructive bloody-mindedness', illustrated by the phrase 'thus far and no further'. Many of us who love England, and see how carelessly our rulers have surrendered our liberties and sovereignty, while encouraging phoney nationalism in Scotland and Wales, feel that we have reached the 'thus far' point. I certainly do. Labour's regionalisation proposals pushed me over the edge. It was clear that the creation of elected regional assemblies in England were simply an attempt to break us up and destroy us – as Charles Kennedy said, to 'call into question the idea of England itself'.

I'm not a politician but, in the 2005 General Election, I stood for the English Democrats in the Greenwich and Woolwich constituency. Why? To help kick up a stink about the mess Labour's devolution botch-job has made of democracy in the UK. I was campaigning, in short, for equality for the English. I'm not anti-Scottish; I merely demanded the right for the English to run our own country as the Scots do theirs, while pointing out that an English parliament would become meaningless and impotent if we remained under EU rules. Inevitably, this was painted as an 'extreme' cause. We had no money and little campaigning time, yet 1,216 south Londoners took the time to turn out and vote for me. Not a great result (although we beat UKIP), but you have to nail your colours to the mast to get noticed. From little acorns the might oak of English liberty will grow.

A year later, a *Daily Telegraph* poll showed that 68 per cent of English voters backed the cause – very nearly seven out of ten people – and subsequent polls have not produced a figure under 60 per cent. Compare that with the vote for the Scottish Parliament of 44 per cent which was described as the 'settled will of the Scottish people', or with the 21 per cent of voters who backed Tony Blair's Government at the last General Election.

Even without regionalisation, the English get a raw deal under the present set-up. Scottish citizens have £1,500 more per head spent on them than do their English counterparts. In England, the Government spend £6,762 per person a year (on health, education and so on); in Scotland, that figure is £8,265. The Scots get free dental and eye checks, free personal care for the elderly, and the free installation of central heating for pensioners. They get life-saving cancer drugs; their students pay no tuition fees; their schoolchildren have more than double the budget for school dinners and some Scottish children between the ages of four and seven get free school meals, with plans to extend that to children of all ages. It's all free! Except none of it is free, of course – the rest of the UK is paying for it.

Why? Back in the 1970s, Lord Barnett came up with his Barnett Formula, which divvied up the national cake unfairly. It was meant to apply for a short period – no more than two years – to kick start the Scottish economy. But 30 years on, it remains in operation. In its defence, some Scots say it costs more to provide services in their rural areas. But England has rural areas, too – Northumbria is just as under-populated as anywhere north of the border. And the North

Sea Oil argument doesn't hold water either – if we were separate countries, by international law England would have a claim to one third of the oil and most of the gas.

There is no coherent argument as to why the Barnett Formula should still be operating; even Barnett himself says it now needs to be scrapped. Successive Governments have kept it going simply to bribe the Scottish electorate not to vote for the SNP. They bought them off for three decades but, finally, English voters are waking up to the injustice. More and more of our people are asking, 'Why do we put up with the Scots spending so much of our money? Why should the English continue to fund better public services in the other nations of the UK?'

To counter the new mood of English nationalism, our new, unelected Prime Minister, Gordon Brown, has wrapped himself up in the Union Jack. 'Britishness' is Labour's new mantra – ironic when you think Labour was responsible for breaking up Britain in the first place, and doubly so if you ever encountered flag-hating, 1980s Labourites, the kind who ended up as social workers, councillors, college lecturers and school teachers.

The response of left-wing teachers to Labour's new red, white and blue offensive was predictable. A survey published early in 2008 found that nine out of ten of these sandal-wearing weird beards and their husbands opposed Gordon's plans for the teaching of British history in schools. The Left-leaning Institute of Education suggested that patriotism should be covered as a 'controversial issue'. Britain's history was, they said, morally ambiguous. 'Are countries really appropriate objects of love?' asked the report's author Michael Hand. It would be funny – Brown hoist by his own petard – if these fools weren't busily engaged in educating our kids to feel guilty about our past. Teaching Britishness, argued one, would encourage 'BNP-type thinking'.

An alternative interpretation would be that patriotism is a natural, healthy state of mind that only turns ugly when it's suppressed. And the double standards over patriotism don't help us either – why are we urged to forgive Germany for invading Poland while we flagellate ourselves about the Opium Wars?

Strangely, Brown's 'Britishness' lessons are only taught in English schools, not in Scotland or Wales. Having unleashed the beast of Scottish nationalism, Labour now seeks to blind us to its consequences.

But where do Gordon Brown's true loyalties lie? He was one of the signatories of the Scottish Claim of Right which states 'in all our actions and deliberations [the] interests [of the Scottish people] shall be paramount.' This was also signed and approved by Menzies Campbell, Alistair Darling, John Reid and George Galloway.

Is it a coincidence that Brown's last act as Chancellor was to cut the English NHS building budget from £6.2 to £4.2 billion, while the Scots and Welsh budgets were left intact?

Brown's Britishness offensive is a con-trick designed to distract us from the inequalities and injustices created by Labour's wonky devolution strategy. Tam Dalyell called it the 'West Lothian Question'. The left-wing Scot asked, 'For how long will English constituencies and English Honourable Members tolerate... at least 119 Honourable

Members from Scotland, Wales and Northern Ireland exercising an important, and probably often decisive, effect on British politics while they themselves have no say in the same matters in Scotland, Wales and Northern Ireland?' It's a good question, for which the Government has no answer.

Gordon Brown, who represents a Scottish constituency, is imposing Labour policies on English voters, with the help of the votes of Scottish MPs, and he is doing it in areas where he has no authority to make law in Scotland. How can that be right? Why should Scottish MPs have a vote on purely English matters while England's MPs can't discuss Scotland?

The English put up with a lot, but there is a limit to how long the people of the UK's biggest and richest country will suffer being treated like second-class citizens. So many issues are now devolved in Scotland and Wales that we can't talk about British education, transport or health policy any more. The current arrangement is unfair to English voters. Scotland and Wales have their own Parliament and Assembly but they are still over-represented in the House of Commons. Scottish and Welsh MPs preside over English matters; English MPs have no reciprocal right. As we've seen, the Barnett formula gives about one-third extra spending to Scotland for *equal* need. This set-up is completely out of kilter, and the only constitutionally workable solution is the creation of a wholly English Parliament.

An English Parliament would ensure that legislation affecting England was proposed and implemented by MPs accountable to the English electorate. It would allow for proper parliamentary time to be allotted for the debate of English matters and scrutiny of English legislation. It would kick the West Lothian Question into touch. It would also ensure that ministers were directly politically accountable to the constituency that their department serves. It is wrong that Scottish constituency MPs are given English portfolios – one example of this is Douglas Alexander, Secretary of State for Transport in 2006, who tried during his tenure to impose an England-only road pricing scheme, which was 'accidentally' reported by the BBC as if it were a UK-wide issue.

An English Parliament would create a more inclusive, civic sense of English identity and national purpose, and it would give England political leadership. Scotland has a First Minister, while England does not. Why then should Gordon Brown become, in effect, First Minister of England? Gordon Brown has no democratic mandate on important matters such as Education, Health and Transport – his constituents in Scotland don't elect him to represent them in these areas, and neither do any voters in England.

An English Parliament would also kill off Labour's still-percolating plans for unwanted regional assemblies in England.

And it's the only long-term hope of preserving the United Kingdom, which, to exist at all, must be independent of the European Union. Our future doesn't lie in Europe, being over-regulated and bossed about by petty-minded Continental bureaucrats. Let's fight for an independent England shaping its own destiny and trading with whoever we please as part, once again, of a greater

Anglosphere of English-speaking peoples dedicated to freedom, liberty and enterprise.

When he was sentenced in 1834, Tolpuddle Martyr George Loveless wrote, 'God is our guide, from field, from wave, from plough, from anvil and from loom; we come our country's rights to save, and speak a tyrant faction's doom. We raise the watch-word liberty; we will, we will, we will be free!'

Now is the time to echo those words and fight to win back the freedoms we have lost. Once again, let's raise the watch-word – liberty.

We will, we will, we will be free.

*   *   *

BACK in the early 1990s, I asked why our television networks never celebrated St George's Day. The response was phenomenal, and overwhelmingly supportive, although Kelvin MacKenzie thought at the time that I was being 'extreme'. But, as an Englishman, I don't hate other nationalities; I just wish to preserve and build on my heritage.

In 1996, I dedicated one of my ITV shows to St George's Day; Chas & Dave played in my back room, and I delivered various bits to camera. Again, the public response was positive. Cab drivers refused to take any money from me, and strangers started buying me drinks in pubs. That same year, Euro '96 reflected this new mood of English patriotism – the terraces were awash with the flag of St George. Thirty years before, when England won the World Cup, all you saw were Union flags. Now the English had adopted a new symbol, and this demand for something of ours was coming from the grass roots up.

I carried on asking why TV did nothing for St George, especially when the BBC regions never forget St David's Day or Burns Night. Finally, in response, in 2000, BBC2 decided to debate Englishness and, although they did it in a typically condescending and sneering way, it was a start. In 2001, Channel 5 devoted an evening to English films.

BBC1 remained reluctant, though. Their top-rated show, *EastEnders*, had managed to hold parties for St Patrick's Day, American Independence Day and even for Diwali, the Hindu festival of lights, without ever mentioning England's patron saint. I invited readers to place bets on what foreign country would get the Queen Vic seal of approval next. Possibly, I suggested, a knees-up for migrant Albanian peasants loyal to the memory of their glorious leader, Enver Hoxha, to drink to the golden days of tractors and austerity before the fall of Communism.

In the real world, the day was increasingly celebrated not just in genuine East End pubs but all over the country, with breweries getting in on the fun. The situation was becoming so absurd that even Ally Ross, the *Sun*'s England-hating columnist, picked up on it. And, eventually, in 2005, Alfie Moon finally had a St George's Day Russell Harty in the Vic, if only to shut us up.

That same year, Red Ken Livingstone, who'd been happily donating huge chunks of public money to St Patrick's Day celebration organisers for years, hastily endorsed some feeble St George's Day events to take the steam out of a planned mass walk on the GLA. I also organised a Variety Festival of England which was screened on 23 April by the satellite channel Sound TV. This took place at the Queen's Hotel, Blackpool, with the great Yorkshire funnyman Johnnie Casson topping the bill and guest appearances from Richard Digance and Bobby Ball. Punters queued round the block and we had to turn a third of them away.

The night ended with the 500-strong capacity crowd enjoying a mass sing-song of patriotic songs led by club singer Joe Wildey, an immaculately tailored Irishman who could see nothing wrong with the English having one day a year when we can celebrate our identity with good humour, as other peoples do. It took me back to my own childhood when we'd always have St George's Day parties at Charlton social clubs, with women wearing red roses on their lapels.

The following year, we doubled the size of the venue. Nearly 900 turned up for a rock and variety show at the Circus Tavern, the 'home of darts', in Essex. The bill, which I put together, was a schizophrenic mix of acts ranging from Brian Conley to the Cockney Rejects, via Right Said Fred, Rick Wakeman, the Artful Dodger and Neville Staple. Mad but exhilarating.

By now, people from all over the country were contacting me with their own St George's Day events; the most impressive was an unofficial motorised parade organised by the 1066 Motorcycle Club in Solihull, while the Stone Cross St George Association (just outside of West Bromwich, West Midlands) assembled the largest St George's Day parade in England.

In 2007, I had my English party on TalkSPORT radio and the switchboard was jammed by appreciative callers. The only exception was a surly Scot who believed that being English was in itself 'racist'. He wasn't best pleased to be reminded that the Ku Klux Klan had been kreated by Sweaty Socks.

In 2008, at least four major St George's Day bashes have been planned, including a punk and ska night in The Garage, in north London. Indeed, the music industry has finally woken up to the idea of the possibilities of our rich English heritage, with more and more bands bringing out patriotic anthems. In their song, 'Roots' West Country folk band Show of Hands sing about English identity being submerged in the Union Jack. The cross of St George needs to be recovered, they say, and resurrected. (The full video is available on YouTube). English clothing companies are sprouting up everywhere, with none as stylish as Longshanks, a company founded by various West Ham herberts who made their money on the 1980s rave scene.

The message is clear – the market is there, the will of the people is there, and St George's Day can become a major event if everyday English folk want it. So what can we do? Take St George's Day off for a start. If enough people treat the day as a national holiday, eventually they will have to make it official. Bombard radio and TV stations (especially the BBC) with letters and petitions calling for English theme nights to mark our special day. And switch off any channel that doesn't include English programming on 23 April every year.

Just as importantly, celebrate St George's Day yourself.

If you can't get to one of the big gigs, organise your own do in your street, your pub or your social club. Get together with people who feel the same way as you and get something going.

It's time for the English to wake up and reclaim our birthright. As Shelley wrote (and my band, The Gonads, set to music): 'Men of England, rise like lions from your slumber, in unvanquishable number; shake to earth your chains like dew, that in your sleep has fallen upon you. We are many. They are few.'

* * *

To be born English is to have won first prize in the lottery of life. To be English is to be part of the world's richest culture. From this sceptred isle sprang talents as diverse as Orwell and Chaplin, Kipling and Shakespeare, Nelson and Joe Strummer. In every field, in every era, the evidence of English greatness is there for all to see, from the enduring genius of Elgar to the magic of Michael Owen's goal against Argentina ... As Ian Dury once noted, England's glory is like the crown of a great monarch, studded with far too many gems to be detailed in a three-minute pop song. OK, not many of us know more than the first two lines of 'There'll Always Be An England', but we do know that our country gave the world football, cricket, rugby, tennis, the Beatles and Dickens. As a people we are not given to chest-beating. Reserve and restraint are as much English qualities as inventiveness and enterprise. But we do resent the way Englishness is put down at by the chattering classes. For them, the cross of St George is tainted by memories of empire (even though the Royal Navy smashed the slave trade). It has been like this for decades.

But my England is not a source of shame.

My England is bubble and squeak and foaming pints of Boddingtons. It is Les Dawson and Barbara Windsor, Max Miller and Page Three. My England is pie and mash and Aston Martins, Derby day and Arfur Daley, Mods and Suedeheads, Rockers and Skinheads, Lenny McLean and Carry On films. My England stretches from Dennis Skinner to Roger Scruton, from Peggy Mount to Beki Bondage, from Constable to the Bryant & May match-girls' strike. It's Blackpool beach, Ray Davies, Charlie Drake, Charlton Athletic FC, roast beef, imperial measurements and vindaloo. It's defiance. Whether it be King Alfred standing up to the Vikings, Colonel H at Goose Green, or the Metric Martyrs giving the finger to Brussels. No-one likes us! We don't care!

Whether your England is summed up by a bowler hat or a pit helmet, punk rock or Morris dancers, there are few national tapestries as rich as ours. And of course it is a national disgrace that TV gives St George a blank. But what do they know? How often do they get anything right? If you are English, turn off the TV on 23rd April and get down the pub, preferably in a fine Longshanks shirt. As Chesterton wrote: 'St George he was for England and before he

slew the dragon, he drank a pint of English ale out of an English flagon.' Enjoy yourself this St. George's Day. And remember, there will always be an England.
(St George's Day speech, 2001)

The Top Ten Modern English Anthems
1) 'England Belongs to Me' by Cock Sparrer
2) 'England My Land' by Sarah Vezmar
3) 'The Power and the Glory' by the Cockney Rejects
4) 'England's Glory' by Kilburn and the High Roads
5) 'Roots' by Show of Hands
6) 'Waterloo Sunset' by The Kinks
7) 'World in Motion' by New Order
8) '(What's the Story?) England's Glory' by The Gonads
9) 'Hurry Up, England' by Motty's Sheepskins
10) 'England' by the Angelic Upstarts

3

Nanny Knows Best –
All Light Up

*'I can't give up smoking but I'm careful. I never
smoke these fags that say 'Smoking Kills'. No. I only
smoke the ones that seriously damage your health.'*
Buddy Lee

The smoking ban kicked in on 1 July 2007. It's being
touted as a blessing for public health, but isn't it just
another infringement of our civil liberties? The fag end of
the wedge?

I don't smoke, largely because I don't fancy having lungs
like Shredded Wheat, teeth the colour of sweetcorn, breath
like an ashtray and a gaping hole in my trachea. I don't
mind the company of smokers, though – I like to cough.
And this ban concerns me for several good reasons – 1) it's
undemocratic; 2) it removes freedom of choice; and 3) it is
shamelessly based on misinformation. In other words, it's
all passive smoke and mirrors.

Big Brother is lying to us again.

There is no medical proof that secondary smoking
causes cancer – none at all. There has been a massive
amount of research in this area, millions of pounds have
been spent and, time after time, the same result comes back

– there is no scientific evidence. Smoking damages the smoker's health, full stop.

Many of you will feel the need at this point to say, 'Whoa, back up there, Gal, what about Roy Castle?' For the benefit of younger readers, Roy Castle was a non-smoking entertainer who died of lung cancer after a long career playing smoky clubs. But I don't have access to Roy's autopsy notes and neither have you. Besides, there are thousands of entertainers playing smoky back-street hell-holes and there was only one Roy Castle. It's not much of a case.

Facts won't slow the advance of the Nanny State, though. Since the ban was imposed, you will be fined £50 for lighting up in a pub, while the landlord could cop a £2,500 fine for letting you. Cigar smokers can't even enjoy a quiet puff in a private cigar smoking club, and this is against a backdrop of decriminalising ganja. Even laboratory beagles will have to step outside the lab to light up. Probably.

You could say smokers have brought the ban on themselves from years of being selfish and inconsiderate, but if smokers wish to congregate in well-ventilated private members' clubs, why on earth should it be any business of the Government's? If a publican chooses to operate his pub as a smoking establishment, why the hell shouldn't he? He wouldn't get my business, but that would be his choice and mine as free individuals in a free society.

Yes, pubs and clubs smell different. They now reek of stale piss and other people's BO and, if you're really lucky, you'll be able to savour a lungful of old codger halitosis.

Drinking establishments are much emptier, too, as business nose-dives; for some, catastrophically. Smokers now have to indulge their habit outside. That's fine if a pub has a beer garden, but it's not so clever when mobs of tipsy smokers spill out into our high streets and obstruct the pavement.

On the plus side, your clothes don't smell of smoke the morning after, and you don't have to eat in a restaurant with some inconsiderate git puffing away over your mutton madras. But we are less free... we have less choice... we're more controlled. Baaa. Baaa. Baaa.

Smokers are a burden on the NHS, it's said, but taxation on cigarettes in this country is ludicrously high. Tax accounts for nearly 90 per cent of the cost of a packet of fags, and British smokers cough up £10 billion a year – six times the cost of treating smoke-related illnesses. We pay more tax than anyone else in the world; it rocketed up by 50 per cent in Brown's ten years at the Treasury; which has been a terrific boon... for the smuggling industry. Smokers pay more than enough for their health care, and it's not stretching the point too far to say that they are effectively subsidising the NHS for the rest of us.

In January 2008, Dawn Primarolo, the government Minister who resembles a young Dot Cotton without the joie de vivre, was putting it about that the pub trade hasn't suffered from the smoking ban. Really? Read local papers, or better still look around your local. All over the country, business is down, pubs are going bust, and people are still dying.

As the weather gets colder a new smoking-related illness has emerged, 'smoker's flu' – a condition caused by constantly leaving a hot pub to stand for ten minutes in the pissing rain and cold before returning to the hot pub. You won't pop your clogs with emphysema any more, you'll die of pneumonia, or from burns caused by blundering into the beer garden patio heater while plastered during a force nine gale.

The oddest side-effect is that non-smokers are still exposed to other people's fags because given the choice between going outside with the smokers or sitting in the pub watching their bags; most of us prefer the company. Outside pub banter is the new cool, and 'smirting' – flirting while smoking outdoors – is the hottest way to pull.

To pile on the anti-smoking pressure – or, more precisely, to add extra revenue to the Government's coffers – in February 2008 it was suggested that smokers should have to apply for a £10 smoking licence – complete with photo ID of course. Professor Julian Le Grand – I'm not making this up – of the Government advisory body Health England believes that a smoking licence would make it harder for smokers to start, or restart. This is a way to squeeze yet more tax money out of smokers and, of course, we'll need a new department of civil servants to process all the information. More admin, more bureaucracy, agents to enforce it... all the revenue it raises will be eaten up, and more besides. The Professor also wants to make the form as complex as possible, which will have the effect of penalising the dim, dyslexic or less well-educated. And when people realise that being a licensed smoker may affect what treatments they can receive on the NHS, they'll surely turn to tobacco smugglers.

So what's next? A licence to drink? A licence to eat crisps or have a flutter on the gee-gees? You'll probably need to ask Gordon's permission to tell State-approved jokes in your local... that's if there are any left, of course.

The big question underpinning this entire debate is: do our bodies belong to us or to the State? The Nazis saw an individual's right to do what he or she wants with their own body as a 'liberal perversion', saying that there is an 'obligation to be healthy'.

Britain is fast becoming a Gestapo Khazi, a place of dull, timid conformity, ruled by people who see 1984 not so much as a novel but as an instruction manual. And we sit back waving goodbye to centuries of hard-won freedoms. Little by little, inch by inch, our personal liberties are being eaten away.

Alcohol has become the next big target, of course. Incredibly, the Government which brought in 24-hour drinking in pubs is now grumbling about people boozing too much. We've already had them moaning about 'middle-class' wine drinkers – are we to assume, then, that other classes don't drink wine?

Will it be a case of: first they came for the *Telegraph* readers and their Pouilly-Fuissé, and I did not speak out because I was not a *Telegraph* reader; then they came for the *Spectator* Wine Club, and I did not speak out for I was not a member; then they came for the saloon bar bores drinking gin and it, and I did not speak out because I do not drink gin and it then they came for me and my six pints of light and bitter with a JD chaser... and there was no one left to speak out for me.

Inevitably, the Government will whack up duty on booze 'for our own good'. Well, if people stop smoking, Gordon will need to replace the lost revenue somehow. Expect horror stories about problem drinkers followed by politicians and health professionals demanding that laws should be passed telling us how many alcoholic drinks we can consume in a pub or a restaurant in any one session. And to keep check on those 'middle-class' wine drinkers, why not introduce night-time home visits as the booze police target us for random breathalyzer tests?

They seem to have forgotten that everybody has to die of something and, if smoking or drinking takes a couple of years off your life, then they will be the boring years when you're old and infirm, or immobile and drooling, and death will come as a blessed relief from the living hell of being trapped in a home watching daytime TV on a five-channel set.

Newsflash – living is bad for you. In my experience, it inevitably causes death. Despite her best assurances, even Gloria Gaynor will not survive indefinitely. So I intend to die with a pint of Bombardier in one hand, eating a medium rare steak and smoking a big fat cigar. And if any carnal acts are on offer, I'll have them, too, please.

The thing to do is enjoy Life while you can; you only have one shot at it and, although some major religions beg to differ, I'm not taking chances. So if eating a bucketful of doughnuts floats your boat, then dive in. It's no skin off my nose, and it's definitely no damn business of Gordon Brown's either. If we don't stand up to this 'health' onslaught, there will be a food cop on duty at every supermarket check-out confiscating pork pies, and a 'fat tax' will be whacked on bags of chips 'for your own good'.

Obesity starts at home, of course, so how about inspectors popping round and check what books we've got? It'll start with Nigella Lawson's recipe books – 'All that sugar, cream and butter... the woman is peddling death on a plate. Oh, and what's this you have here, sir? George Orwell? Better confiscate that one... don't want your kids getting ideas.' Once we let the State into our private lives, there will be no end to it.

There's always a 'good reason' to surrender our freedoms; it always sounds so reasonable. Freedom of speech should be set in stone, but that's been chipped away for decades. Our right to privacy has gone down the gurgler, too. We're on camera now every time we leave our homes. How long before the Government takes the logical next step and insists on cameras *in* the home, too? They'll do it for very good reasons – it will be instigated under the guise of preventing child abuse or domestic violence, and certain papers will chip in and say, 'If you've got nothing to hide, why would you object?' The same arguments have been used in the ID card debate, and when we were forced to give up our right to keep our bank details private. Now, on the dubious grounds that any one of us could theoretically be laundering drug money, bank officials have been empowered and are obliged to report you for any 'suspicious' transactions that you make on your account.

This is how the Police State begins; we give up our freedoms in the name of the greater good, when what politicians really want is greater control, greater bureaucracy and more stringent taxes to pay for it all.

So what do we do? Fight back. Anyone who believes in liberty should oppose the smoking ban. But how? One possible drawback is that any protest march would no doubt have to be abandoned halfway due to shortness of breath. We could play them at their own game, I suppose, and demand legal protection from anti-smoking persecution. In fact, why not design your own posters and march on Downing Street? Your slogans might include: 'Look Baccy in Anger'… 'The Grapes of Rothmans'… or 'Who's Afraid of Virginia Slims'?

If I smoked, I'd set up 'smoke-easy' clubs like the speakeasies that sprung up under Prohibition in the USA… and I'd put a picture of Gordon Brown in every ashtray. I suppose the least you should do if you're concerned is download the new single by those ancient rockers The Pretty Things called 'All Light Up'… and petition Walker's to produce a new line of nicotine-flavoured crisps.

- What would Churchill have to say about this? Or Strummer, Keef, Einstein, Sinatra, Sartre, Groucho Marx, Orwell, Johnny Cash, Oscar Wilde, Bill Hicks, JFK, Jack Kerouac, Monet or any of the other famous, brilliant and creative smokers?

  Joe Strummer once said: 'If you took cigarettes away we wouldn't have the writers anyone worships.'

  Winnie lit up. Hitler didn't. The Sex Pistols smoked, the Bee-Gees didn't. John Lennon liked a puff. Mark Chapman? You're way ahead of me.

Hitler was also largely vegetarian and a teetotaller, but it would be wrong to draw any conclusions from that; wouldn't it?

- My pal Billy is devastated by the smoking ban; coughing in our local was the only exercise he got.

- In September 2007 newspapers reported that the smoking ban had cut heart attacks in Scotland by 17 percent. MPs trumpeted the good news to the world. It was claimed as a major success and a vindication of Government Policy. Then six weeks later official data more than halved the drop — to 8 percent — compared to a trend immediately before the ban of a 5 or 6 percent drop. And a fall a few years ago of eleven... All of which makes it hard to be sure if the ban has had any effect at all.

Naturally this wasn't publicised half as well.

You Are What You Eat

If we're all so unhealthy, how come we're living longer? I mention this quietly as I don't want to disturb the health busybodies as they go about their business of sticking their noses in to other people's lives and spreading contradictory scare stories.

One of the worst is 'Doctor' Gillian McKeith, as welcome in my living room as the Ebola virus, who has made a fortune out of preaching her dietary beliefs to the nation – beliefs that scientists, having carefully considered, have duly declared as mumbo jumbo.

Her show is called *You Are What You Eat*; if that's true, McKeith must be gorging on nettles and lemons.

Hardly a week goes by without us being nagged about

what we should eat and drink, and what bad people we are if we don't force-feed our children with alfalfa, pumpkin seeds and sun-dried tomatoes. You wouldn't mind so much if the 'experts' didn't change their mind every five minutes. When I was a kid, we were told that we should go to work on an egg, that Guinness was good for you, that we should drink a pint of milk a day; that nothing beats a Sunday roast and that an apple a day keeps the doctor away. That all went down the gurgler in the nineties. Suddenly, eggs were bad for us, milk was full of fat, red meat would clog up your arteries, and don't you dare eat that apple 'cos it's been plastered with pesticides.

Avoid roast beef and eat salads, they said – only now this week we're told that we should avoid certain salads because their salt content is higher than the much-maligned McDonald's burger. It is OK to eat eggs again, though – for now – and the latest studies show that even chocolate is good for you. Really, scientists say that eating chocolate may be beneficial for your heart. It doesn't do your arse any good, but that's the choice you have to make.

Then there's coffee. For years, we were told to avoid it because the caffeine is bad for you; now we're told to swig coffee and jog if we want to beat cancer! Caffeine might help with Alzheimer's, too, apparently. If you remember where you left your cup.

What about the sun? 'Stay out of the sunlight,' the experts said, 'it'll give you skin cancer.' The threat has been so exaggerated that many simple-minded people are now terrified of going outdoors without a burqa. As a result, the West is experiencing a rise of epidemic proportions of

Vitamin D deficiency, increasing bone conditions such as rickets and osteoporosis, not to mention the risk of MS, diabetes and possibly autism.

The papers frequently peddle the idea of the amazing health benefits of 'super-foods', which often result in a major sales boost for the featured fruit or veg. Often, these reports turn out to be based on research paid for by an interested party. For example, in 2006, the BBC reported claims that pomegranate juice can 'slow prostate cancer'. The study, by the University of California in Los Angeles, maintained that pomegranates contain a cocktail of chemicals which minimise cell damage, and potentially kill off cancer cells. But when you examine the small print, it turns out that the research was: a) paid for by a company that makes pomegranate juice; and b) based on just 50 male cancer patients, a group too small to be significant.

According to a *Horizon* report, health claims made for novelty fruits like goji and pro-biotic yoghurt drinks don't stand up to scrutiny either. You're filling your guts with bacteria when you'd be better off with a nice pie.

You'd be forgiven for concluding that nobody knows anything, and that the best way to live your life may very well be to ignore the fads and the health freaks altogether.

Some things have been proven beyond doubt to be good for us, though. If we have diets rich in fresh fruit and veg, drink red wine moderately, avoid obesity and take physical exercise, we can protect ourselves against some cancers and heart disease. Billions of pounds of research has established that Granny knew best. It all boils down to eating your greens, and 'a little of what you fancy does you good'; enjoy everything in moderation and move about a bit and you'll be fine.

Hour after hour of TV time is devoted to shows whose messages can be summed up in two sentences – lose weight and smarten yourself up and you'll look younger; eat better food and exercise and you'll live longer. It's not rocket science, common sense is all it takes. But common sense is in short supply in the lucrative health market.

Nutritionists have to make diets sound more complicated to justify their existence. The result is that we are bombarded with faddish, new-age nonsense by people who are the scientific equivalent of Mystic Meg. But when you ask them to produce proof, actual scientific evidence for their claims, they tend to go quiet. Everything from antioxidant supplements to 'Doctor' Gillian McKeith's extraordinary claims for plant enzymes from 'live' raw food has been scientifically proven to be useless. And all this mumbo-jumbo supposedly beamed into our living rooms and endorsed by qualified 'experts'? Things are not always what they seem.

In February 2007, McKeith agreed that she would no longer call herself 'Doctor' in her adverts. It turns out that she has a less-than-impressive doctorate in holistic nutrition obtained via a postal course from an unaccredited backwater US college. McKeith was taken to the Advertising Standards Authority and ended up agreeing 'voluntarily' to drop the title.

Elsewhere, biologists have exposed her for 'science' loaded with dubious claims. One wrote: 'McKeith is a menace to the public understanding of science. She seems to misunderstand not nuances, but the most basic aspects of biology – things that a 14-year-old could put her straight on.'

She's not a medical doctor, a botanist or a biologist. Yet the 'diet doctor' had Channel 4 – and millions of gullible viewers – eating out of her hands for years.

Her very first show back in 2004 set the template for every subsequent one. McKeith's prey was junk-food addict Yvonne Grant, 32, a cheery Scot who drank a pint of Irn-Bru for breakfast and scoffed up to ten packets of crisps a day, in between microwave meals, chips and sponge cakes, which she often polished off in one sitting. Yvonne was 5ft 2in, fat and flatulent. She weighed 17.5st, but was no soft target – except if you poked her in the Pillsbury Doughboy sense. She wasn't getting any other poking ('Sex life, what's that?')

Yet she was funnier and far more likeable than nagging Gillian. 'I think I'm bulimic… I just forget to throw up,' she quipped. But it's hard to maintain your dignity when someone is irrigating your colon on television, especially when 'no-nonsense nutritionist' McKeith used a glass tube so viewers could see for themselves there was no fibre in her waste. Thanks. This became her trademark stunt. But why would anyone agree to have a televised enema? And why would any sniggering smarty-pants of a TV exec think we'd want to watch one, except as a means of belittling the target? 'Look,' they say, 'look how desperate these people are to be on telly. They'll do anything.' And yet, like gullible punters at a fairground, the mugs keep on coming with their messy homes, fat guts and swearing brats for their short burst of TV infamy.

IN Victorian times, middle class missionaries would venture into working class areas to save the honest poor with heady talk of temperance, religion or revolution. Nowadays they come with a camera crew for the purpose of national humiliation.

Whatever you've got, TV will mock it – your clothes, house, spouse, lifestyle, even your dreams. And in the process if they can get you to strip off and break down in tears, so much the better.

Roll up, roll up for the great degradation show.

Bushell On The Blog
March 2007

1 March The *Sun* and the *Daily Mail* today banned an advert which spelled out how open borders were imposed on the UK with no discussion in the British Parliament. The Free Movement of People directive, which allows unlimited immigration within Europe, was never debated in the Commons. Instead it was discussed behind closed doors by the New Labour-run European Scrutiny Committee. This directive means that all EU countries are now effectively one nation (the old Mosley dream!). It's a scandal, and an affront to democracy, and yet the papers refused to run the ad claiming absurdly that it was 'potentially racist' and 'inflammatory.' Welcome to Europa, where free speech is rationed.

2 March Is there any real difference between George Osborne and Gordon Brown? The Tories' Shadow Chancellor missed another great chance yesterday to spell out an alternative policy to Brown's crippling high-tax, high-spend approach. It's particularly galling because Gordon isn't working. 'Prudent' Brown makes Sharon Osbourne look like Scrooge's more frugal aunty. He slings fortunes at public services, yet to nobody's surprise the NHS is struggling again. Why? Because the Government makes a lousy boss; always has done, always will. Gordon's answer is to leave politicians, pen-pushers and paper-shufflers in charge of public services while he squeezes every spare penny out of hard-working families. Direct taxation creeps up annually, surpassed only by sneaky 'stealth' taxes. Council tax is exorbitant, fuel prices are through the roof. Joe Public gets walloped at every turn.

Has George Osborne got a solution? No. Gormless Geo says the Tories will 'share the proceeds of growth between public spending and tax cuts.' D'oh! Tax cuts cause economic growth. Tax cuts are the alternative to Big Government, Jurassic thinking and the lower productivity that comes with it. Slashing taxes won't threaten economic stability, as Osborne claims. On the contrary they will attract investment, boost employment and swell Treasury coffers.

3 March Birdseye are going to cut down on using cod in their fish fingers. Well, plenty more fish in the sea...

6 March The weasels that run British television have been caught red-handed with their hands in our pockets. The premium-rate phone line fraud has crossed the line between exploitation and greed, and spread into downright theft. Viewers have been scammed, deceived and conned, and those responsible should at least lose their jobs. But they won't. ITV has so much chutzpah, I keep expecting Kate Thornton to pop up on the ITN news saying 'If you think premium rates should be axed, phone 0898-666666...calls cost £100 a minute or the soul of your first born.' Phone votes shouldn't be banned. They add to the excitement of popular shows like *I'm A Celebrity...*, but they don't have to be so dear. US shows like *American Idol* use toll-free numbers and there's no reason why our TV shows shouldn't use local rate calls for phone-ins.

8 March Michael Grade is right to say that ITV's copycat TV shows are 'creatively bankrupt.' Saturday nights aside, the ITV schedules are a sorry mix of soap and second-hand formats. Its one thing to nick an idea and do it better (*Dancing On Ice*), and quite another to churn out clueless copies of the BBC originals – see Fortune: Million Pound Give-Away, Bonkers and You Don't Know You're Born. ITV comedies like *Benidorm* (good) and *The Abbey* (ropey) have the feel of BBC3 or C4 shows, with viewing figures to match. If Grade wants his network to flourish once more he'd be better off looking at the kind of unique programmes ITV once made and steal from them. Better to emulate *Minder* or *The Sweeney* than Trinny and ruddy Susannah. Not to mention *Widows*, *The Avengers*, *On The Buses*, *The Comedians*, and *The Prisoner* – arguably Uncle Lou's finest hour.

9 March Patrick Mercer, the Tory MP for Newark has been forced to resign from David Cameron's Shadow Cabinet for speaking frankly about army life. Mercer, decorated for his own military service, said that under-achieving recruits from ethnic minorities would be abused by sergeants – just like everyone else. 'That's the way it is in the Army,' he said. 'If someone is slow on the assault course, you'd get people shouting: 'Come on you fat ****, come on you ginger ****, come on you black ****.' Patrick Mercer is not a racist; nor was he advocating racism. (Black soldier Owen Lewis describes Mercer as 'the finest Colonel I ever served under.') He was merely pointing out that NCOs target slackers and will find anything about their physical appearance to bully them along – something that anyone who watched *Bad Lads Army* knew already. The effect is to make or break. It's brutal but it works. Maybe Cameron thinks good soldiers can be made with hugs, empathy and a daily reading from the *Guardian*. It says a lot about today's Non-Conservative Party that they'd make a good man leave for telling the truth.

• Great C4 documentary on global warming swindle last night. Backed by an impressive array of experts, Martin Durkin argued persuasively that temperatures are rising because of solar activity, not carbon emissions. Al Gore's *An Inconvenient Truth* turns out to be more like a convenient springboard to career-resuscitation. See Bjorn Lomborg's website www.lomborg.com for honest, sceptical environmentalism.

16 March Red Nose Day. Even more irritating than the great green swindle for three main reasons: 1) Only about a fifth of it is funny. 2) It avoids Africa's real problem: bad government. 3) It brought back Kate Thornton, a woman whose broadcasting career is more mysterious than the Turin Shroud. She's like a vacuum with nipples. Over the past four decades Africa has received more foreign aid in real terms than the Marshall Plan – most of it swallowed up by civil wars and corrupt politicians. Real change in Africa can only begin in Africa. People are saying how sporting it was of Tony Blair to appear with Catherine Tate doing her 'Am I bovvered?' line. But I'd like to know why Tone doesn't seem bovvered about Zimbabwe. Blair could do more for Africa by speaking out against that evil genocidal maniac Robert Mugabe than appearing in a comedy skit. Sending our troops to Iraq and

Afghanistan, Blair said he would 'confront evil wherever he found it.' Yet he doesn't seem to see it in this former British colony where opposition politicians are beaten up and murdered, torture and false imprisonment are widespread, and farmers with names like Smith, Brown and Thomas are being killed and robbed for the 'crime' of being white. At the very least, Tone should be spearheading a moral crusade against this tyrant.

Hot on Red Nose Day: Harry Hill, Ricky Gervais, Peter Kay and the firing of Piers Morgan. Rot: the never-funny Davina, Chris Evans, Dibley, Moyles and the honking squawking cacophony of *Fame Academy*. Never mind a red nose, I'd pay £50 to see someone give Richard Park a black eye.

18 March I lost my talk radio virginity tonight, standing in for George Galloway on Talk-SPORT. Not sure what I was standing in, but it smelt like it had come out of the wrong end of a goat. I'm not getting cash for this – I'm expecting to get paid in virgins. I think 72 is the going rate. Knowing my luck they'll all look like Bela Emberg. I was quite touched that old showbiz pals like Billy Murray and Bobby Ball bothered to ring in. And you might have heard my jaw hit the floor when 'Shirley from Marylebone' came on – it was my old arch-enemy Wendy Richard. Thanks to everyone who called up. Even the cretinous Scot who thought being English in itself was 'racist'. Great logic. It was Scottish emigrants who founded the KKK.

22 March Dropped in to Filthy McNasty's by the Angel for their punk posters exhibition. The place is blitzed with memories: vintage flyers from early Clash, Jam, Buzzcocks and Pistols gigs and tours. Spizz performed and the soundtrack pogoed from X-Ray Spex to ATV. Punk's past recycled as nostalgia. Some of the posters were selling for £1K a pop. Propping up the bar was Steve Connolly, once known as Roadent, who I hadn't seen since a Clash rehearsal room back in 1978. 'If I'd known then how much these posters would be worth...,' he said. Tell me about it. Incidentally, there's now a very rare Gonads US tour poster available with a buy-it-now price of £500, no questions asked.

23 March Fifteen British servicemen have been kidnapped by the Iranians. So far there's been a deafening silence from Tony Blair. Words would be a start, but action is what is needed here. Think 'What would Nelson do?' and do it, pronto.

25 March Here we go again. Now we're told that the British people should apologise for the slave trade. Why? Of course slavery was appalling and shameful but let's not try to pretend the British invented it. Our own people were enslaved by the Romans two thousand years ago. The Arabs were running the African slave trade for centuries before any Westerner was involved and they carried on doing it well into the last century.

Slavery has been practised by all races throughout history. The British slave traffickers of the 18th century traded goods for slaves who were supplied by black Africans – principally the Ashanti tribe. Instead of beating ourselves up about that, we should celebrate the fact that English evangelists successfully campaigned to abolish the Atlantic slave trade and the Royal

Navy sank it. England abolished slavery nearly fifty years before the Yanks and more than 100 years before China.

This demand for saying sorry about the sins of the past, real or imagined, is just another method, devised by the far Left, of trying to make us feel bad about ourselves and our country. And if there's any apologising to be done let's start with the aristocracy and British politicians apologising to the working class of this country for centuries of exploitation and misrule. How about saying sorry to us because of the way our forefathers were forced up chimneys and into the workhouse? It was only a few hundred years ago that the English poor were forced into servitude – or villeinage as it was then known. This mad new cult of apology is all about self-loathing. Well I don't loathe our country or my ancestors I loathe the useless class of politicians who have misgoverned us and lived off the fat of the land for the last sixty years. How about having Blair, his grasping wife and his pack of gutless cronies saying sorry to the British people for making a mockery of democracy in this country?

- Why has it taken two days for Tony Blair to condemn the Iranian kidnapping of fifteen British naval personnel? It was 'unjustified and wrong' on Friday when it happened. It's likely that the Iranians are just baring their teeth and posturing like they did in 2004. But the swift dispatch of a gun-boat would let them know how seriously we take the wrongful abduction of our people. Our ambassador to Iran looks like a smirking Marcus Brigstocke clone. Is he capable of letting Ahmadinejad know how angry the kidnapping has made us? The very least we should do is intensify sanctions. The Iranians have been arming insurgents in Southern Iraq and violating Iraqi waters. They no doubt see us as weak and unwilling to add a further dimension to Bush and Blair's Middle East misadventures. We must leave them in no doubt of our seriousness and our ability to protect our people.

27 March Day five of the new Iranian hostage crisis. What the hell is the Foreign Office doing? Fifteen British sailors and Marines are being held illegally by the Iranians. Instead of 'monitoring the situation' and having 'businesslike' meetings, our officials should give Tehran an immediate deadline for the safe return of our servicemen – and leave them in no doubt of the severity of our response if they are not released on time and unharmed.

28 March I recorded my latest Total Rock podcast today with the help of Rhoda Dakar and Beki Bondage, two of the rudest women in rock. Me, Beki and Rhoda trapped in a hot Soho garret for 90 minutes: 25 years ago that was my wildest dream... and the ending was a little different. Beki wasn't threatening to do me damage with a vegetarian sausage for starters. Anyway, the show includes brand new tracks from Maninblack, the Strawberry Blondes, the Cause, the Cockney Rejects and Rhoda, along with quality numbers from the excellent Skaville UK, The Big, Shibby, Crashed Out, Gripshift, Nobodies Heroes, and Go Jimmy Go.

29 March Finally Iran makes the front pages. In the old *Sun* days, Kelvin MacKenzie would have splashed on this shocking story on Monday. For all his many faults, that old rogue cared more about having a finger on the public pulse than sucking up to our useless ruling elite.

- Available now, the new Shia SatNav system, as used by the Revolutionary Guard. Guarantees to give your position two miles closer to Iran than any rival product.

- I'm addicted to *Kidnapped* on C4, a show with more twists than Quasimodo's braces. Why has it had such a luke-warm reception from TV critics? Probably because most professional reviewers don't watch telly like the public do. It's the same with movie critics who are totally out of touch with filmgoers. Look at the lousy reception 300 has had. This is a great, unpretentious comic book war film about courage with an unfashionable message: it dares to say that war and sacrifice can be noble and can have a point (values that were commonplace a few decades ago.) Critics like the *Sunday Telegraph*'s resident wet feminist panned it. But the movie wasn't made for people like her (and nor incidentally is the *Sunday Telegraph*). Broadsheet reviewing has been colonised by liberals who see everything from a dreary Hampstead viewpoint, while the tabs employ 'celebrity' critics who more often than not don't even bother to see the films themselves. What movie lovers need is a website that appreciates action films and tells it like it is.

30 March Our weakness in the Iran hostage situation is utterly embarrassing. It makes Tony Blair look even more plastic than usual. He struts the globe playing the great statesman but the disturbing truth is that the Iranians have sailed up to our sailors and marines and captured them, confident that we would not retaliate. There was a time when British citizenship guaranteed some protection from foreign persecution. Lord Palmerston famously said that a British subject abroad could feel 'confident the watchful eye and strong arm of England' would protect them from injustice. Now Britain can't respond militarily. Our Armed Forces are chronically over-stretched fighting other people's wars. Budgets have been slashed and squeezed. Millions have been squandered on the useless euro-fighter while our ex-service personnel live in poverty waiting years for injury compensation; it's shocking and humiliating. Our government's talk of diplomatic pressure is a cover for their own weakness and lack of will. We need to move from hand-wringing to the threat of military action, accelerating to actual strikes against military targets and petrol production plants if the Iranians don't release our people unharmed immediately. We may not want to fight but by jingo we had better show our teeth if Britain wishes to retain any status in the world. Who would have thought there would ever come a time when Freddie Flintoff in his pedalo would put up more of a fight than the Royal Navy?

• I-ran, I-raq, I-rate...it sounds like a Latin verb, meaning to steam at the ears. Funny how these mouth-foaming mullahs are all teetotal. Would they be a little less crazy if we dumped a few barrels of navy rum in their water supply?

4

Merry Winterval

Merry Christmas! Are we still allowed to say that? Christmas is on the hit-list for the hard-line thought-police of Political Correctness. In Stoke, neo-fruitcake councillors want to replace Christmas with 'Winterfest'. Brummie nitwits prefer the term 'Winterval'. In Cornwall, the Grinches who run the Eden Project have banned Christmas in favour of celebrating the 'Time of Gifts', while, in Brent, they're talking about banning nativity plays, but that may just be because they're having trouble finding three wise men and a virgin.

More and more councils and businesses send out cards saying 'Happy Holidays' rather than 'Merry Christmas' for fear, they say, of 'causing offence'. It isn't just happening in Britain either. In Italy, town councils are banning public displays of the nativity on the grounds that they 'may offend' Muslims, who may, in turn, declare a fatwa on any passing fat bloke in a Santa suit. And militant atheists in New Jersey have taken legal action to ban not only the singing of carols (including instrumental versions) at schools, but also a planned trip to see Dickens's *A Christmas Carol*. They've even out-Scrooged Scrooge.

The Twelve Days of Christmas are a thing of the past, my friends; we are living through its last days. But why? Well, there may be a reasonable Socialist case to be made against Santa; he exploits those elves and reindeers something shocking. Claus gets all the glory, while the workers – whom he patronisingly describes as his 'little helpers' – get a few raw carrots and a sniff of left-over port. No wonder he's so bloody jolly.

He's also a fake, adapted and adopted by cynical ad men working for Coca-Cola in 1931 to promote their gut-rotting pop. He's jingling those bells all the way, all right – all the way to the bank.

The Health and Safety aspect can't be ignored either. Your turkey has probably got bird 'flu; pouring a tot of brandy on your pudding and setting it alight is clearly a fire hazard on a par with recklessly setting off your own fireworks in your back garden. And don't even think of putting a 5p coin in the pudding – someone could choke.

There's a substantial religious argument to be heard, too, of course. These days, the only 'Christ' in Christmas is likely to be your response to the credit card bill. The Christian bedrock of the holiday is increasingly played down, with Jesus, Mary and Joseph replaced by a new Holy Trinity of Santa, Rudolph and a fat bird throwing up in the back of a mini-cab.

Nowhere in the moving tale of the Messiah's birth is there even a Da Vinci-style coded suggestion that the faithful might properly celebrate by getting legless and photocopying their hairy arses at the office party. (And the men are just as bad.) You never caught the Lamb of God snogging Mary Magdalene under the mistletoe; his disciples never left out mince pies for a tipsy, bearded intruder, erected a moulting tree inside the house or made a last-minute Christmas Eve dash to the corner shop to find the right-sized batteries for an over-priced singing doll that's odds-on to be broken by Boxing Day anyway by their ungrateful, spoilt brat of a child.

Christmas over-indulgence offends the new Puritanism abroad in the nation. All that hedonism, drinking and eating… don't you know how many calories are in a Christmas pud? It's enough to give Gillian McKeith ulcers. And as for all that cash we splash about… Oliver Cromwell must be spinning in his tin.

Rampant commercial exploitation is the curse of modern Christmas. If the virgin birth happened today, it'd be sponsored by Richard Branson, complete with a televised make-over called *Changing Stables*. The Wise Men would have set up a stall down Brick Lane offering a three-for-the-price-of-two deal on gold, frankincense and myrrh.

Christmas should be about family, not profiteering.

And if that were the reason the hard Left of what used to be the people's party opposes the ho-ho-hopelessness of modern festivities, they'd have some kind of a point. But the real motives behind the backlash are more disturbing.

The library at High Wycombe, Bucks, banned posters

for Yuletide celebrations on the grounds that it would be wrong to single out Christian festivals for special treatment. They were then found, days before, to have hosted a party to celebrate Eid, the Muslim knees-up marking the breaking of the fast of Ramadan.

These days, Christian festivals get singled out for special mistreatment. The curtain is falling on school nativity plays all over the country, as Heads do away with the traditional Christmas story for fear of upsetting pupils of other faiths. Only one in five primary schools put on nativities in 2007. A generation of kids will miss out on the heady joys of dressing up as shepherds in old bed sheets.

In 2007, the Health and Safety killjoys stepped up their war on Christmas. In Halesowen, in the West Midlands, Santa was told he had to be belted into his sleigh and go no faster than 5mph or face exorbitant insurance charges. Imagine the fit they'd throw if he went near a chimney.

In Llandudno, north Wales, a security guard and a community cop stopped children singing carols in the shopping precinct on the grounds that were too loud. Children … singing carols! Not playing Motorhead at full pelt, or happy-slapping coffin dodgers to the sweet sounds of grime.

In Windsor, the authorities stopped reindeer pulling Santa's sleigh because all movement of livestock had been banned because of the Blue Tongue outbreak. All together: *'Rudolph the red-nosed reindeer, Has a very scary tongue, Clearly the best place for him, Is inside a burger bun…'*

In Barking, east London, Jesus and Mary have been usurped by a Czech winter play. 'We are an ethnically diverse school,' a spokesman told the *Telegraph*. 'We want to learn about other cultures.' Yes, heaven forefend that kids whose parents have recently arrived from Somalia should learn about ours. So out goes 'Silent Night' and in comes some unfamiliar, joyless dirge.

Why? Because, it is said, our Christmas traditions may offend someone from another religion. In response, the British people would feel perfectly justified in replying 'So what? This is how we do things here and, if you don't like it, go home.' Since when has the right 'not to be offended' become the central plank of British society?

Yet the argument that the nativity offends other religions is spurious old cobblers. I've yet to meet a Sikh, Jew, Hindu or liberal Muslim who objects to British people enjoying British customs in Britain. Jesus is viewed as a prophet in Islam, and his birth is described in the Koran. Besides, if Christian kids in inner-city schools are encouraged to celebrate Diwali as a Hindu festival and Eid as a Muslim one, why shouldn't Hindu and Muslim kids get to see a nativity play? What makes Christmas uniquely undesirable?

The real battlefield is a political one, of course. The middle-class Marxist Left objects to Christmas: a) because it is a Christian tradition, and the one thing they detest more than Christianity is tradition itself; and b) because it represents our shamefully mono-cultural past, when Britain was in a state of darkness. In other words, Christmas is incompatible with the new faith of multi-culturalism.

This well-meaning but wrong-headed creed is built on double-think. Its supporters are intellectually schizophrenic, being fervently opposed to Western values, but gung-ho in favour of minority faiths and loyalties. Therefore – our religion bad, any recently imported religion good; our history bad, any other history good (except, of course, that of the Great Satan, the USA).

The same kind of logic explains why BBC TV idents include colourful dancing Asians, Africans and Latinos but not a single Pearly King, spotty Mod or Yorkshire colliery band. It also explains why my daughter, when she was three years old, came home from nursery school parroting Vietnamese phrases; why Tower Hamlets council in East London axed Bonfire Night in favour of a Bengali tiger procession, effectively including other cultures by abandoning our own; and why the dedicated agitators of the Socialist Workers Party, passionate advocates of gay rights, female emancipation and abortion on demand, are happy to link arms with the extremely illiberal Muslim Association of Britain. Incredibly, some on the Left believe that al-Qaeda's medieval 'holy war against infidels' must be intrinsically 'progressive' because their enemy is Western civilisation and the West is automatically the oppressor.

This cultural self-loathing is growing like a cancerous tumour and, naturally, the BBC play their part in the war on Christmas by ensuring that the festive episode of *EastEnders* is the most miserable of the year. Good will to all men? Bollocks to that! Let's have Peggy Mitchell smashing up the Vic with a baseball bat. In Albert Square, the big question is shall we hang the holly, or hang ourselves?

It isn't merely a case of liberal politeness gone potty or the guilt-driven need to 'apologise' for the imagined sins of empire. We are facing folk set on undermining everything British people hold dear. As Alexander Solzhenitsyn once observed, 'To destroy a people, you must first sever their roots.'

Clever Marxists, having failed to win power by the ballot box, have been successfully subverting the institutions for decades. In schools and universities, British history is ignored or derided, while Western achievements are written off as the work of the dreaded 'dead white males', many of them British. 'Who controls the past controls the future,' wrote Orwell in *1984*. 'Who controls the present controls the past.'

We could, of course, roll over and agree to see our traditions as reactionary and out-dated, turn our backs on all Anglo-Saxon, Christian-based customs and hand over our redundant turkey-basters to the nearest lesbian artificial insemination collective. We could try and cut a deal with them: let us celebrate Christmas and we'll agree to pretend that you didn't make up Kwanzaa. We could do what we Brits always do, ignore the meddling pests and carry on doing things our way until something better comes along.

Or we could fight back at every level – cultural, political, ideological and financial. Boycott any firm that wishes us 'Happy Holidays', bling up your house and maybe do something even more extraordinary – pop along to church and join in the carol service with gusto, not forgetting to sling some shrapnel in the collecting tin. Hallelujah, Noel, be it Heaven or Hell, the Christmas we get, we deserve.

The World According to Garry Bushell

Top Five Ways To Celebrate A Modern Christmas in London

- In Soho. Prancer, Donna, Vixen and Blitzen are available to be petted for a small fee. They're lap-dancers employed by Santa's love-child, Peter Stringfellow.
- In Peckham. Those after-dinner bangs may not be crackers thanks to Frosty The Hit Man. In South London, Santa's sleigh is armoured.
- On Hampstead Heath. Tread gingerly, unless you want to come across two blokes in turkey suits stuffing each other.
- In Hackney. Jacob Marley can be found with his brother Bob sleeping off the ghost of ganja past.
- In Knightsbridge. Jack Frost will be happy to nip at your nose. He's a cosmetic surgeon specialising in rhinoplasty. A snip at £5,000...

Genuine Christmas Gifts on Sale in December 2007

- Jesus on a Harley Davidson
- 'Thongs of Praise' – skimpy undies packaged with a picture of the Madonna and child on the front)
- The Pope's Cologne – allegedly based on a formula favoured by Pious IX with subtle hints of violet and citrus
- A hip-flask Bible
- A 'Holy Toast' stamp that imprints an image of the Virgin Mary on your bread before you pop it in the toaster. Merry Kitschmas!

5

A-Haunting We
Will Go

When it comes to the afterlife, I'm strictly agnostic. I don't believe ghosts exist, but I'm open-minded about it. So when the call came through from my agent for me to appear on *I'm Famous and Frightened*, spending a weekend at Chillingham Castle, which is said to be haunted by distinguished royals, I was intrigued enough to go along for the ride.

Why? To confront the unknown, conquer my fear and find out how much of *Sunday Sport* legend Linsey Dawn McKenzie goes goose-pimply when she's scared. And if Anne Boleyn fancied popping round to my boudoir one night for an out-of-bodice experience, I'd be prepared to give it a go. The flesh would be willing even if the spirits were weak.

And, of course, the fat fee helped.

So we trekked up to the allegedly haunted castle in Northumberland, near the Scottish border. We were told that it was going to be like *I'm A Celebrity...Get Me Out Of Here!* with the snakes and creepy-crawlies replaced in theory by spooks and heebie-jeebies. We would be confronting the unknown, with the help of a platoon of 'psychics', fortune tellers and a phalanx of Living TV people. (Why are so many shows about dead people on a channel called Living by the way?)

The most frequently appearing spectres at Chillingham are said to be the Blue Boy, John Sage, a former torturer and Lady Mary Berkeley – none of whom would have been half as scary as the show's self-appointed star Julie Goodyear. The former *Coronation Street* legend is famous for: a) playing Bet Lynch; and b) for her varied love-life, prompting me at one time to dub her the 'Each Way Bet' – she never forgave me. Julie kept aloof from the rest of us, who were the expected mix of faded celebs, a sitcom actress and several wannabes: Linda Robson, Keith Chegwin, Cheryl Baker, Toby Anstis, Terry Nutkins and the aforementioned fabulous floozy Linsey Dawn McKenzie, a retired lap-dancer who is an all-natural 34GGG.

We were contracted to spend three days and three nights here. I told Linsey that she'd know the spirits were real if she woke up to find two white fivers and a groat tucked in her garter. Not for the last time, she hit me. We all approached the weekend challenge in the spirit of sceptical fun, except for Julie, who was clearly determined that if one thing was raised from the dead at Chillingham it would be her TV career.

Lo and behold, she breezed to victory with her amazing psychic insights. She was Julie Good-Seer... or so it appeared. It would be churlish to suggest that the former soap star was faking it, but consider this. On our first night, four celebs were sent to investigate the Grey Room, apparently haunted by the spirit of Lady Berkeley. En route, walking across the courtyard and unaware her words were being broadcast live on TV, Julie told Chegwin, 'I'll you what, Keith, I hope Lady Mary smokes.'

Three minutes later, she stood before her portrait, her brow furrowed in a mix of concentration and ham anguish. Finally, Julie spoke. 'Mary,' she said. 'Am I right? I feel Mary.' Presenter Tim Vincent confirmed that Lady Berkeley was indeed a Mary and Julie's premonition was immediately trumpeted as proof of her mystic powers. But everyone watching the show at home knew that she already knew the name. She is about as psychic as Stan Ogden's Y-fronts.

Julie later starred in a séance where she was contacted by the spirit of Pat Phoenix who conveniently advised her to go back to *Corrie*.

Do I sound cynical? I didn't set out to be; I went along with an open mind but the only spirit to possess me came out of Cheryl Baker's Smirnoff bottle. Nothing supernatural happened there – despite laughable 'evidence' served up by the production team. These included the noises made by burning wood, cold feelings in the courtyard – we were outside, for God's sake! – and 'orbs', small glows said to be early signs of spirit activity, which were clearly insects caught in the TV lights. The only orbs on display at the castle were the ones bursting out of Linsey's skimpy tops.

Brave LDM spent a night alone in the castle's apparently haunted Pink Room, where something clearly put the willies up her. Insert your own joke here.

I was the first to be evicted. I'd spent more than a day there, felt nothing, and my cynicism clearly wound up the home viewers. But the show was full of moments of unintentional hilarity, such as self-styled medium Ian Lawman who was 'possessed' in the courtyard and later claimed to have had an unlikely encounter with the ghost of Henry VIII.

'Would Henry VIII turn up for Living TV?' asked a gob-smacked Cheryl Baker. Of course not, he'd be on Men and Motors.

Nothing that happened that weekend suggested that Chillingham had any supernatural presence; it was hokum, plain and simple. And every day something happened that underlined the gullibility of those who take it seriously. One of the TV mediums claimed to feel the pain of tortured spirits in the dungeon area, but a bit of research quickly established that the dungeon wasn't a real gaol at all; it was a bit of 'gritty atmosphere' built for the tourist trade. We were actually standing in what had been the castle's stables.

The worst aspect of the entire enterprise was the live ouija board, ill-judged in an entertainment show. The glass moved eerily to spell out a message: WQ2SW... so either the ghost was dyslexic, or Polish.

Maybe I'm a sucker for punishment, but I also appeared on *Mystic Challenge* where a pretty blonde psychic made her début. The producers had high hopes for her sustaining a lengthy TV career. Unfortunately, it all went pear-shaped when she attempted to identify a hooded man by touch alone. She decided the powerfully-built geezer was an athlete, a footballer in fact; she 'saw' him in a red shirt, 'the red shirt of Man United' she decided. It turned out the guy was a one-legged stuntman. D'oh!

Years later, we're still chasing spirits on TV. It's medieval. On *Most Haunted*, Yvette Fielding and her team of 'psychics' claimed they were being stalked by a one-eyed man. Was it Gordon Brown? Cos if any of these places actually were haunted, you can bet your life he'd slap a ghost tax on 'em.

Strangely, the spooks never turn up on camera. They must be awfully shy…

Former *Blue Peter* star Yvette has become a millionaire through paranormal television. Her company, Antix Productions, has churned out hours of this guff for Living TV since 2002 with nothing concrete to show for it. All we ever see are 'orbs' – insects, to you and me. Sometimes, stones are mysteriously thrown (by the production team?), and people have cold feelings – surprising that, in old, unheated buildings. There are séances, always in the dark for maximum effect, and the table is banged or shaken; but you never have locked-off cameras above and below showing everyone's hands (knock twice for a tea break …). Yet that doesn't stop the opening voice-over from promising 'poltergeists, deaths and military phantoms'.

Like a herpes sore, *Most Haunted* keeps coming back – even though one of Yvette's own team exposed it. Parapsychologist Ciaran O'Keefe conned television medium Derek Acorah by feeding him the names of invented dead people. The ghosts of Kreed Kafir, Rik

Eedles and Ged Harken – anagrams of 'Derek Faker', 'Derek Lies' and 'Hang Derek' – duly possessed Mr Acorah, a former Liverpool FC reserve. He was subsequently rumbled and has since departed to be replaced by a chunky female medium called Johnnie Firori.

In one show, Yvette and her team, which includes her husband, visited Coalhouse Fort in Essex, 'a claustrophobic warren of paranormal activity' (translation: it had underground tunnels). Frankly, I've been to a Travelodge that looked more frightening, but never mind. Here, Yvette had a conversation with a blinking light. 'They're learning to communicate,' she deduced. Yeah, either that or it was an electrical fault. At one point, the team claimed to smell something like sulphur. Don't worry, chaps – it's only the bullshit.

Johnnie said the fort was haunted by pirates, even though it stands on the site of a military blockhouse built by Henry VIII in 1540. If there were any genuine 'brigands' here, she would have wobbled out faster than you can say 'Who ate all the ectoplasm?'

So what, you might say, it's just harmless hogwash. What's the big deal? The truth of the matter is, there is an entire industry of fake mediums out there preying on the vulnerable and the grieving. And, all right, I'll admit that some psychics bring comfort to the bereaved and some, like Gordon Smith, Glasgow's psychic barber, seem amazingly accurate. But many are sharks.

John Edward on US show *Crossing Over* is a medium who uses the old magician's cold-reading technique to bamboozle his audience.

'Has anyone lost someone?' he asks. Of course they have – that's why they're there! Edward uses a scattergun approach, also employed by Mary, the medium featured on BBC2's *Everyman* investigation. You sling out snippets of information – names, initials or other clues – and hope enough of it clicks with some mug in the audience. If any hiccups occur, you fast-talk your way out of it.

Psychic 'expert': 'I'm getting an M.'
Distressed wife: 'His name was Jack Puttock.'
Psychic 'expert': '*Mister* Jack Puttock... I'm sensing he died of natural causes... '
Distressed wife: 'He was run down by a tram on Blackpool prom.'
Psychic 'expert': 'So naturally he's dead... '

Back in 1922, a medium in Atlantic City claimed to have made contact with Harry Houdini's mother, Celia Weiss. Her spirit came through and started talking in fluent English. Houdini was amazed as his mum had only ever spoken Yiddish. When he pointed this out, the medium curtly informed him that, in Heaven, everyone speaks English.

Cold-readers often repeat back information their 'mark' – or gullible victim – has already given them, making it sound as if the info is coming from 'the other side'. Believers remember the bits that work for them and forget the stuff that doesn't. But surely, if the spirits could talk to us, they'd have more to say than how much they liked biscuits, or that you need a new carpet. It's a national disgrace that we still broadcast this garbage.

- Jennifer Love Hewitt is the Ghost Whisperer, the best-looking psychic on TV. Is it any wonder spirits are attracted to her? That body alone could raise the dead.

Bushell on the Blog
April 2007

3 April A French high-speed train has smashed the world record for a train on conventional rails, reaching 356mph. In a related story, a buffet car operated by Connex South East also broke a world record – by running out of cheese sandwiches within two minutes of leaving Folkestone.

4 April Live Earth...brought to you by the people who ended famine and world poverty...

5 April Our boys (and girl) are back and safe, and for that thank God. But what's the deal with those suits? Talk about Iran at C&A! They're not so much Top Gun as Top Man. Come to think of it, Saddam's suits never hung well either. Well, not as well as he did... The real reason Iran released our servicemen? They heard Davina was coming over to host a Friday night eviction.

8 April The Ministry of Defence is letting our sailors and marines held hostage in Iran sell their stories. Doesn't this stink? Firstly it's shocking that the MoD is comparing the captives to Victoria Cross heroes. And secondly it's an obvious smoke-screen. The government think their sob stories will distract us from asking tough questions, like how the crisis happened and who is to blame.

The MoD has changed the rules because of 'exceptional circumstances.' I'd say there were exceptional circumstances all right – the appalling way our people were allowed to be captured, and then were used as propaganda by the Iranians, ending up looking like ushers at a bad wedding in cheap whistles. Why should they profit from this disaster? The message it sends out is a bad one: do your job wrong and get caught and you'll make more money than if you do it right and get injured serving your country. It's absurd. Of course I'm relieved our people are safe. But should they really be rewarded for getting caught? I'm dismayed by the way this humiliating story has unfolded. Why weren't our military personnel trained to just give name, rank and serial number? Why are they forced to work under UN ridiculous rules of engagement which mean they can't ever fire first? The new drill seems to be surrender first, apologise later and make a mint selling your story – as if you'd just come out of *Big Brother*. It's inappropriate – and particularly distasteful after a week when six more of our soldiers have been slaughtered needlessly in Iraq. Their families aren't selling stories. The British bulldog has been castrated on the world stage. The defence secretary should fall on his sword, and the commanding officers should face an inquiry at the very least. As for the money being made from the sale of these stories, surely most of it should go to forces charities.

- It used to be a wife in every port. With today's Royal Navy it's a literary agent.

9 April Idiots still claim our marines and sailors were in Iran's territorial waters when they were taken hostage. These people hate this country so much that if Iran claimed the boat race had been in Iranian waters they'd believe them.

- For reasons that defy all reason, some lunatic has started an on-line petition calling on the BBC to make me the 14th Doctor Who (http://www.petitiononline.com/14drgal/petition.html). This is bizarre. However, if it gets me closer to Martha Jones I'm backing it to the hilt.

10 April What a shame to see Richard Littlejohn calling Faye Turney, 'Tugboat' Turney. I didn't agree with the way the MoD handled the hostages' stories but this personal abuse was uncalled for. What has she done to deserve that? Besides, the last time I saw Rich he was the size of the Woolwich Ferry.

- On tonight's *EastEnders*, grandad Jim went to a lap-dancing club in Dartford, Kent, where he was charged £112 for a pint of flat lager and two glasses of cheap bubbly. This sort of scam operated in Soho to fleece tourists years ago, but Dartford? You don't get tourists in Dartford, or lap-dancing clubs. The nearest one is through the tunnel in Purfleet where it's a tenner a dance. Besides, the women in Dartford High Street wear fewer clothes than that did in that club.

13 April Scientists have discovered an obesity gene...not to be confused with Lenny Henry's missus. She's obesity Dawn...

14 April *The Mark of Cain* was a searing drama by the playwright Tony Marchant which appeared to be based on those completely discredited, faked pictures published by Piers Morgan in the *Daily Mirror*. This was a docu-drama – in other words weasel TV. The docu-drama wants it both ways. It's a work of fiction that looks real and claims to be 'based on extensive research' but so many viewers will perceive it to be a work of fact. It showed Iraqi detainees abused by British soldiers and our squaddies being bullied and beaten by their comrades. It has already been screened in the Middle East and is likely to result in yet more British deaths, courtesy of C4. Of course the Army has its share of sadists and abusers – like every other section of society. No one is pretending otherwise. But the Army also has many more men and women who are professionals. We do not see plays on TV about those servicemen who do their duty, who step up to the mark and give their all in the service of their country – 106 have died so far in the sickening mess that is Iraq while the politicians who lied to send them there strut the world stage and look forward to lucrative publishing deals. We don't see many plays about our Army heroes either. The BBC, another state-backed broadcaster, has just axed a drama based on the true bravery of Johnson Beharry, whose two acts of outstanding gallantry earned him the Victoria Cross in 2005. They axed it because it showed the conflict in 'too positive' a light. WHY do the people who run the BBC and C4 have a problem in showing a British soldier in a positive light when they are quick to screen plays that do the opposite? Why do they seem to hate our country, our troops and our values so much? Could it be that the rather superior types who run British TV are out of step with the rest of the country? Is it harsh to conclude that a percentage of them are self-loathing, middle-class traitors who lack 'moral clarity' far more than our armed forces do? I'm not calling for censorship, but a bit of balance would be welcome. *The Mark of Cain* had some partial truth. To claim it showed the whole picture is sickeningly irresponsible.

15 April I went along to the filming of a new rock show today. Club Chaos featured an array of great young bands, including the Fallen, the excellent Koopa and Blackpool punkettes Pink Hearse whose singer had a touch of the Siouxsie about her. Goth-glam shock rock band Spit Like This – great image, so-so songs, and a real stage presence. They made me nostalgic for my old *Sounds* days. Back then, if I'd seen a band this enjoyably outrageous they'd have been reviewed within the week and Vikki Spit would have been on the cover a month or so later. Happy days...

16 April What a beautiful day. 75 and sunny. Just like Camilla. It seems a shame to spoil it by talking about paedophiles on the radio. Sarah's Law wouldn't be an issue if these sickoes were dealt with properly by the courts in the first place

- William and Kate are over. It's the biggest Royal split since Fergie tried on Diana's Bellville Sassoon blue-and-white going-away number. Poor Kate Middleton. She'll hesitate before kissing her next frog, just in case he has commitment problems. The worst aspect of this story is the snobbery. Bloated weasel James Whittaker says Kate 'didn't have the breeding' to make a Royal. (Did Fergie?) The evidence: Kate's Mum chewed gum in front of the Queen. Larks a mercy. Off with her head. Isn't it more likely that the Palace pressurised the Prince after Kate went running to the PCC?

  Kate's better off in the long run. That girl was getting popular. Better to end it now than a few years and a couple of kids down the line. The world's not ready for another race through Paris with a drunk driver...

17 April Bryan Ferry is in heiss wasser over some innocuous remarks about Nazi art. (Cue new Roxy Music discography: Hess Is The Drug, Eva Plain, Pyjamaryan, All I Want Is You...And a 1,000 Year Reich.) Isn't this nuts? Ferry was saying that the films of Leni Riefenstahl and the buildings of Albert Speer were stunning, not that he endorsed Hitler's odious politics. Odd that no-one raises an eyeball when bands and performers use the iconography of repressive Communist regimes. Do the deaths of people killed by Stalinists mean less than those butchered by National Socialists? If everyone who preferred Breker's sculptures to Henry Moore's eyesores was forced to apologise we'd be here until doomsday.

22 April Sandra Aitken rang in to my TalkSPORT show, with Mark Wyeth of Foxy's Ruts, to say that the plaque for Laurel Aitken, RIP, has been successfully erected on the great man's old Leicester council house. Great to hear too, that 15,000 turned up for unofficial St George's Day parade in the Midlands.

23 April Happy St George's Day. We had a party for St Geo on TalkSPORT last night. Thanks to all who rang in, especially Jethro and Sandra Aitken. The arguments against the English celebrating St George's Day become increasingly perverse. One malignant Scot caller claimed that the red in the cross of St George is a symbol of bloody slaughter. This is an argument that could be made against virtually any national flag – but isn't. The French Revolution, for example, came with a price tag of two million deaths. The Irish tricolour could be linked to terror, co-operation with the Nazis, and widespread paedophilia within the Catholic Church. And oddly, those who moan about English patriotism go strangely quiet when the crimes of Communism are mentioned. The legacy of Marxism-Leninism is more than 100million deaths. The self-loathing of the hard Left gives succour to the far Right, suppression of honest patriotism fuels less benign forms of nationalism. There is nothing wrong with loving your country, and nothing wrong with the English having one day a year when we can celebrate the great things our people have achieved.

- Raw sewage has been pumping into the filthy Firth of Forth for two days. Does this explain why so many Scottish callers to my radio show are full of crap? Millions of gallons of waste – it's like Gillian McKeith The Movie. PS. If you're eating out north of the border, avoid the brown trout...

25 April The despicable Tory Euro-traitor Ted Heath has been accused of propositioning men for sex. And there was me thinking he was called Hamsptead Heath because of his teeth...If Ted was gay, it must have helped that he had such a tight inner circle. Those guys in his cabinet bent over backwards for him. So was Ted the first Tory to hug a hoodie? Did he put the gross in Grocer? And how safe was his seat? I've no idea but at least we now know why he encouraged all those black-outs...Ted brought in the three-day week, no prizes for guessing what he got up to on the other four...The unfortunate consequence of all this is that our future PM became EEC-positive. His condition degenerated in to full-blown EU mania before his death.

26 April An 'Earth-like' planet has been found 20 light years away called 581C. What kind of name is that for a planet? It sounds more like a Docklands apartment. Here's how earth-like it is: it already has the council tax, a congestion charge and a Simon Cowell TV show.

28 April Tory MP Iain Dale says the 'fanciability factor' matters when people decide who to vote for. Well it certainly explains why Ann Widdecombe keeps getting elected

29 April The new *Sunday Times* Rich List shows that the gap between rich and poor is now at its greatest since 1886. I'm puzzled by the Sky News claim that it shows 'a huge leap in British billionaires.' Most of the Top Ten are foreign nationals who live here because they pay no tax to do so, other than council tax. At number one is Indian born steel baron Lakshmi Mittal. This bloke is so loaded that his dog is at number five. London is now one of the best places in the world to avoid tax legally. We've become a haven for super-rich parasites. Is that something to be proud of?

6

Don't Get Fooled Again

'A single death is a tragedy, a million
deaths is a statistic.'
Joseph Stalin

'If Left is right, then Right is wrong,' said Tom Robinson.
Nice one, Einstein. But for Tom and thousands like him,
that 'if' was redundant. For decades, there has been an in-
built assumption among the great and good that the Left
have right on their side.

The belief is hard-wired into Socialist brains. Unlike the
craven Tories, who are busy feathering their own nests, the
political Left are the good guys – rebels with a cause. The
Left are for the people and for progress; they are, by self-
definition, 'progressive'. They're fighting for change, for
social justice and for a better life for the working class.

French scholars estimate that the great Communist
experiment of the 20th century came with a price tag of
100 million corpses. But it doesn't seem to matter how
many are murdered and tortured, how many promises are
broken, or how many Socialist icons turn out to have feet
of clay. From Joe Stalin to Gerry Healy, the Left make

heroes of despicable creeps. And even when their crimes are discovered, it never shakes the conviction that Communism was 'less evil' than Nazism. The belief corrupts our thinking, lingering on like a bad smell. The stench of death...

Ernesto Guevara de la Serna (Che Guevara) was a psychopath, yet he remains a perennial emblem of cool. The stalls of trendy Camden Market are still blitzed with his Christ-like image. Silver-tongued Galloway kissed the backside of genocidal mass murderer Saddam Hussein but, hey, he's anti-war, so let's make him a celebrity. Stalin – Uncle Joe! – slaughtered millions more people in the cold light of peace than Hitler did in the hot furnace of war, yet there are no special anniversaries to remember the crimes of Communism.

The Russian Revolution was a disastrous failure, a hell on earth distinguished by repression, corruption and inefficiency. But take a trip to Tate Modern and you'll find an exhibition devoted to Soviet realism. (Try putting on an exhibition of the iconic sculptures of Arno Breker and see how long your gallery stays in business.) The Gulags, show trials and mass executions are apparently of little significance. In Lithuania, they've got a Stalin theme park! It must have the world's longest ghost train.

The Chinese Revolution was even more blood-stained; Jung Chang has detailed all of Chairman Mao's murderous deeds, yet Tony Benn called him 'the greatest man of the 20th century'.

You will never see a BBC4 documentary on former Mosleyites with the same uncritical tone as their nostalgic

2006 series *Lefties*. If a Nazi sympathiser was discovered working at the Beeb he would be hounded out of a job, but there are never any protests when leading Marxists occupy positions inside the Corporation, or in schools and universities. Socialism gets the benefit of the doubt because its intentions are good.

What was that about the road to hell again?

Keyser Söze, the mythical master criminal in *The Usual Suspects*, said the greatest trick the Devil ever played was to convince the world he doesn't exist. The greatest trick the Hard Left has pulled off is to paint itself as a benign force for good, and I say this as a former hard-line Trotskyist who spent years campaigning for the cause – a cause I no longer believe in.

The simple truth is Socialism hasn't worked, doesn't work and can't work. Socialists do not have a monopoly on sense, compassion or moral superiority, and the human animal is not perfectible. Living standards and literacy can improve, but human nature never changes. We are what we are; we have to learn to deal with it, but it took me decades to work that out.

When I was a kid, I was naturally of the Left. I'd grown up in a solid Labour, south London household. Mum, Dad, Nan and Grandad all voted Labour; Grandad, a painter and decorator, was in the TGWU. Dad was a fireman, and a member of the Fire Brigade Union. Nan had lost the fingers on her right hand in an industrial accident; the Union had fought her case and won. We were Labour through and through, except for my favourite uncle, Sam – he was a Communist. So almost inevitably I became a teenage street-fighter, battling the cops and later the National Front on demos and protests. From Red Lion Square to Grunwicks, I was there. It didn't matter that we frequently broke the law, because we were on the side of the angels; we were the people, we were strong and we were righteous.

Impatient for change, at eighteen I joined the International Socialists, which had quite a few dock workers in their East London branch (not to mention the stunning actress Carol Harrison, later of *EastEnders* fame). After some illegal fly-pitching, we descended on a friendly East End pub for a beer. One old dear made the mistake of playing 'Una Paloma Blanca' on the juke-box. The dockers went nuts; one of them, a hulking great bloke, single-handedly picked up that big heavy machine and dropped it, wrecking it in the process. Not because it was a crap, throw-away ditty sung by the not-then-disgraced Jonathan King, but as a protest against the detested Generalissimo Franco. Any song that made Spain sound like a cool place was unconsciously bolstering the fascist Government. How we cheered. The publican who objected was dismissed as a bit of a Paloma Blanca himself.

In the fight against fascism, small things like personal property, were insignificant; to worry about them was bourgeois. If we saw the National Front, we attacked them. If they were holding a lawful meeting, we would try our damnedest to smash it up. In a democracy, all views are valid, but ours were more valid than theirs.

And we didn't stop with the far Right either. Pretty much everyone from the right of the Labour Party to Enoch

Powell via Conservative professors were denounced as 'fascists', condemned and, as often as possible, silenced. We fought in the name of tolerance, our hearts beating with moral certainty and our eyes ablaze with pure hatred. You might wonder who the real fascists were.

The International Socialists were a small Trotskyist sect but they appealed to me because they had a credible explanation for why Socialism had failed. At school, we'd got in trouble for distributing Chairman Mao's *Little Red Book* but, after Soviet tanks had rolled into Czechoslovakia, even as kids we could see that the Stalinist States weren't the bastions of progress that they were made out to be in the *Morning Star*. Other Trot sects like the Socialist Labour League (later the Workers Revolutionary Party) were stuck in the 1930s.

The International Socialists had developed their Marxism to make sense of the post-war world. Their analysis saw the Soviet countries as 'state capitalist' not Socialist or deformed workers' States, and they argued that the West's 'permanent war economy' was keeping the capitalist depression at bay. (The Socialist Labour League believed that the next big slump had been imminent since 1945 and was still likely to happen next week, if not sooner.) The IS slogan was: 'Neither Washington nor Moscow but International Socialism.' A plague on both their houses.

Above all, what impressed me about them was their humanity. I ended up doing my journalistic training on the *Socialist Worker*, alongside people like Paul Foot, a funny and passionate man, and Laurie Flynn, a fine investigative reporter. Some of the comrades were strange; Chris Harman, a hugely intelligent man and the party's leading intellectual, once left his own baby in a hold-all under the table at a political meeting; but their leader, Tony Cliff (Ygael Gluckstein), was a tremendous public speaker, unblemished by the kind of sex scandals that dogged SLL leader and serial rapist Gerry Healy.

It took a while for my feeling of affinity with the IS to wear off. The first real crisis of conscience came in 1974, when the IRA planted a bomb in the King's Arms pub in Woolwich, murdering two men – a sales clerk and an army gunner. Selling *Socialist Worker* in Woolwich that Saturday, I was approached by a middle-aged woman who sneered, 'Still support the IRA now, do ya?' I had nothing to say to her, because I never did. I didn't believe terror could ever be justified in a democratic society.

That same month, four people were killed and fifty injured by bombs in Guildford, and twenty-one youngsters were slaughtered in two Birmingham pubs. These weren't military targets; the bombers were hitting the English working class. The IS position of supporting the terrorists 'critically but unconditionally' suddenly seemed like shocking nonsense. What do you say to some teenage car mechanic with half of his leg blown off? 'We're critical of how this happened, mate, but we still support the bastards who did it unconditionally; come and join us on the next Troops Out march... bring your wheelchair – I'll push'?

Our support for the Paedophile Information Exchange disturbed me, too. IS activists were sent to protect these child-molesting perverts from local East London parents who were protesting outside their meeting. My sympathies were entirely with the parents.

Other niggling doubts started to trouble me, like the growing self-delusion and lack of democracy in the organisation. The big change came at the 1975 Conference. Faced with an internal challenge, the leadership just changed the rules and turned itself into a self-perpetuating clique. From that day on, the membership were effectively excluded from changing party policy. This was justified as 'democratic centralism', as practised by the Bolsheviks in 1917. It occurred to quite a few of us that there were major differences between a party about to engage in armed revolution in Tsarist Russia, and a few thousand lefties in Great Britain under a Labour Government.

The same democratic centralism was used as a ruse to expel dissidents and forbid factions. It was all centre and no democracy. You might wonder how liberating this revolution could possibly be if its first requirement was the suppression of debate and dissent. I know I did.

A year later, against all logic, the IS declared itself and its 3,000 members to be 'the Socialist Workers' Party', the vanguard party for the revolution, which, more than 30 years on, looks even less likely than it did at the time.

At the height of its success in 1974, when 50,000 copies of *Socialist Worker* were being sold every week, the IS had a clear focus on the working class. The only people who could bring about the liberation of society were the proles themselves, they said. But genuine proles were some of the first to be expelled – including Birmingham engineering workers who disagreed with the decision to run candidates against the Broad Left (Labour/Communists) in the AUEW. In an echo of Stalinism, the Party began to be seen as more important than any principle or policy; the Party was the path to Liberation. And if the Leadership *is* the Party, you couldn't question one without challenging the other. Ipso facto, any dissent was a betrayal of the Cause. The flexibility that had marked the early International Socialists had been replaced by cynical political opportunism.

Like the Communist Party, the Socialist Workers' Party built itself by becoming the driving force inside wider protests, such as the Right to Work Campaign and, later, the Anti-Nazi League. Through these front organisations, they could speak to thousands of non-aligned activists and pull them into the Party. But the defeat of the miners in 1985 spelt the death of the class struggle for decades. The workers were emasculated; the ruling class had won.

Reeling from the shock, the SWP, in common with the rest of the Left, threw itself into any protest going from Greenham Common to crusty anti-globalisation tear-ups, all of which would have smacked of 'substitutionism' to the IS 'cadre' of 1974. This was to culminate in the obscenity of 'Respect', which saw the comrades teaming up with George Galloway and turning mental somersaults to apologise for and justify militant Islam. The SWP, a party committed to equality, feminism and the end of the 'false consciousness' of religion, was marching arm in arm with right-wing nut-jobs who advocate medieval barbarity, believe that women are second-class citizens who should wear the *burqa*, and that any Muslim who converts to another religion should be killed.

In 'riding the Islamic tiger', these self-styled anti-fascists who had marched and fought against the National Front and the British National Party got into bed with Muslims whose social views made neo-Nazi John Tyndall look like a limp-wristed liberal.

They weren't the first or even the worst. The SLL had become the Workers' Revolutionary Party. To keep the organisation afloat, Gerry Healy took back-handers first from Saddam Hussein and then from Colonel Gaddafi. In return, the party's daily paper *News Line* started churning out crude anti-Semitic propaganda – it was nothing more than crypto-fascist filth. The Jews apparently controlled everything from the CIA to the BBC via the Labour and Tory parties. Only the WRP was safe. *News Line* photographers even spied on pro-democracy Iraqis. Healy took Saddam's money while the Iraqi dictator was preparing to exterminate tens of thousands of Kurds using poison gas.

In the 1980s, I found myself increasingly disillusioned with the Left. The Parliamentary Labour Party included scores of MPs who thought the Eastern European States were in some way Socialist. It was hard to see how; anyone visiting East Berlin before the Wall came down, as I did, would have been struck by the overwhelming stench of austerity, poverty and oppression.

An East German punk I knew had a joke about it: 'What would happen if a Socialist republic were set up in the middle of the Sahara,' she asked? 'Within three years, it would have to import sand.'

Our own nationalised industries were hardly beacons of

efficiency either. So if State-control of the economy wasn't the answer, what did Socialism actually mean? I went back to basics and re-read Marx.

It rapidly became clear that old Karl would have laughed until his boils ached at the suggestion that Socialism could be established in a backward, feudal society such as Tsarist Russia. Marx believed that Socialism could only exist after capitalism had advanced to its maximum potential (and even then there was nothing 'inevitable' about it if you re-read Volume III of *Das Kapital*).

So the millions of murders carried out in Marx's name had been for nothing. Lenin had falsified Marxist theory to suit his ends and Stalin twisted it further to justify mass murder. In place of abundance and liberation, the revolution brought terror, misery, torture and despair.

In the name of the classless, stateless society, the Russian revolutionaries created a new boss class – the Party – sustained by an awesome apparatus of State repression. And everywhere Marxism-Leninism has blossomed, the outcome has been tragic. Russia, Poland, Hungary, Ukraine, Czechoslovakia, Bulgaria, Yugoslavia, Albania, Lithuania, Latvia, Laos, Estonia, Romania, Vietnam, Cambodia, North Korea, Angola, Afghanistan, Uzbekistan, Tajikistan, Kazakhstan, Ethiopia, Mozambique, Nicaragua, Chile, Cuba... the roll-call of countries that have tried to build Communism is long and varied. And every single one of them failed to deliver a workers' paradise.

Would it have been any different if the revolution had happened first in industrialised Britain? It seems unlikely. Marx argued that Socialism would lay the brickwork for true communism, which would mean the withering away of the State. But there is no logic behind this assertion. No oligarchy surrenders power voluntarily and the evidence of history suggests that there would always be a reason for a totalitarian State to hang on to it.

Christianity offers heaven as a reward for a just life; Communism offers heaven on earth at some unspecified time in the future. And that glorious (impossible) end justifies 'any means necessary', from ballot-rigging to concentration camps.

As we see time and time again, talk is meaningless, and political promises are cheap. We have to judge people on their actions and the vast majority of Socialist leaders have been flawed in some major way. All of them talk grandly about 'the proletariat' while having next to no experience of everyday life for those at the bottom of the heap. Che Guevara was as working class as the Duke of Kent; his mother Celia was Argentinean high society; and his dad was descended from Spanish and Irish nobility. Fidel Castro, the son of a prosperous sugar plantation owner, said his revolution was 'by the humble, for the humble'. But it wasn't; all the leaders of Fidel's 1959 coup d'état were upper-middle-class.

Both Pol Pot and Leon Trotsky came from wealthy farming families; Leon may have dreamed of a future cleansed of evil, oppression and violence but 'the good Bolshevik' personally led the troops who butchered the Kronsdadt sailors, having the heroes of the revolution shot 'like partridges'.

Lenin's dad was a successful, upper-middle-class,

provincial civil servant who was created a hereditary noble (a title his son inherited but kept hushed up). Marx, a rabbi's son, was kept afloat by his rich industrialist comrade, Friedrich Engels – Marx's work was subsidised by the sweat of Manchester textile workers.

Blue blood flowed through the veins of many of Britain's most illustrious Marxists. Paul Foot's father was Lord Caradon, the last governor of Cyprus, and the UK Ambassador to the United Nations; Paul was educated at posh Shrewsbury School. Vanessa Redgrave, the pin-up of the WRP, went to a public school in Worcester. Her father, Sir Michael Redgrave, was raised by his mother and stepfather, a wealthy tea-planter, and was also educated at public school. Tony Benn was born Anthony Neil Wedgwood Benn. The aristocrat formerly known as the second Viscount Stansgate, was educated at Westminster School. Some of them were decent people, but their experience of 'the workers' was largely theoretical.

Not that being working class in itself was any guarantee of integrity. Gerry Healy was a jumped-up, womanising bully who enjoyed seeing people beaten up and who forced his attentions on female Party members saying, 'You are doing this for the party... and I *am* the Party!'

In 1985, 26 women members accused Comrade Healy of 'cruel and systematic debauchery' on Party premises. One woman from Oxford described her Leader's sexual technique: 'Healy came towards me,' she said, 'he was hovering over me. He was not listening to a word I was saying. He wanted only one thing from me – my sexual submission. For a moment, I just stared at him – fat, ugly, red-faced. Was this the price I was supposed to pay? Something snapped in me. I guess it was my faith, my belief. The dream that drove me forward now seemed unreal and reality entered – tawdry, petty, dirty, seamy reality.' Birds, eh, Gel?

Arthur Scargill is a vain, pompous man whose refusal to hold a ballot undermined the 1984–85 miners' strike and led to the most colossal defeat of the English working class since the General Strike of 1926. No Party was big enough to recognise Arthur's leadership skills so he formed his own.

In 2000, Londoners got the chance to vote for 'Socialist Labour Party – leader Arthur Scargill'. They managed a whopping 0.8%. Asked his opinion of the blood-thirsty tyrant Stalin in a radio interview, Arthur replied that Joe had been a 'very good leader', especially during the Second World War. It was true that he had committed 'many, many errors', but, there again, 'Churchill in Britain was also criticised'.

You never hear Arthur say a bad word about Cuba, though – he adores the place. His Party makes trade with Cuba the central plank of their foreign policy. For the Old Left, the country is a cause célèbre. To hear them speak about Fidel Castro, you'd think he was a benign uncle who has preserved his country as a sun-kissed Utopia free of that oppressive Yankee influence. This baffling belief has scores of adherents in the Labour Party, too. When Castro announced he was retiring in February 2008, 65 Labour MPs signed a Commons motion absurdly praising Fidel's achievements. Harriet Harman, Labour's Deputy Leader, pronounced him a 'hero of the Left'.

In fact, Castro was a ruthless dictator who has

suppressed democracy and ruined his country. Cuba is a khazi. 'Stalinism with pineapples' didn't work either. Food is rationed, shops are empty and half of Havana's crumbling housing stock is on the verge of collapse. There are holes in everything.

Yes, life was tough under Battista, but the economy compared favourably with many neighbouring countries and the annual income per head of population was just under £1,000. In 1996, the figure was nearer £600. The minimum wage in Cuba is 225 pesos (just over £5.00) a month.

When Fidel took power in 1959, Cuba was among the five richest countries in Latin America. Nearly 50 years on, it's one of the poorest. Now State control of the economy is about as absolute as it can be; only North Korea is less free. Private restaurants are allowed, but they can have no more than 12 seats, and are only permitted to employ family members. There is no graffiti on the walls 'cos there's nowhere to buy the paint.

The economy has shrunk by between 30–40 per cent in the last 25 years, largely because the collapse of the Soviet bloc put an end to subsidies, Cuba's export markets and a handy supply of oil. Poverty abounds in the people's paradise; there are decent houses down at Miramar but they're all owned by the Government or foreign embassies.

In 'Socialist' Cuba, political prisoners are kept in solitary and gays are sent to 're-education' camps. Castro has more prisoners per head of population than the USA. In the name of Socialism, 30,000 dissidents were executed. Thousands more were jailed, many of them trade unionists. Even Jehovah's Witnesses were slung behind bars.

Draconian laws make any dissent a nickable offence and union activists are harassed to this day. Yet on its fortieth anniversary, the BBC ran a whole week of programming to celebrate the legacy of the Cuban Revolution. *Hasta la vista*, journalism.

The 'heroes' of today's British Left are just as suspect. George Galloway was a flash political bully-boy whose Labour Party career was languishing in the doldrums. But the insignificant backbencher found recognition and adulation in the Arab dictatorships. The reinvention of Gorgeous George started with him going down on one knee in front of Saddam on Iraqi TV and climaxed with him pretending to be a cat on *Celebrity Big Brother*. Comrade Puss told the Iraqi despot, 'Sir, I salute your courage, your strength and your indefatigability. And I want you to know that we are with you until victory, until victory, until Jerusalem.' The lifelong fan of Soviet Russia had found another despot to idolise. Galloway became pals with Tariq Aziz and sucked up to Saddam's psycho son Uday. George went on to back Syria and, inevitably, Hezbollah, who, he said, were 'never a terrorist organisation'. He was expelled by Labour for bringing the Party into disrepute. It was unnecessary, really, as Tony Blair was able to achieve that all on his own.

A man of such high principle was a natural draw for the deformed Trot group the SWP. In January 2004, the Party was instrumental in the launch of Respect, installing long-time activist and SWP member John Rees as leader. Respect campaigned on a Stop The War ticket and was comprised of SWP cadre, members of the reactionary Muslim Brotherhood of Britain and the Muslim Council of Britain (so much for women's rights and secularism). The far Left's journey from Marxism had ended up with a form of communalism – their main targets were now immigrant communities united by their religion and ethnicity. There are a lot of Islamist votes in Bethnal Green & Bow.

Galloway was a founding member and, in 2005, he became the Party's first and only MP, defeating sitting member Oona King (one of the country's few black MPs) for the east London seat. But there were too many egos and internal contradictions in Respect for it to last. In 2007, Galloway and his supporters broke away from the SWP and launched a rival Respect Renewal faction. This left the comrades in an awkward position; if they told the truth about Galloway's opportunism and grubby ambition, it would mean revealing that they had covered for him for years.

In Tower Hamlets, councillor Ahmad Hussain split with the Galloway faction but has since left SWP-Respect to join the Conservative Party. Such principle, such integrity. The good news is that, as a Tory, Ahmad is still to the Left of New Labour …

Talking of principles and integrity, let's not forget WRP fellow traveller, Ken Livingstone, recently exposed by Channel 4's *The Court of Ken*. The *Dispatches* documentary, written and presented by Martin Bright of the left-wing *New Statesman*, accused Red Ken of financial extravagance, cronyism, boozing and of having links to Socialist Action, a post-WRP Trot faction, many of whom ended up on the pay-roll. It also revealed that public money was used to smear Livingstone's enemies and that GLA staff raised funds for his re-election.

The smear is Ken's favourite weapon; anyone who criticised the corrupt London Development Agency and Lee Jasper's elastic relationship with public money was called 'racist', even when they were black themselves. When Trevor Phillips argued that multi-culturalism was a failed creed, Ken accused him of being about to join the far-Right BNP.

In the 1980s, Livingstone condemned critics of the WRP as 'Zionists'; the women raped by his mate Gerry Healy were written off as 'dupes' of MI5. Now he likens Martin Bright to 'a 40-year-old virgin still living at home with his parents'. So what exactly is Ken trying to say, that Mr Bright might be a homosexual? Clearly, if you're against Ken and his mates, you must be either Jewish, a racist or gay, possibly all three, and probably taking back-handers from MI5 to boot.

Livingstone has been allowed to portray himself as a cheeky chap rebel, an honest outsider who happens to be a bit eccentric. He isn't – in my opinion, he's a power-crazed egomaniac, a swaggering bully-boy who has saddled London with a chaotic and unfair congestion charge which has hammered many small businesses out of existence. 'I hate cars,' Ken once said. 'If I ever get any powers again, I'd ban the lot.' He couldn't get away with that, but he's done the next best thing, persecuting motorists with dubious emission charges and gridlocked roads.

Is Ken a loveable Londoner? Or an arrogant bully? You decide. He's squandered fortunes in public money on self-aggrandising junkets to India, China and Venezuela. He has also demeaned our capital and our country by publicly cuddling Yusuf al-Qaradawi, the Qatari-based Islamic nut-job who supports child suicide bombers and believes that female genital mutilation is OK, wife-beating is permissible and that anyone who renounces Islam should be killed (along with homosexuals).

*   *   *

IN power, Left politicians have proved just as corrupt and unprincipled as any right-wing ones; and in absolute power, just as murderous. The Left's commitment to democracy is a matter of expediency, and you're now more likely to find authoritarians, conspiracy theorists and anti-Semites on the political Left than you are on the Right.

The Left no longer represents the views or the interests of the British working class. The constituency Labour Parties have been taken over by middle-class professionals and white-collar office workers – lawyers, lecturers, social workers, teachers, council paper-shufflers. New Labour represented a retreat from Clause 4 socialism to a spin-driven, woolly-minded form of statism. Their various follies – from the Dome to the Iraq War – would take a rainforest worth of paper to document here.

Working class people who continue to vote Labour should be aware that the people's Party has no time for them. All of Socialism's achievements are in the past, and even the things they crow about are flawed. The National Health System was created by the post-War Labour Government (although Lord Beveridge, on whose report the NHS was based, was a Liberal). To hear some Labourites talk, you'd think the NHS had built the bulk of our hospitals – they didn't. They merely nationalised them, and closed down a lot of small ones; they didn't construct new ones for years.

In 1948, Labour argued that 'efficient' central planning would replace the pre-NHS 'unplanned medley of public and voluntary institutions'. Back then, lengthy waiting lists and virulent hospital infections didn't even merit a mention, because they weren't problems; it took decades of central planning to achieve that.

The last forty years have been the golden age of the meddling do-gooders. The Welfare State was supposed to be a safety net for the poor. It's turned into a hammock, supporting the idle and work-shy. Benefits and brutal re-housing policies accelerated the decline in the two-parent family and the break-up of the old extended, working-class family.

Years of campaigning by Leftist lawyers and teachers have bequeathed a system where crime isn't punished, children aren't properly educated and truancy has gone through the roof. Result? A steady rise in crime and a decline in manners and civility, as generations grow up dependent on State hand-outs.

The working class has suffered most from the Left's policies of failed social engineering, economic incompetence and liberal pipe-dreams. But when they oppose endless immigration because of the impact it has on their wages and Social Services, they find themselves labelled 'racist' by Labour papers written by middle-class graduates whose only experience of immigration is a Polish barmaid in their wine bar and a dirt-cheap cleaner from Estonia.

I was tucking in to some stewed eels in a pie and mash shop in Shadwell some years ago when I was approached by an elderly Cockney woman. Her eyes brimming with tears, the old dear told me that she had voted Labour all her life but, whenever there was a problem between the native white council tenants and their Muslim neighbours, the Labour council always and without exception took the side of the immigrants. The distress and the pain of betrayal that this nice old lady felt were tangible.

Is it surprising, then, that when the British National Party target white working-class areas in Barking, Barnsley or the Isle of Dogs, they find an audience ready to listen? Of course, when those forgotten people respond by protest-voting BNP, they find themselves dismissed as 'fascists' by white, middle-class activists with 'ologies in navel-gazing.

So who speaks for the workers now? Not the Trades Union Congress. The TUC claims to fight for 'a fair deal at work and for social justice abroad'. But when it comes to the great scandals of today – from mass immigration to hospital super-bugs, from exorbitant council tax demands to piss-poor education – there is a deafening silence from the brethren. They have no wish to rock New Labour's boat.

It's not the Tories, either, with their Blair Lite policies. Nor the Lib Dems – everything the Labour and Tory parties are wrong about, the Lib Dims are even more wrong about. And if you trust the BNP, more fool you. That Party's approach to book-keeping makes Robert Maxwell look honest and Ken Dodd look meticulous.

Don't Get Fooled Again

In the Britain of 2008, the old Left/Right division has become a meaningless pantomime. The real division is between the rulers and the ruled. It's Us v Them – the political élite who have transformed society against the will of the people.

We need to learn from the mistakes of the past, and to value those priceless liberties the authoritarians would take from us – free speech, free association and the right to protest. Only then can we move forward as a people breathing the righteous air of freedom, tempered with a healthy measure of cynicism.

* * *

CHE Guevara believed that Socialism would usher a New Man into existence. Leon Trotsky agreed. Trotsky wrote that 'Communist Man ... will become immeasurably stronger, wiser and subtler; his body will become more harmonised, his movements more rhythmic, his voice more musical. The forms of life will become dynamically dramatic. The average human type will rise to the heights of an Aristotle, a Goethe, or a Marx.' Why, Leon, why? He never said. Trotsky's vision of the new enhanced human was consistent with the type of garbage we were told by the Comrades when I was a teenage Marxist. All people, we were assured, had the potential to be geniuses because humans 'only use one tenth of our brains.' This was a myth long since debunked by scientists, and you don't even need ten per cent of your mental powers to work it out for yourself. Just watch the Jeremy Kyle Show any morning...

*   *   *

GEORGE Galloway joined the cast of TV's *Celebrity Big Brother* in January 2006. It was priceless. Unforgettable moments included the MP for Baghdad imitating a cat by crouching on all fours, purring and licking imaginary milk from the hands of the actress Rula Lenska. That pussy furore will live forever on TV clip shows. George's eventual eviction could only have been more glorious if they'd made him crawl out through a giant cat-flap.

To me, 'Genial Geo' seemed to emerge as something of a bully and a bore. Brilliant at the Senate, he went bonkers in the House. He seemed to be quick to accuse others of double standards, while remaining unaware of his own failings. He portrayed himself as the protector of the weak, but sided consistently with the strong.

George claimed he was there 'to try and heal the wounds' and 'to keep the boat stable'. Yet, to me, he seemed to help destabilise it, goading the alcoholic Barrymore by saying to him, 'Poor me, poor me, pour me a drink.'

Geo was right to go on the show – it's the biggest pop-culture soap-box available. But he failed to realise that *Big Brother* reveals all your faults and magnifies your frailties. The highlight was when he accused dull rocker Preston of becoming 'a lying plutocrat.' It was as if he'd caught him selling the souls of the poor to Montgomery Burns rather than tucking in to cake and bubbly on a TV game show.

George broke the rules and was prevented from nominating other celebrities. His response left him sounding like one of his favourite tyrants. 'If I get the chance to repay those who took my rights away I will,' he seethed, adding: 'One way or another, either in here or outside ...'

What was he planning to do, set Hamas on the Ordinary Boys?

The row ended with Galloway poring over a copy of the Communist Manifesto while singing along to *Unchained Melody* – the Righteous Brothers meet the Self-Righteous Brother.

By picking on non-celebrity Chantelle Houghton, George and Pete Burns helped her shine. She may be uneducated but she had spirit and common sense. In the end the fake celebrity beat a near-nonentity. But so what? Never mind the winner, the loser is the one we'll remember. The man who set the socialist cause back decades. George Galloway. Purrer to the People!

7

Cosmetic Surgery Live!

Have you ever wanted your arse whitened? I only ask because anal bleaching was the hot, new procedure on last year's *Cosmetic Surgery Live!* It's easy enough to picture someone looking in the mirror and deciding they want their teeth fixed or a shapelier nose, but how much time and money must you have on your hands, and what company must you be keeping, if spray-painting your backside becomes a matter of medical urgency?

When it started, *Cosmetic Surgery Live!* raised some eyebrows... it also lifted cheeks, sliced open a few guts and tortured more privates than a sadistic sergeant-major. But after that first series, I thought nothing could surprise us – I was wrong. Anal bleaching seems almost quaint compared to the freakish procedures we're seeing on the latest run of the Channel Five show.

Take Brazilian nutcase Alexandri Barbosa. He had his manhood sliced open and, I quote, 'widened with the skin of the dead'. What was the sales pitch for that operation? Stay harder longer with rigor mortis?

Then there was a lunatic lady-boy who had his face pulled clean away from his skull as part of an operation to look 'more feminine', while Tammy had 'a bra made out of her own skin'. At least it won't shrink in the wash.

We saw buttock implants (talk about saving your arse), vaginal tightening and people hacked open like meat on a butcher's slab. We also had a good look at the world's biggest plonkers – Vanessa Feltz and Dr Jan Adams.

The presenters' gushingly uncritical approach feels deeply suspect to this viewer. Feltz and Adams come over as cheerleaders for the multi-billion pound cosmetic surgery industry, but no scalpel can make the truth any prettier: Channel Five is peddling a lie. The show plays down all the risks and plugs the myth that happiness can be bought; that pricey 'reconstruction' will make you a better human being.

But consider the evidence. 'Tomorrow,' trilled Vanessa, 'how porn star looks can get you ahead.' Cut to a shot of a crazy Yank with barrage-balloon breasts – her own personal silicon valley. Lola Ferrari from *Eurotrash* had the same absurd implants and they killed her.

Channel Five markets these ghoulish images as a public service. They're just letting us in on all the latest hip ops, they say, with a nudge and a wink. It's all a laugh, innit?

Well, no, not really... it stinks. The series is as horrible as it is depressing. A lot of these freakish operations were inspired by the Brazilian transsexual scene, and they just underline the obscene waste of money and medical know-how on display. Breast augmentation for men, scrotum reduction, sexier belly-buttons... this has gone beyond vanity. It's plain nuts. As opposed to the synthetic ones offered to female-to-male gender-benders in Florida. Whatever happened to diet, exercise and a little raising of self-esteem?

Originally, plastic surgery had an honourable purpose – to repair people horribly damaged in war, accidents and disasters. But in its modern cosmetic incarnation, it has become a form of fraud. Someone who looks like a troglodyte is transformed by the surgeon's knife in to a supposed object of desire... although Pete Burns and Lesley Ash don't necessarily add weight to this argument. Once split open, plumped with silicon sewed back up and sent on their merry way, these 'enhanced' superbeings will then attract a mate, marry them, have a baby... and lo and behold, the kid turns out to be a minger, too. Isn't that worse than being mugged? A mugger couldn't give a stuff about you. Your spouse, the love of your life, has tricked you into reproducing the genes they hated to begin with. It's criminal deception. Besides, when you've been on *Extreme Makeover* and had your complete head and body transplant, who exactly are you?

We can't stop the cosmetic surgery industry; it's a free country and people can spend their dough however they like. But what bothers me is the effect shows like this have on young kids. They had a survey in a girlie magazine recently which found that one in three teenage girls 'want' surgery. This shallow craze should be questioned long and hard. Or, in Alexandri's case, long and wide.

Bushell on the Blog
May 2007

Mayday New film *This Is England* is a huge let-down, wrong on countless levels. Unforgivably, given its subject matter, it's also incredibly boring. Nothing about it seems right. The gang, with their mix of ages, styles and accents, don't feel real. The little kid Shaun with the older punk girlfriend looks farcical and perverse. The film feels out of time too. The young skinhead's Dad had died in Falklands conflict, setting the film in late '82/'83 by which time skins were well on the decline and casual was everywhere. The anti-war theme would work now with Iraq but far-right skins in the early 1980s were very pro the Falklands – as most people were. Besides, the racist NF back then was a British party (still is) so they wouldn't have been making speeches about England and quoting Churchill. Is this another attempt to smear those of us fighting for an English parliament? All the snooty reviewers, whose knowledge of skins could be tattooed on a midget's foreskin, are saying how rare it was to see a multi-racial gang at this time. Eh? Skinheads were back big-time '78; there were plenty of Afro boys about in '79, and far more in 1980 after 2-Tone hit the charts. There were lot of black Rude Boys and skins on the scene then – just like there were the first time around. The media can't get over their own cherished and oft-repeated prejudice that all skinheads were Nazis. Only a tiny minority ever were. And God knows where the movie is supposed to be set – the accents here are Scouse, Yorkshire and Midlands. The language doesn't sound right either. Surely the Australian 'no worries' only caught on here after *Neighbours* took hold in the mid-eighties, and no-one in 1983 was saying 'chill'. The best things about this film are the soundtrack and the acting – Stephen Graham sparkles as ex-con Combo, a psychopathic racist, Joseph Gilgun makes a very likeable kind-hearted Woody, and Thomas Turgoose is obviously a star.

2 May Posh-boy Paul got the boot from *The Apprentice*. Good. The jumped-up Yuppie had it coming. Paul's campaign was so full of intelligence failures it could have been masterminded by MI5. His biggest clanger was a peach: Paul tried to sell pork sausages to a Halal kebab house, run by a strict Muslim, during Ramadan. It's just a relief he didn't offer a free Danish cartoon with every purchase...

5 May A lot of celebrities support green supermarkets who are replacing cheap, disposable carriers with long lasting ones. Even Richard Madeley has got himself a Bag For Life.

7 May That five course US Presidential banquet for the Queen in full – hot-dogs, ribs, grits, KFC bucket, quarter pounder with cheese, followed by Mom's apple pie. All washed down with your choice of Coke Zero, Bud Ice or Root Beer. You all come back again, y'hear?

8 May Loved Jessie Wallace as Marie Lloyd on BBC4. Edwardian London clearly had a lot in common with Albert Square. For starters they had the same wallpaper.

9 May Thanks to *The Apprentice* for explaining what 'Nigella seed' is. I'd assumed it was something spilt by male viewers during a TV cookery show.

12 May Channel 4's offensive comedy week was as funny as woodworm in a cripple's crutch (Bernard Manning, 1974). They tried to stitch-up Chubby Brown, but his kind of humour – stag comedy – has become the norm. This week a BBC show included the rather dubious gag: 'You can lead a horse to water, but you can't get a dog to suck you off.' So you suspect Chubby's biggest crime in the eyes of the TV establishment is being working class and not buying the *Guardian*. I like filth as much as the next bloke, as long as the next bloke is Frank Skinner, but I find TV's lazy reliance on shock depressing. As my old vicar once told me, if you need to swear to get a laugh you're probably a ****.

13 May Why do we persist with the ridiculous charade of Eurovision? It's a pointless cheese-fest and we haven't got a hope in hell of winning. There's only one way we could do it: stop entering as the UK and start entering songs from England, Wales, Scotland, Ulster, the Isle of Wight, Rutland, the Isle of Man, the Hebrides etc – and then vote for each other. It's how they do it in the Balkans.

15 May Absurdly, Chris Tarrant has been nicked for horseplay in an Indian restaurant. Chris is alleged to have thrown cutlery on to another diner's table. He'd been joking with the guy and no-one was hurt, so why did it take four cops to arrest him? Why arrest him at all? There are only three celebrities whose proximity to tableware should cause panic: Freddie Starr, Uri Geller and O.J. Simpson.

16 May Scientists say that Monet painted the way he did because he had cataracts. A further study reveals that Picasso was on acid and Lichtenstein did it for a bet.

21 May Janet Street-Porter consumed horse rump steak on TV, leading cruel wags to conclude you are what you eat. That's grossly unfair. On horses. Have another look at Janet. The jerky movements, the awkward gait...she's much more like Muffin The Mule.

23 May David Beckham, Ginger Spice, Ranulph Fiennes...Greatest Britons had quite a line-up. ITV should write it down and post it to the 1990s when we might have been impressed.

29 May That's all we need on TV, another bunch of cranks, weirdos, self-publicists and wannabes. Not *Big Brother* but the contenders for Labour's Deputy Leader on *Newsnight*. Did you watch it tonight? You could barely see little Hazel Blears over her lectern. She looked like an eight year old. But at least she seems half-human, unlike humourless Harriet Halfwit (Deputy Dawg?), and Hilary Benn who could walk in to an empty room and blend right in. Not exactly inspirational are they? Peter Hain is a career bore who makes Alistair Darling seem charismatic. Alan Johnson wants more tax and amnesty for illegal immigrants, so he can get stuffed. And then there's Jon Crud, standard left-wing hypocrite: MP for Dagenham, lives in Notting Hill, sends kid to an elite school but seeks to deny other children a chance of selective education. Gertcha. Which one is the weakest link? Trick question: it's all of them.

30 May Here they come then, this year's *Big Brother* contenders. First up, twins: Sam and Amanda, stupidity in stereo, screaming and squawking. Wonder if they always make such a racket on entry. I pity the bloke who has to find out. And these girls are training to be social workers? Ye Gods!

2) Lesley, 60. A 'retired head-hunter' – maybe she'll come out of retirement and shrink Chris Moyles's big fat head. 'We're twins,' squawk the Squeaky Girls. 'No,' replies Lesley, deadpan. I like that. She can't possibly win though.

3) Charley, 'an unemployed lap-dancer.' Wants money. Well try working, love. Booed on arrival. Great legs, shame about the boat race. Looks like Sugar Ray.

4) Tracy. A raver. But not a bather by the look of it. Strewth. What is she on? She's like Bez but more mashed. And more masculine. She's like Tory policy on grammar schools: all over the shop and completely mucked up. But what a coat. She could be Joseph!

5) Chanelle. Kinnell, she's gorgeous. 'I based my image on Victoria Beckham,' she says. Yeah, face like Victoria, but unfortunately legs like David...Her first words on entering house: 'F*** me up the bum'. Enough said?

6) Shabnam, Another unemployed layabout. She's struggling to keep all those teeth in her mouth. Bad skin.

7) Emily, a drama student. Peaches Geldof lookalike. Thinks she's intelligent. Very up herself. No chance of winning.

8) Laura. Stone me, it's Taffy Pollard. A Welsh version of Vicki. Peter Kay in drag. Breasts like zeppelins. Seems genuine, though. Not just fame-chasing shallow scum.

9) Nicky, 27. Bank worker. Hates men. Quite like her.

10) The last one, Carole, 53 from East London. It's Millie Tant from Viz! Or Boss Hogg in drag. An 'unemployed sexual health worker'. What's that then? Bet she's always looking for openings ... An SWP member, wants to stand for Respect – it's Galloway's Page 3 Girl! Her husband cheated on her – you don't say? An obvious hate figure for male TV critics, but think on lads. Carole is a left-wing agitator, Charley is an unemployed lap-dancer. Carole must fight for her right to work! But keep your own clothes on, please love. You'd certainly down a few tools. Not sure I like the all-women twist. C4 have bottled it.

8

Art Is Dead – Long Live Money!

In 1997, a large mosaic of Myra Hindley's face was displayed at the Royal Academy as part of the exciting new Sensations exhibition. This despicable baggage was one of the Moors Murderers; she and lover Ian Brady had killed five young victims, aged between 10 and 17. The picture of Hindley, by Marcus Harvey, was made up of kids' hand prints. Do you see what he'd done there? A child-killer re-imagined through the hands of innocent children. Very profound.

Norman Rosenthal, the RA's exhibitions secretary, proudly wrote in the catalogue that art should 'jolt us out of our complacency'. He went on to insist that it was the artist's job to 'conquer territory that hitherto has been taboo'.

Two members of the public had their complacency well and truly jolted. Peter Fisher threw ink at Myra's portrait, while Jacques Role chucked eggs at it. To keep it safe, the sick junk had to be mounted behind Perspex and guarded permanently. The art world, meanwhile, reacted angrily. The men who had defaced the portrait were 'philistines', they said, narrow-minded morons motivated by fear.

I disagree. To me, they are art heroes; they are the true rebels, the only ones bucking the system.

The Young British Art scene, in common with most post-modern art, hides behind the illusion of radicalism. But, at heart, it is as empty as it is élitist. It has nothing genuinely challenging or valuable to say. It is a highly profitable, culture-wrecking con.

The Sensations exhibition was the high-water mark of the Young British Art phenomenon. It showcased the best of the UK's new artists, making media stars of many and a fortune for the patron, millionaire Tory Charles Saatchi. So what exactly did it stand for?

As a work of art, there's nothing particularly interesting about Marcus Harvey's 'Myra'. The only point it makes is that Hindley's status as a national hate figure is built on murdered children, which is something we knew already. The work had no more significance than a toddler's attention-grabbing temper tantrum, and nothing to say other than 'Look at me, ain't I bold?'

Yet it wasn't even the most hateful piece on display. That dubious honour belongs to a Chapman brothers' work called 'Zygotic Acceleration', which consists of child mannequins with sexual organs on their faces. Some noses are penises; some mouths vaginas; others anuses. The only territory this seeks to 'conquer' is our natural revulsion to paedophilia.

Another Jake and Dinos Chapman piece, 'Great Deeds

against the Dead', shows two castrated figures tied to a tree trunk, with a third one hanging over a branch, castrated, decapitated and with its arms hacked off. The severed head is impaled on another branch. This image was based on a stunning Goya etching which brilliantly illustrates the savage treatment Napoleon's army of occupation dished out to Spanish peasants.

Goya's work, with its mounds of butchered, mutilated corpses, is genuinely shocking, all the more so for being utterly devoid of sensationalism. The brutality of war has rarely been captured with more power. In his *Disasters of War* series of 85 etchings, Goya gave the world authentic new art for an age of doubt. God was dead, he seemed to say, and all that remained was a loveless world full of murder and mutilation.

The Chapmans took Goya's vision and tore all the humanity out of it, stripping it of its strengths and reducing true horror to cheap shock. In place of flesh and blood, they delivered torture kitsch, artless throw-away pap. Sado-porn.

Other deliberately headline-chasing Sensations works included Chris Ofali's 'Holy Virgin Mary', which surrounded a black Madonna with vaginas cut from pornographic magazines. From a distance, and this is a sweet touch, they looked like cherubs. For good measure, Ofali embellished the painting with elephant faeces. You can imagine art pseuds flocking round it, admiringly: 'Look, Camilla, see how the majestic symbolism of the portrait is off-set by the perceived vulgarity of the vaginas.'

'No, Tarquin, you're missing the point... the religious

iconicity is worthless and crass; it's the shit that makes it beautiful.'

When the exhibition moved to New York's publicly-funded Brooklyn Museum, this dung-ho debasement of the mother of Christ generated the same level of public hostility as child-killer Myra had in London. The Big Apple's Left intelligentsia were quick to leap to Ofali's defence through accusing critics, who included Mayor Giuliani, of being reactionary 'Christian fascists'. And yet it's hard to discern any merit – radical, spiritual or artistic – in 'Holy Virgin Mary'. Rather, like Harvey and the Chapman brothers' work, it sums up the mechanics of Young British Art in a nutshell – cynical art school twonk dreams up something they know will infuriate Joe Soap, make the tabloids froth at the mouth, and the self-proclaimed *culturati* steam in to defend them, guaranteeing acres of free publicity, attendances shoot through the roof and Charlie Saatchi laughs all the way to the bank. *Vive la révolution*!

Damien Hirst had been hailed as a genius but in my opinion, he's the biggest cynic of them all. Hirst's shark-in-formaldehyde (entitled 'The Physical Impossibility of Death in the Mind of Someone Living') was part of Sensations. In 1990, he came to the art world's attention with a work called 'A Thousand Years'. This included maggots hatching inside a white box which then turned into flies and fed on a severed cow's head.

In 1993, Hirst exhibited 'Mother and Child Divided' – a cow and a calf, sliced up and displayed in sections, which looked like it had been copied from a biological supply catalogue. A year later, he gave the world a sheep in formaldehyde ('Away from the Flock'). In 1995, we got 'Two Fucking and Two Watching' featuring a rotting cow and bull.

Are we seeing a pattern yet? Dead animals + pretentious title = filthy lucre. Having made millions through pickling animal corpses, Hirst moved on to 'Hymn', a monumental 20ft-high sculpture copy of his son's young scientist anatomy set, which weighed six tons. Me learned friends became involved and in the end, he paid the original designer, Norman Emms, a goodwill payment and made donations to two children's charities.

In 2006, graphic artist Robert Dixon said that Hirst's print 'Valium' had 'unmistakable similarities' to one of his own designs. A spokesman for Hirst rebutted the claim, saying that the inspiration came from the Penguin *Dictionary of Curious and Interesting Geometry* – not realising that this was the very book that had published Dixon's pattern back in 1991.

In 2007, Hirst's skull studded with diamonds was found to be strikingly similar to a pendant mass-produced in China, not to mention the glittering skull jewellery on sale and prominently displayed at West End fashion jewellers Butler and Wilson.

The limits of Damien's artistic vision become ever clearer; the kindest thing I would say is that he's an accomplished pretender.... That hasn't affected his earnings, though; Hirst's sparkling skull was sold for £50 million. Forget art – what matters is marketing.

Art is dead – long live money.

* * *

THE financial value of art seems to have less and less to do with its intrinsic quality. Ben Lewis, writing in *Prospect* magazine in 2005, showed how a handful of wealthy collectors, curators, critics and dealers connive to drive up the prices of certain favoured artists. One rich collector told him, 'The exciting thing about collecting contemporary art is that there is no real body of validation.' And so something worthless can become virtually priceless.

Post-modern art is built on bluff, chutzpah and profit. Its genius is to convince a lot of gullible, wealthy nitwits that something artistically worthless has a great inherent value. It makes junk a must-have accessory; it makes millionaires out of charlatans and then has the audacity to sneer at anyone who refuses to play along. If you don't get it, it's not for you; you're obviously thick, bigoted or reactionary, unlike today's hip and happening *dilettanti* who understand, man, and who consider themselves chic, smart and fashionable.

Ironically, this 'cutting edge' art is now completely institutionalised. The avant-garde has become the official art of our times. It's the only work that those who run public institutions deem to be of any importance and the only art that they invest in. The general public themselves are excluded from the game.

In 2006, the Tate was strongly criticised by the Charity Commission when it emerged that it had bought seven works by five artists who were serving trustees, thereby breaching charity law. Another audit revealed that the Tate had acquired more than seventy other works by serving trustees since 1955. This was particularly scandalous, considering the huge impact of what the Tate buys and chooses to exhibit on the standing and finances of the artists involved. The scope for conflict of interest and insider trading is enormous. In any other business, this kind of scandal, mostly involving public money, would have made front-page news. At the Tate, said the *Telegraph*, ethics are on the canvas.

* * *

THE roots of the Great Art Con go all the way back to 1919, when Marcel Duchamp produced his famous urinal, which he called 'Fountain'. Duchamp had intended to send up the art world; instead, his work was to become the model for most of the art created since the 1960s. Duchamp's subversive pisser became the spiritual godfather of post-modernism.

Historically, art was the servant of the rich – European royalty, nobles or the Church – whose patronage kept the artists afloat. Later, the well-to-do bourgeoisie paid the piper and called the tune. Old standards of art went out the window in the 1920s when Modern Art came to prominence. A new breed of artist emerged, whose purpose seemed to be vigorously to subvert all that had gone before. Fresh ideas abounded – symbolism, Fauvism, Post-Impressionism, Dada, Surrealism and Cubism, whose greatest exponent was Pablo Picasso.

Picasso was, of course, a genius. Everyone agrees, don't they? No one would question his technical skill; the Spaniard changed the course of European art. Yet, as the great English neo-romantic painter Michael Ayrton argued, changing something's course doesn't necessarily improve it. 'Such men as Hitler have changed the course of human history to the disadvantage of mankind,' he said. 'And I believe that Picasso... has been of very negative service to art.'

Ayrton went on to attack Picasso for making a fetish of originality while actually pirating from the past at will. 'What he does,' Ayrton wrote, 'is to engulf an existing formula... it may be a Negro sculpture, Greek vase painting or the drawings of Ingres. This formula, once digested, he regurgitates... accentuating certain characteristics and obliterating others.' By challenging the way Picasso deconstructed images, Ayrton provoked a formidable backlash and was forced to resign as the *Spectator*'s art critic.

Picasso's biggest and most famous canvas – 'Guernica' – is still considered iconic by the radical Left. Picasso had been paid $6,000 by the embattled Republican Government of Spain to come up with the work for the Paris World Exposition. Initially, the artist had hit a creative block. What to do? Then, in April 1937, Hitler despatched the fascist Condor Legion to bomb the heart out of the Basque town of Guernica in northern Spain, killing 1,500 civilians. The Western world was shocked by this appalling act of savagery and Picasso had his inspiration. Yet compared to the Goya work mentioned earlier, Picasso's 'Guernica' seems strangely dispassionate and remote from its subject. There is no town, no planes in the skies, no bombs, just a jumbled mess of corpses, a gored and injured horse, visions of death from a bull-fight, something that had long haunted his imagination, and a half-hidden harlequin face. The imagery seems devoid of meaning or relevance – and Picasso refused to explain it. More interestingly, 'Guernica' closely echoes one of his drawings from 1934 – three years before the Condor Legion's attack.

The Republican Government was not impressed. For them, 'Guernica' failed to convey the horror of the carpet-bombing, the agony of civil war or the struggle against Franco's fascists. The painting was rolled up and returned to Picasso, who, unabashed, toured it around the world. It was swiftly dubbed a masterpiece, and Pablo became not just *the* painter of the 20th century but also a living saint.

Arguably, Salvador Dali had more to say. His 'Self Construction with Boiled Beans (Premonition of Civil War)', completed six months before the conflict began, showed Spain tearing itself apart. His earlier works displayed a profound understanding of man's mortality and in-built decay.

Dali would be considered a genius of at least Picasso's equal had he not been suspected of secretly harbouring fascist sympathies. He also watered down his genius with playful self-parody, collaborating with everyone from Walt Disney to Alice Cooper. In 1972, Dali even made a TV advert for Alka-Seltzer. 'Look,' he seemed to be saying, 'art's a big joke now… let's milk its absurdities for all they're worth.'

* * *

IF Modern Art has a message, it is an élitist one. Each new development has been claimed as a new way of seeing that only the *culturati* could ever appreciate. 'Any art that can be understood is the product of a journalist,' sneered Tristan Tzara's 1930s Dada manifesto. In other words, if you don't get it, you're not meant to, you thick pleb.

The rich loved it; Modern Art became so fashionable in the USA that corporations were queuing up to invest in it. In the Depression-blitzed 1930s, Cubism's triumphant reign was edged aside, especially in New York, by Left-led social realism. But after the Second World War, Modern Art reasserted its hold. Abstract Expressionism was to seize the reins; for the next 15 years, art was completely Pollock's. The three-dimensional realism of old art was replaced by the glorious flatness of the new order.

The intellectual driving forces behind the new art were New York critics Clement Greenberg and Harold Rosenberg, who ushered in action painting, which reigned supreme until the dawning of Pop Art. Jasper Johns started that with his simple but effective 1958 work, 'Flag'. Critics like Leo Sternberg and William Rubin saw Johns' work as something newer and more perfect than Abstract Expressionism. Swiftly, Pop Art became the new cool, giving the New York art scene a fresh burst of life. Roy Lichtenstein and Andy Warhol became the next art gods by reproducing comic book images and soup cans respectively. Pop Art was fun – childlike, if you like – and accessible, yet still extremely commercial.

But in a world driven by ceaseless innovation, Pop Art was soon challenged by Op Art; then Abstraction, then Minimalists and then Conceptualists. The heady excitement peaked in 1970 when Laurence Weiner announced that a work of art 'need not be built'. The new art didn't even have to exist; emptiness now had significance.

In the mid-1970s, the English artist Jamie Reid lent an extra dimension to the exciting new punk rock phenomenon with his radical designs. Reid, whose main inspiration were the early 20th-century Situationists, used ransom-note style letterings cut from newspapers and safety-pin reconstructions of the Queen's face and the Union Jack to make an instant impact.

Video art and photography came to the fore in the 1980s, breaking the tyranny of canvasses and sculptures, before abstract art made a comeback in the 1990s. The most influential artists of the period were Gilbert & George, whose works were distinguished chiefly by virtue of being deliberately devoid of taste. Their 1977 'Dirty Words' series was exactly what it said on the tin – public toilet graffiti loaded with obscenities. It was a sign of things to come.

In 1987, their exhibition at the Hayward Gallery – all vast, flat squares and oblongs – came with names designed to shock: 'Tongue Fuck Cocks', 'Friendship Pissing', 'Shit Faith'. That same year they caused a furore at the Royal Academy with gigantic photo pieces called 'Wanker', 'Bummed' and 'Prick Arse'. Taken at face value, it was dire. But Gilbert & George understood the value of outrage and were brilliant at hyping and marketing themselves. They'd already won the Turner Prize and were busy laying the foundations for the coming YBA wave. Their protégés, The Chapman Brothers, worked as their assistants before branching out in their own right in 1992.

You can't help but be impressed by both the emptiness of their work and the scale of their cheek. Of their own style, they write, 'We uphold Traditional Values... we honour the High-Mindedness of Man... Beauty is Our Art.' Like Stalinists, they invert the meanings of words. There is no beauty in their work, no high-mindedness; they put ugliness on a pedestal and worship shit.

In January 2008, the Tate Modern celebrated Gilbert & George's 40-year partnership with a retrospective that takes in such works as 'Cunt Scum', 'New Horny Pictures' (rent-boy adverts) and 'Naked Shit', featuring their own excrement. Not that this stopped esteemed art commentators like Belfast gallery director Hugh Mulholland dubbing them 'unquestionably among the most important and original artists of our times'

Gilbert & George set the tone for the art that followed them. If graffiti and turds can be art, then anything can be art. And if anything can be art, then nothing is art.

So what is art? Anything the new art establishment says it is. Porn is a frequent factor – see Marcus Harvey's 'Proud of His Wife' and 'Like What You See?' The Chapman Brothers' latest wheeze is to 'update' Hogarth's 'A Rake's Progress' by defacing it, changing human heads for animals and cartoon grotesques.

Often, dreaming up a new gimmick is enough to put you ahead. Winners of the Turner Prize include Martin Creed's flickering illuminations, 'The Lights Going On... and Off', to which art critic Rachel Campbell-Johnson responded, 'His flickering installation may mean everything or it may mean nothing.' Ain't that the truth?

Then there was Simon Starling and 'Shedboatshed' – a shed that he turned into a boat. Starling found a wooden shack in Switzerland, made a boat out of it, paddled it down the Rhine to Basel and then rebuilt it back in to a shed. Is that art or woodwork? Tate Gallery curator Martin Myrone had no hesitation in declaring Starling's botched DIY job 'a buttress against the compression of time and space characteristic of modernity and of global capitalism'. Of course! Let's hear it for the most underrated artist of the 20th Centruy – Bob the Builder.

Starling won £25,000 for 'Shedboatshed' – now that's what I call a nice little Turner. But if a battered boat and a creaky wooden shed qualifies as art, why doesn't Big Mo Harris win the Turner prize?

In 1998, our old mate Chris Ofili won it with 'Captain Shit', a black superhero realised in elephant dung and resin. (He just loves painting with pachyderm poo, this guy; but does anyone shake his hand afterwards?)

In 2007, the Turner Prize winner was Mark Wallinger, whose 'State Britain' meticulously recreates peace campaigner Brian Haw's anti-war protest in Parliament Square. A return to social realism? Unlikely, as Wallinger is best known for his film *Sleeper* – 154 minutes of footage of the artist wandering around a deserted German gallery disguised as a bear. Still, the Tate was impressed, saying that there were parallels between Wallinger in Berlin and Michelangelo and the Sistine Chapel: 'Both artists were interested in transforming spaces.' Yes, absolutely. And there are similar parallels between Jon Gaunt and William Shakespeare, both being keen on stringing some words together.

Other commentators are even more gung-ho in their defence of everything Young British Art has to throw at us.

The Marxist Terry Eagleton, Professor of Culture, no less, at Manchester University, has written, 'To the avant-garde, truth is a lie, morality stinks and beauty is shit.' Those members of the public moved to attack degenerate or decadent art instalments are motivated by fear, he says: 'An art which too radically disrupts our identity and the panic this breeds finds its outlet in aggression.'

Not for the first time, the People's Professor is talking out of his over-educated arse. It wasn't fear or panic that made Peter Fisher sling ink at 'Myra'; he said he wanted to take a stand against a picture that was 'glorifying the crimes of a monster', while egg-chucker Jacques Role said, 'There is a limit when an artist profits in terms of fame or money from the death or torture of children.'

These men were motivated by a sense of decency, something the fashionable art world has long forgotten.

Today's art has no soul, no merit and no imagination. It is obsessed with stunts, gags and sixth-form satire. Graffiti, spray-painting and fly-posting are now considered artistic enough to go under the hammer at posh auction houses, which just serves to underline how shallow and adolescent contemporary art has become.

In my opinion, one of the greatest art charlatans at large is Robert Banks, the graffiti nuisance known as Banksy. Posh people call him a 'conceptual artist', and these days his work sells for around £200,000 a pop. He must be laughing all the way to the Banksy. But what concept is he illustrating? That a fool and his money are soon parted, or that the line between being very clever and remarkably dim is wafer thin?

Today's Art would like us to believe it is significant and

challenging, when it's actually as deep as a toddler's play-pool; all it challenges is the patience. Compared with Picasso, Matisse, Derain and the rest, today's shock-artists are infantile underachievers devoid of point and meaning. They can't even entertain us the way that Lichtenstein and Warhol did. They are an incestuous collection of conmen and show-offs more interested in perpetuating the myth of their own brilliance than they are in producing anything aesthetically pleasing or culturally significant. You buy one of their pieces to prove how rich and hip you are. It's not art, it's a status symbol.

Today's establishment artists are limited in vision, intelligence and skill but, as we've seen, that doesn't matter a light – all that matters is that they are marketed and hyped efficiently, that they generate enough fuss to wind up the public and hook those rich mug punters. (I have high hopes for my own shortly to be unveiled installation, incidentally: 'Dead Rodent in A Skip', a diced and sliced sewer rat wearing a tiara, symbolising the fall from grace of royal butler Paul Burrell.)

The new art is easy to understand for one simple reason – there is nothing in it to understand.

We can't turn back the clock; we can't go back to portraits and landscapes, and stark social realism. But we – and particularly public-funded institutions – need to find and develop artists motivated by a love of humanity and not the puerile desire to shock a maiden aunt. We need art that recognises there is morality, truth and beauty in the world that isn't 'bourgeois'; art that takes a hammer to all that is ugly, poisonous and degenerate; art that means something.

The case against art subsidies

All art subsidies should be abolished for three very good reasons: 1) because anything any good should not need subsidising; 2) because only art that panders to the tastes of the metropolitan élite is ever subsidised; and 3) because the very act of subsidising ensures that the arts remain élitist. If we took away the free money, if we removed the dead hand of the chinless wonders from the tiller, British Art would not wither and die – it would be reborn.

Subsidies remove art from the masses; they mean that artists no longer have to worry about attracting an audience. Instead, they have to please the committees who award the subsidies. The people who receive the money are not necessarily the ones who need or deserve it most, but simply the ones who are most adept at getting funding, which is why the ballet is feather-bedded and music hall, punk rock and morris dancing aren't.

Compare and contrast the British music industry and the British film industry. Pop isn't subsidised and British rock and pop are genuinely influential all over the world far beyond our size. Movie-making is subsidised and British films are a cottage industry that we try and pretend matters.

Art is distorted by subsidy. If I worked for Camelot and my private tastes involved, for example, being tied up and spanked on Little Mo's ironing board, then film-makers and artists would be pitching projects to appeal to my peculiarities rather than to public taste. To honest Joe Public, a dead sheep isn't art, it's a kebab, but in today's commercial climate, there's no point bleating about it. If a committee of rich snobs says Tracy Emin's unmade bed is

*art, nobody believes them except for other rich snobs...
and so art is removed from the people. This is not healthy
for art. Wouldn't it make more sense to follow the Irish
example and abolish tax for all artists, instead of feather-
bedding them? People tend to be a whole lot shrewder
when they're spending their own money. Ladies and
Gentlemen, I put it to you that subsidies do for art what
Angus Deayton did to his hooker.*

9

The Male Eunuch

'Every man, deep down, knows he's a
worthless piece of shit.'
Valerie Solanas

Forty years ago, the feminist Valerie Solanas wrote her
SCUM (Society for Cutting Up Men) manifesto. Men were
emotional cripples, she argued, 'walking abortions...
trapped in a twilight zone halfway between humans and
apes.' To be male was be 'completely egocentric... incapable
of love... a walking dildo... incapable of mental passion.'
Most men, she concluded, should simply be killed.

Today's feminists would shy away from such an extreme
stance, not because they disagree with it, but merely
because they no longer need to say it. The battle of the
sexes is over. Women have won.

Modern men are mixed up, socially emasculated and
thoroughly under the thumb. Germaine Greer's *The Female
Eunuch* has made way for something worse – a fearful,
tearful hesitant wimp. Behold, the Male Eunuch.

The last four decades have seen the triumph of the
wimmen's movement, and the complete collapse of male

confidence. Men, we have been told repeatedly, are all bastards, brutal oppressors and potential rapists, while women, although terribly persecuted and long-suffering, are the kinder, gentler, fairer and more tolerant sex.

It would be churlish at this point to bring up Lizzie Borden, Winnie Mandela, Myra Hindley, Rose West, Agrippina the Younger, and the rest. They may have been evil, but patriarchal society was to blame. Blokes are the bad guys by virtue of, well, being guys.

And if that sounds 'sexist' and discriminatory, brace yourself; it gets worse.

Feminist thinking has become the new orthodoxy. Women and their treacherous, limp-wristed lap-dogs have seized the media, with British culture becoming thoroughly feminised.

In TV advertising, women are portrayed as intelligent, assertive and caring; attractive über-women. Men, on the other hand, are more often painted as lazy, useless wimps; flabby invertebrates.

You want evidence? How about the Gold Blend ad where a woman in an art gallery lassoes a fella and drags him across the floor... or the bespectacled berk in the Mr Muscle ad... or the Lee jeans ad with a woman resting her stiletto on the arse of a naked man, weak, prostrate and conquered? Then there was Pot Noodles nude dude stuck dumbly in cat flap with a bike parked up his backside... the helpless twit in the bin in the Capital One ad... and, of course, the Lambrini poster where a woman tells her friend she's lost a lot of useless fat. 'So you dumped him then?' her friend replies.

Laugh? I nearly slapped on an oestrogen patch. But while

Advert Man is an incompetent, brow-beaten slob, he has a rival in misery – the dickless wretch who is Soap Man.

In TV soap operas, female sexuality is portrayed as liberating. Women shown out on hen nights ogling male strippers are always portrayed as enjoying a wholesome, life-affirming experience. Male sexual desire, on the other hand, is seedy and perverted. Poor old grandad Jim on *EastEnders* was depicted as a dirty old man for wanting sex with his wife on their wedding night. Big Mo, 70, on the same show, is entitled to have a 'right old laugh' for lusting after fellas and holding riotous Ann Summers parties.

In 2007, Charlie Stubbs became the first man bludgeoned to death by a woman on *Coronation Street* since, ooh, at least 2005. Did he deserve it? Of course not! Charlie was a love rat, a control freak and a bully, but he wasn't Fred West. His girlfriend/killer, Tracy Barlow, has done a lot worse – she seduced her mum's boyfriend, cheated on her first husband, blackmailed the Croppers, tried to frame Steve, nearly ripped off Penny, tricked Charlie into thinking she was pregnant... She was the devious yin to Charlie's lecherous yang, a woman so poisonous, it's a wonder the Snakeheads haven't tried to recruit her.

So why was he bumped off and not her? Because he was guilty of a greater crime – he was a bloke. And what was worse, Charlie was an old-fashioned bloke, a building worker, as unreconstructed as Stonehenge.

In the soaps, it's always the same story – female misbehaviour equals fun; male misbehaviour is always reprehensible. Female desire is good; male desire is sexist. Female values are wholesome, while male values are prehistoric.

In February 2007, I debated masculinity on an ITV show in the Midlands. One opponent was the feminist agony aunt, Suzie Hayman, who welcomed the new mood of 'metrosexuality' afflicting younger males. Suzie said she was glad that men were becoming 'more human'... offensively equating humanity with femininity.

Ah yes. To hell with men and their trivial contributions to civilisation, like telephones, radio, television, the Internet, electricity, computers, fax machines, rock music, space rockets, trains, planes, cars, telescopes, nuclear fusion and engineering. (That's proper engineering, not the social kind beloved by women like Susie and Janet Shrek-Porter and Polly Bloody-Toynbee.) The gap between reality and the world as it is perceived by feminists is wide enough to dump a billion burning bras.

* * *

THE problem with women is that they are two-faced, indecisive, manipulative bitches. Not all of them, of course... just the nice ones.

Admit it, men – every woman you've ever met, read or spoken to has been, at worst, a hormonal nightmare and, at best, deceitful and probably deranged.

In the TV show *Heroes*, they had a female character who was sweet and gentle some of the time, and a violent, argumentative nutter the rest. That's not a superpower, it's like every bird you've ever encountered.

It's increasingly apparent that most women who aren't

part of the man-hating sisterhood only play the feminist card when it suits them. If we were on a sinking ship right now and the captain hollered, 'To the lifeboats, women and children first…' how many feminists would turn round and berate him for his shameless display of naked male chauvinism? I'll tell you – absolutely none of them. They'd be queuing up as quickly and as happily as if it were sales day at Bluewater.

Women want to be treated as equals… but only when it's convenient. In restaurants, I've yet to be wrestled to the floor by a feminist demanding to pay her half of the bill. They'll fight, rightly, for equal pay for equal work, but rarely for an equal share of the bar tab. Men are still required to change car tyres and remove the spider from the bath. And woe betide the male wretch who doesn't stand back and hold a door open for his date. Stride ahead of her and you'll be labelled a pig.

Women are your equal, until you divorce one. Then they expect you to carry on paying for them for the rest of their lives and, if you don't, some emasculated toad of a judge will lock you up and take your house away.

Why? 'It's pay-back time,' gloats Janet Street-Porter. 'We've earned it.'

Equality! Fellas, when you tell your sons about the birds and the bees, don't forget to mention the wasps and the pigeons that come along later to sting and crap on you.

In all things, and at all times, women want it all ways.

Worse than that, they want to change *us*, but they're never sure what to. Women say they want men to be caring and cuddly, to weep, to emote, to be in touch with their feminine side. So you end up stuck in the bathroom mucking about with a tube of exfoliating gel, while they're lying in bed going weak at the knees over Ray Winstone or Sean Bean – proper geezers who can get things done without recourse to a pedicure.

Weep and share your feelings with your girlfriend and she'll dump you for a hairy-arsed plumber with his car radio permanently tuned to TalkSPORT. Straight women don't want their men to be wimps – they only say they do.

In reality, deep down, women want a man who will stand up for them, stand up to them and understand the importance of foreplay. It's possible to be bright *and* two-fisted, macho and gentle; to be assertive, without being a knuckle-dragging bully.

*　　*　　*

NOT all feminists are badly-dressed, hairy-legged, man-hating lunatics with too many cats. Not any more. Modern feminists are often worse. You knew where you were with Andrea Dworkin. Now women want the right to wear short skirts and low-cut tops and still blow a fuse if blokes look at them. No wonder adult males raised in this culture are as confused as the proverbial blind lesbian at Billingsgate fish market.

On *The X Factor*, we see young men weeping publicly because they have failed to pass a talent show audition. Three generations ago, fellas their age were climbing into Spitfires and risking their lives to keep this country free. If they cried, they did it behind closed doors. They didn't emote; they didn't peck each other on the cheeks; they shook hands and got on with the job.

Now, of course, feminists want women to fly jet-fighters too, which is fine. (Any woman who wants to know what the effect force G will have on their private parts would be advised to type 'baboon's anus' into Google and hit image search). We're expected to over-look the likely effects of menstruation on the mood of a female flying a heavily-armed £25million air-craft for one week out of every four, but no matter. I have no objection to any woman doing any job they choose to do. What I do object to is:

1) Women being promoted on the basis of their gender rather than their merits. How many of Blair's babes would have got their Parliamentary seats on the basis of their political skills alone? Most of them have gone through more glass ceilings than a multi-storey greenhouse simply by virtue of possessing a vagina.

2) The way motherhood is undervalued by the 'wimmen' as a lifestyle choice for women. Young parents aren't told that children dumped in day-care by working mums are more likely to be insecure and prone to attention deficit disorders than those cared for full-time by their mothers.

3) The widespread idea that domestic violence is always male-on-female. (My own brother Terry was beaten up by one of the women in his life. He took some stick for that. His nickname was Tempura Tel cos he was lightly battered...)

4) Female comics being applauded for man-hating gags. Like Jo Brand with her hilarious little jokes like 'the way to a man's heart is with a knife through his breast pocket.' Or

'It only takes four men to wallpaper a house, but you have to slice them thinly.' Any bloke who told mean-spirited gags like that about women on TV would never get booked again. And they'd certainly never get away with suggesting that the way to Jo's heart is with a Kango, through 15in of blubber.

*　　*　　*

IN the 1980s and 1990s, feminists tried to tell us that men and women were essentially the same, and that all of the differences between the sexes were learnt – socially imposed by patriarchal society. It was nonsense, but it didn't stop feminists dressing their sons in skirts and giving their daughters train sets.

Now, of course, scientists have confirmed that male and female brains are wired differently. (For example, a woman will listen to a conversation with her whole brain while a man only listens with half of his; the other half is wondering what she looks like in a bikini.)

So feminists have changed tack, and have tried to redefine social roles. My father grew up with male heroes like John Wayne and Errol Flynn; I had Brando, Clint, Regan and Carter; my son has Sean Tully, Ian Beale and that tongue-tied, stuttering fop Hugh Grant. I don't call that progress and neither, I suspect, would most women.

We have to acknowledge that men and women are different – gloriously so. Women emote – men grunt; women multi-task – men are single-minded; King Alfred burnt the cakes, but he also battered the Vikings.

We are not the same! We should cherish that fact, make

the effort to understand how each other thinks, and learn some mutual respect. Girls – quit your nagging; guys – hide your porn mags.

And governments should stop social engineering. Even now, you hear Ministers fretting about 'sexist' career guidance. Smug schools minister Ed Balls says he wants more young women encouraged to be engineers and 'more young men encouraged to have a career in childcare'. Why? Does he really think that 'gender stereotyping' is keeping a generation of 16-year-old girls from realising their long-held ambitions to plunge their hands into sump oil and break their nails on a carburettor?

There is nothing good to be gained by pretending that the sexes are the same; quite the opposite. The idiot gender-blenders have created a generation of women who burp, belch and drink pints, while their male equivalents squander fortunes on moisturisers and male cosmetics, creating a new breed of 'geezer birds' and girly men.

Masculinity has had a make-over with the male-grooming industry going into overdrive; fellas now spend £750 million a year on beauty products.

David Beckham is probably to blame. He's fêted as a football icon but he's not exactly Bobby Moore, is he? He never brought home a World Cup.

Even Jonathan Ross fell for the metrosexuality con-trick. He's a smart guy. A straight guy. A funny guy. But he went out, in public, in a Jean-Paul Gaultier kilt. Jonathan thought he looked hip, stylish and modern. Wrong. At that moment he didn't only possess the biggest plonker in showbiz, he also looked like one.

This disease is catching. Today's young men spend longer in front of the bathroom mirror than their women. They have facials, they get waxed… they're not gay, they're just glad to be fey.

Take Scott Alexander, arguably Britain's vainest man. He cheerfully admits to pumping his body full of growth hormones twice a day and splashing out on manicures, facials, porcelain teeth from Japan, regular Botox injections and the like. He spends over £100,000 a year preening himself, and for what? To end up with a face like a Tangoed hamster, with choppers like tombstones and eyebrows that wouldn't disgrace a Bangkok lady-boy. This self-absorbed show-off blows his own trumpet like Satchmo on pay-per-note, and he has a portrait of himself in his living room, pictures of his abs as a screen saver, and more snaps of himself on his mobile phone. He'd put Narcissus out of a job.

Scott boasts that he has never had a relationship with a woman that has lasted more than six months. Of course not; no woman could compete with that type of deep, all-consuming love he's found in his mirror.

What kind of deep-seated insecurity drives this absurd behaviour? There is more to masculinity than posing and pumping iron. Real machismo has higher values – loyalty, courage, chivalry and self-discipline. There's a difference between being clean and dressing smartly and becoming a perfumed dandy, vain to the point of absurdity.

Maybe I'm old-fashioned, but I reckon blokes would be better off using their spare time to go to football and have a pie and a pint rather than booking in to a surgery to have their lips thickened and a spot of lipo.

The Male Eunuch

It's time for men to throw out the exfoliator, hang up their aprons, dry their tears, take a deep breath… and fight back.

Men need to be men again. And that's not just my opinion – it's also my wife's.

* Buddy Lee: 'Of course men can multi-task. Why only last night while making love to my wife, I was happily thinking of her sister.'

Why It's Great to Be a Bloke

1) You never have to fake an orgasm.
2) You can go to the toilet without a support group.
3) You never need to take more than one suitcase to go on holiday.
4) You don't turn into a hysterical carpet-chewing psychopath for one week out of every four.
5) You have no compulsion to ask how big your bum looks in whatever you're wearing.

New Rules for Modern Men

1) Never propose during a lap-dance.
2) Penis enlargement pills don't work, and never try and sue the mail order company you bought them from. If you do, you will be publicly exposed as a gullible mug… with a very small penis.
3) Honesty is the key to any relationship; if you can fake that, fellas, you've got it made.
4) In Thailand, it is not only permissible, but advisable, to check to see if your date has an Adam's apple. When possible, ask to see a birth certificate, too.

5) In nine out of ten cases, that very suggestive, 18-year-old single woman with the perfect figure you are talking to over the Internet will be a 40-something gay man with a beer gut and rampant halitosis.

6) Super Viagra tablets are a waste of money. They give you an erection for 36 hours, but why would you want that? I can't even smile for 36 hours.

7) No matter what he might tell you, Dale Winton is not and never has been a government-approved sperm tester.

Bushell On the Blog
June 2007

2 June Charles Shaar Murray praised Punk on The Seven Ages Of Rock tonight; surely not the same Charles Shaar Murray who once described the Clash as 'the kind of garage band who should be speedily returned to the garage, preferably with the engine running'?

5 June So the Olympics logo: over-priced, ridiculous, pretentious, a bit pink, cheesy, disjointed and falling apart ... all in all then, a perfect symbol for modern Britain after ten years of Tony Blah. A triumph for pseuds, bullshitters and chattering-class tosspots everywhere. Never mind drug-testing the athletes, they ought to drug test the people who designed this – and the idiots who shelled out £400 000 for it.

7 June Emily Parr was kicked out of the *Big Brother* house of horrors in the middle of the night. Her crime was to use the N-word, which in her case should really stand for naïve, nit-witted nonentity. Now Emily, a middle-class white girl from Bristol used the word in friendly conversation with Charley, the beautiful black unemployed lap-dancer. She didn't use it in a racist sense, she used it in the hip-hop sense because she was desperately trying to appear 'street'. Reason enough to boot her out, you might think. What disturbed me more was the orgy of self-righteous claptrap that followed and the hypocrisy of Channel 4. This conversation wasn't even broadcast on the E4 live feed. Producers Endemol leaped on it to stir up a major fuss, with them cast as the good guys. It seems obvious to me that Emily Parr has been made a scapegoat for the Shilpa Shetty debacle. Cue an avalanche of condemnation from those arseholes who go through life hoping to be offended. The N-word is ugly. I wouldn't use it, but Emily wasn't being racist – she was trying to act black. Crucially, Charley wasn't upset by the word. She was a bit taken aback but she wasn't enraged like she was when Lesley suggested she might be stupid. Seven hours after the incident, Emily was called from her bed in the middle of the night and cross-examined. Very apt. The PC lobby increasingly resembles the Stasi. Emily was guilty – not of racism, but of thought crime.

11 June *EastEnders*. Keith lost the remote – again – and I lost the will to live. There are fleas in the Vic, but the script is full of itches you can't scratch. How does Sean make a living? How did he afford his world tour? How can Bradley go for promotion when he never works? Is this soap beyond saving?

12 June George Bush had his watch stolen in Albania. Sleight of hand meets slight of mind.

16 June. BRITAIN'S GOT PERVERTS, announces the *Sun* splash today after a contestant was revealed to be on the sex offenders' register. Yeah. It's Opportunity Nonce.

- Tonight on TV the story of a very ordinary man who becomes a monster. And if you don't want to watch Piers Morgan on *Britain's Got Talent*, I understand Jekyll is on the other side.

18 June I am standing for London Mayor, according to articles in the *Independent* and the London *Evening Standard* today. This is premature. I am considering the possibility. An election of this nature has to be taken extremely seriously. And you have to have the cash to fight an effective campaign. It concerns me that London, my home and the capital city of this great country, suffers from such levels of crime, grime, pollution and poverty. And it infuriates me that so much of London's tax revenues are siphoned off to pay for better public services in Scotland and Wales when there is so much to be done here. London and Londoners have been ignored or taken for granted for too long by the established political parties. We're shelling out more than £13billion a year to the rest of the country when London has ten of the poorest wards in all of Britain. I want to speak up for London and the people of London. The forgotten Londoners, over-taxed and under-served. We need to safeguard our hospitals, build affordable starter homes for our young Londoners and confront the growing menace of knife crime. Only a policy of zero tolerance will do. And we need a Bill Of Rights to restore hard-won traditional liberties such as freedom of speech, freedom of assembly, presumption of innocence, habeus corpus and greater freedom of information.

19 June White men can't run the fire brigade! Ken Livingstone has blocked the appointment of nine white blokes to the London fire authority because he says they are 'unrepresentative' of London. How daft is this? Surely all that should matter is how good they are at their job. I wouldn't care if all nine of them were Watutsis as long as they were the best people available. In a related story, Ken has called for *Trumpton* to be remade. In future, Trumpton Fire Brigade will consist of Pugh! Pugh! Barney McGrew! Singh! Obama! Wang! (And Wang is a pre-op transsexual)

23 June This is hilarious. I seem to have upset Piers Moron when I reviewed him on *Britain's Got Talent*. He hits back in the *Mail* today saying that a pig as ugly as me would demand plastic surgery. This is a great line, right? The only trouble is, as Piers well knows, I wrote it about a soap actress back in 1987. It caused a stir because she promptly sued me. Piers, have a go at me as much as you like mate but use your own jokes – if you have any. It could be Piers expects special treatment because I once employed him. That's not the way my column works. If you do favours you get found out. But out of interest, when I had my own ITV series in 1996 do you know who Morgan got to review it? My arch enemy Jo Brand! What goes around comes around.

24 June Europe is back in the headlines. You know that bit in the horror films when you think the monster's dead, then its eyes blink back to life and it rises up to run amok again ... that's what's happened with the European Constitution. People voted against this Constitution in Holland and in France in 2005. We'd vote against it here given the chance. But the career politicians and bureaucrats don't care about that, they just changed the wording and ploughed on like a juggernaut. And so we get a reform treaty instead, 90 per cent the same as before, just a few words changed. Germany's Chancellor Angela Merkel said the EU would achieve its goal with or without the consent of the citizens. So much for democracy. This whole deal stinks like a Glastonbury

Portaloo after its 1000th visitor. The EU is shown up once again as a liar and a sneak. It's more exposed than Jodie Marsh's mammary glands. Why does this matter? Here's why. Member states have now lost the right to veto legislation they don't like in 52 important areas such as asylum, immigration, welfare, energy policy, transport and decisions on who can take part in EU military operations. There will be greater powers for the European President. There will now be a European foreign minister. Plus, the European Council has decided that the IGF – the Inter Governmental Conference, which represents the interests of the member nations – can only discuss items they say can be discussed. And guess what? Most of the new changes are off the agenda. Zese are your orders and you vill obey zem! NOBODY wants this except the EU's central bureaucracy and a political class who represent no-one but themselves. They radiate contempt for the people of Europe. Their summits make Marrakesh street traders look like beacons of fair play. Our new unelected prime minister Gordon Brown could expose this scandal and oppose it. He could give us the referendum Tony Blair promised us in TWO manifestos, but he won't. Why? Because he knows it can't be won.

- Monday night on *EastEnders*: a disorientated Dawn Swann is lying on a strange bed, writhing and screaming, her wrist shackled to the headboard. Something that doesn't normally happen to her until at least the third date ... Some have slammed the Beeb for broadcasting these scenes. But let's put it in perspective. This soap prides itself on gritty realism and it was high time they tackled the widespread menace of family doctors who abduct patients in order to steal their unborn babes by forced Caesareans. Yes, it was Dr Psycho at your cervix. Myra Hindley's Casebook, with The Stitches Of Salem to follow. And to think people say Enders can't do comedy...

26 June Well, at last he's gone. Tony Blair has finally come to the end of his cringe-making, stage-managed farewell tour. He bowed out today. Bloody good riddance, I say. But what amazed me was the standing ovation he got from MPs in the House of Commons. For what? Has the world gone nuts? Blair presided over the biggest foreign policy cock-up since Suez. Immigration is so out of control that even Labour MPs have noticed, taxes have never been higher, our former Prime Minister has been grilled three times by Scotland Yard over the loans for peerages scandal. Under Phoney Tony our personal freedom and democratic rights have been eaten away; every day brings some fresh nanny state nonsense and his last act of treachery was to agree to the European Constitution surrendering Britain's veto in dozens of areas. The man has turned lying into an art form. Yet, despite all this, MPs in the House of Commons, Labour and Tory, gave this grinning clown a standing ovation. It beggars belief! He should be leaving the Commons in handcuffs!

So where does that leave us? With a new unelected Prime Minister, and a weak and ineffective Opposition. Almost as amazing as Tony Blair's standing ovation was the way Gordon Brown proceeded to try and sell himself as something different. It's time for a new style of government, he said, time for change ... but isn't it more a case of plus ça change, as the French say?

Brown was up to his neck in the Blair government: he was privy to every Cabinet decision, he ran the Treasury for ten years and he is as much responsible for domestic policies as Blair was, if not more, because he controlled the purse strings. And he's got the brass neck to say: 'Now let the work of change begin.' Why didn't anyone laugh? Gordon Brown is the man who stole our future by raiding occupational pensions. His legacy as Chancellor is stealth taxes and budget day sleight of hand. This bloke can't look at a book without wanting to cook it.

In my mind, the only way Brown can make us trust him is to honour Blair's 2004 pledge to give us a referendum on the new EU constitution. Don't hold your breath – this ain't going to happen.

29 June Why isn't the theme tune for *Embarrassing Illnesses* 'It Started With A Cyst'?

30 June Book of the month: *The Yiddish Policemen's Union* by Michael Chabon (Fourth Estate). CD of the month: 'Unforgiven', the Cockney Rejects (G&R Records). Download of the month: 'All Light Up', The Pretty Things. DVD of the month: *Randall & Hopkirk Deceased* box-set.

10

Drop The Celebrity

Freddie Starr has thrown knives at me. Noel Edmonds has dragged up as Teri Hatcher to 'gotcha' me (a memory that is far more mentally scarring). But the only time I was ever genuinely terrified on a TV show was when I signed up for ITV's *Drop The Celebrity*.

Well, I say signed up. Essentially I was conned in to it. My agent, Tony Clayman – terrible man, looks like Penfold in *Dangermouse* – just rang up one morning and asked, 'How do you fancy a big jump with Linda Lusardi?' I had no idea what kind of ordeal I was letting myself in for.

Drop The Celebrity turned out to be disaster cunningly disguised as opportunity. 'It's prime time Saturday night ITV,' said Clayman. 'What could go wrong?'

What could go wrong indeed! How about everything? If they don't like you on *Big Brother*, you get sent home. We were getting slung out off a Hercules at 12,000 feet.

There were six of us: me, Linda Lusardi, Cheryl Baker,

Bobby Davro, Lady Victoria Hervey and Ricardo from Channel 4's *The Salon* – so four minor celebs, a posh bird and a hairdresser. We were taken to a West Country airline hanger and briefed by a parachute crew. We would exit the plane, they said, strapped to an expert, plummeting towards the earth at 120mph. Gulp. That's faster than Clarkson with a cob on! I didn't like the sound of that. Nor the fact that in word association 'plummet' always seems inextricably linked to 'splat'.

All we had to remember was to raise our knees before impact. Sounded fine, in theory. But the reality was far worse. For starters, Cheryl forget to raise her knees and broke her ankle. Then there was the plane itself. Loud, cramped, noisy and there was no food – it was like flying Easyjet. And there was none of that Mile High club stuff going on either. The tight sods didn't even come round with the drinks trolley.

When the tailgate went down for the first eviction all we could see was light streaming in – just like it did before the aliens come for you on the TV show *Taken*. At that point there wasn't one of us whose years didn't flash before our eyes. I was convinced I had all the life expectancy of a turkey on Christmas Eve. This was it, death by television. This show made *I'm A Celebrity* look like *Wish You Were Here*.... The only way it could have been scarier was if ITV had booked Maureen Rees to fly the plane. And to cap it all, after enduring all of that, the only thing that dropped faster than we did was ITV's viewing figures. It was a ratings Chernobyl.

What did we go through? Clouds, mostly. Why did we

do it? Fun, money, exposure, charity – people had different reasons. Our job, apart from jumping, was to convince the voting crowd below which of us was the biggest celebrity. And this was where Lusardi came into her own, shamelessly name-dropping people she had never even met as best mates.

Had the host, Mark Durbrain-Smith asked any tough questions, the whole fancy stitching of her colorful fake life would have unravelled like a love-rat's alibi. But alas he didn't. And so, although I made the final three, Linda Lusardi beat me (four words I like to savour). Yes, I wuz robbed. LWT's sour-faced warm-up man pleaded with the crowd to boot me off, where's the justice? And the votes were clearly counted in Florida. But the jump was exhilarating. What an experience. As soon as I'd finished I wanted to do it again (insert your own Lusardi joke here).

LWT wanted to raise serious 'post-modern' points about the nature of celebrity too and, in a roundabout way, they did. Fame, once a by-product of talent, has now become an end in itself. Ricardo claimed he was 'born a celebrity'. He'd cut hair on *The Salon*! No wonder he was the first out. The guy was lost in showbiz without ever being in it.

Our throwaway culture has produced a glut of people who are recognisable but talent free. We put everyday folk in a house and complain when they don't entertain us. We create instant pop groups who have one manufactured hit and vanish. In our hearts we know they're a poor substitute for the real thing.

Modern celebrity may be about being seen in the right places and dropping the right names. But that's not proper stardom. One Paul O'Grady is worth fifty Ricardos. One Brucie is worth a hundred Davinas, and one Dolly Parton equals a thousand Victoria Beckhams.

- After the show I got a phone call of commiseration from Frank Carson: 'It could have been worse,' he said. 'In the Irish version the pilot got voted off first.'

11

The Bushell-Men of the Kalahari

'To be young, gifted and black, oh what a lovely precious dream.'
Marcia Griffiths

Channel 4 reckons that I am 8 per cent African. I don't know which part it is; possibly my nose. The claim, featured on *100% English*, was broadcast as a proven truth, with their expert saying that the 'probable' explanation was a single black ancestor six generations back on my dad's mother's side. What? In Swalecliffe? You would have thought someone in the family would have noticed.

I'd be delighted if it were true. Think of all the Bushell-Men of the Kalahari gags we could do. It would radically improve my chances of being adopted by Madonna, and it would certainly explain my lifelong love of Ska. Sadly, there's no sign of it being likely.

Channel 4's science was suspect; theories were incorrectly presented as facts. They claimed Carol Thatcher was one-quarter Middle Eastern, when clearly she isn't. And if she was, what would it matter? Only Nazis

– and, it appears, Channel 4 – think of national identity in terms of racial purity.

So what was their documentary all about? After the show was broadcast, many viewers felt that they had just wanted to piss on anyone associated with the cause of English freedom and write us off as Little Englanders or some other variety of nutcase. The unspoken subtext was that anyone who celebrated their English identity and sought to preserve our customs and freedoms had to be some kind of racist. That's why the programme-makers turned away people from recent immigrant backgrounds who wanted to say they felt English and were proud of being English.

It didn't end there, either. Much of the filming was done at the St George's Day Festival of England that I promoted at the Circus Tavern in April 2006. Top of the bill that night was Neville Staple, formerly of The Specials, a black man, born in Jamaica, who grew up in Coventry. Also on the bill was the Artful Dodger, featuring MC Alistair, who is black and English born. Neither were mentioned by Channel 4, nor were they or any black person in the audience asked to contribute their thoughts on why they love England.

Instead, the programme adopted a mocking tone. Presenter Andrew Graham-Dixon, the *Sunday Telegraph* art critic (who looked pretty French to me), took great pleasure in breaking his spurious findings to people whose only crime was to feel English. In some cases, it was like pulling the wings off a butterfly.

Let me tell you how the show came about. In March 2006, a TV production company called Wall To Wall invited me to take part in a documentary for Channel 4 which was then called *Who Are the English?* It would explore what it means to be English, they said, and they would welcome my take on what being English means.

Further down in their email, they mentioned they were asking every contributor to the programme to take an ancestry DNA test. This, they said, would give an insight into where our ancestors were from and the migratory paths they would have taken over thousands of years to arrive in England.

And there's one significant phrase – thousands of years. One DNA test went back 10,000 years, another 20,000, when the country was covered in ice and no one lived here. From that perspective, every one of us is 'foreign'.

The Angles and the Saxons didn't arrive until the 5th century AD. The term Anglo-Saxon was first used 300 years later to distinguish our lot from the Old Saxons on the continent; after the Norman Conquest, chroniclers started to refer to them as the English.

By the way I've always known that I'm not 100 per cent English. My middle name is Llewellyn; it's a bit of a clue. My mum's great-great-grandad was as Welsh as a bucket of leeks, so his ancestors were probably driven west by the incoming Saxons. But I digress.

Wall To Wall's email went on to say, 'It is important to stress that these tests are strictly designed to reveal only the information described above, and are incapable of identifying any personal family data.' So why pretend otherwise? Without genealogical investigation, they can't possibly make such claims about an ancestor 200 years ago.

The people who did the testing, DNAPrint Genomics, are based in Sarasota, Florida. Most anthropologists disagree with their racial classifications and hugely dislike the test, which, incidentally, is popular with US neo-Nazis. They have a 28 per cent margin of error for European DNA and the same DNA has been shown to produce radically different results. To mean anything they'd have to test me, my parents and grandparents.

The other point to bear in mind is that races are defined by DNA mutation. If part of my dad's DNA is showing up as sub-Saharan African, it could just as possibly be an ancient DNA strand that hasn't mutated. It doesn't mean African as we'd understand it today.

I believe that suspect science, coupled to a hidden agenda, produced exactly the result Channel 4 were after. Andrew Graham-Dixon interviewed me at length twice, but none of the things I said about English history or the English cause made the cut because all they wanted were Alf Garnett-type quotes to demolish our case. They also edited out any contribution that stressed positive and progressive English achievements such as trade unions, Parliament, habeas corpus, and so on. They built up a straw man and then demolished it. It was a pointless exercise, clearly politically inspired. Like John Prescott, they're pushing the hoary old chestnut, saying that 'there's no such nationality as English'.

But hold up. You could apply exactly the same tests to the French or Italians and get very similar results, yet no one questions their right to nationhood. Only the English liberal-Left beat themselves up about patriotism.

The production company's motivation was to push the fashionable position – we're all mongrels, there's no English culture to speak of, we'll lose nothing by being sliced up into regions, or dissolving further and faster into the EU. And this self-loathing runs deep; the *Guardian*'s Poly Toynbee even wrote a piece entitled WHO WOULD WANT TO BE ENGLISH?

It's why Greenwich schools have a black history month, but teach nothing about Watt Tyler or Henry VIII, and why Southwark Library displays a brochure proudly detailing every immigrant group who've ever settled in the borough without once mentioning the English.

Of course, a degree of immigration can enrich a culture. But too much, especially when coupled with liberal self-denial, could seriously damage our tradition of tolerance.

The English won't be written out of history; a sense of identity – a knowledge of who you are and where you've come from – is essential for the health of any society. And like it or not, the Bushells have been here for more than 1,500 years... with or without my great-great-great-great aunt Beyonce.

Bushell On The Blog
July 2007

1 July The smoking ban begins – watch it devastate the pub trade. (For the full entry, see All Light Up)

4 July Will Boris Johnson run for London Mayor? It seems he doesn't know. He cares so much about London that he's undecided. Some dismiss Boris as a bumbling clown. This is unfair. Born in New York, educated at Eton and Oxford and passionate about classical Greek, Alexander Boris de Pfeffel Johnson seems just the man to connect with hard-up inner city voters.

7 July Did you watch the big Live Earth concert? Neither did I! I spent the afternoon revving up me 4x4 and barbecuing a penguin on a coal fire. It's nothing new. McDonald's have been selling quarter-pandas for years.

- Global warming's come in handy. I've told the kids that the Bermuda triangle has moved north and Santa has gone missing.

8 July Today, much of South East London ground to a halt because of the Tour De France. What's all that about? It's a great sporting event to be sure, but the Tour De France should be in France. The clue is in the name. It's not Le Tour de Kent is it? What next? The running of the bulls in Peckham High Street? The Kentucky Derby at Lands End? That'd be something, eh? Watch out for the big water jump. The usual nitwits are saying how wonderful is it to have a big international sporting event here. Well, yes. Except we don't need to import French events, do we? Let's have a few more of our own. Why not reinstate the Royal Tournament at Earl's Court, which was abolished by the Labour Government in 1999, and featured the Navy's Field Gun Competition and much more?

Of course the first time Le Tour De France went through England was in 1974 to 'celebrate' the UK being conned into the Common Market. Whoopeedoo. There I suspect is the real reason it started here. To underline all that Europa-a-nation nonsense.

- The Tories are planning to increase tax on beer by up to 7p a pint to pay for the treatment of heroin addicts. Another great vote-winner from the champagne-guzzling chinless wonders. What will they do next, revive the Poll Tax? Two points 1) Shouldn't Tories be about CUTTING taxes? 2) Surely the people they ought to target are the nincompoops who promoted junkie chic for years – moronic rockers, hippies, the NME etc. Hit them, not the honest Joe who likes his pint after a hard day's work.

  It may be admirable to tackle binge drinkers (although I enjoy the occasional binge myself), but clearly the half-cut yobs who blight our high streets aren't buying pints in pubs. They're getting cheap, strong cider from corner shops just as teenagers have always done. Besides, it's already an offence to serve alcohol to anyone who's mashed. If shop-keepers and landlords stuck to that, and the cops and courts backed them up, problem solved.

9 July Peter Mandelson is strongly tipped to be made a lord in Tony Blair's farewell honours list, it was revealed yesterday.

Wouldn't that be a fitting legacy? Nothing says New Labour more than arch manipulator Mandelson. The guy was forced to quit the Cabinet twice – once over his secret loan from Geoffrey Robinson, the second time over the Hinduja brothers' passport scandal. Mandelson masterminded the doomed Millennium Dome – a snip at £600million – which he promised would 'blow your socks off' but which actually sucked like an airplane toilet. He is a man so deceitful you suspect that even when masturbating he fakes his orgasms. Mandelson is the essence of slipperiness decanted into a suit.

12 July What cobblers from Gordon Brown about 'supercasinos'. There are casinos everywhere. A supercasino is merely a larger version with more entertainment built in. A supercasino somewhere like Blackpool would be a fantastic leisure attraction. It would boost tourism and showbiz, attracting the world's greatest entertainers. Banning supercasinos is just a sop to the *Daily Mail*. It won't stop people betting, it just denies Blackpool hundreds of millions of pounds worth of investment. It's nonsense to say this announcement is a blow against gambling. We live in a gambling culture. Every child in the land is exposed to ads for the Lotto. They see scratch-cards in the corner shops, horse racing on the telly and fruit machines in every arcade. At least casinos operate strict age restraints. If I want to go out and play a game of blackjack, what business is it of the government? You'd get better odds playing craps than you would with a Lottery ticket, where the odds of winning are 14 million-1. (Bob Monkhouse's newsagent once told him he had as much chance of being hit by lightning as he did scooping the jackpot, to which Bob replied, 'You have your dream and I'll have mine.')

14 July The BBC was forced to apologise over a trailer that seemed to show the Queen in full garter regalia storming out of a photo session. The Queen throwing a wobbler? That's about as likely as finding Gordon Brown on the craps table at Caesar's Palace with a litre of Mad Dog 20-20 in his hip pocket. The Beeb is now eating all kinds of humble pie. But surely their biggest pretence is political neutrality? The Corporation remains hideously biased against England, the USA and of course Israel. They are biased against the white working class and the countryside, against popular comedy and heterosexual males. And they are biased in favour of the EU, the euro, Hamas and Live Earth propaganda to mention just a few. One bit of trick editing is nothing. The Beeb is institutionally wet – and we're forced by law to fund it.

- The motorways are getting worse. I drove up the M6 today, there was a sign saying 'Keep two chevrons apart'. I nearly killed myself trying to keep up with a Porsche. And that's hard to do in a diesel Sierra.

  My last car was a Skoda but I wrote it off in a crash. It was terrible. Bits of marzipan, chocolate and icing sugar everywhere. You've seen that advert haven't you? What's the point of turning a car into a cake? Does it mean you have to be a fruitcake to buy one? It'd make more sense if the car was a Lada...

16 July Boris Johnson has entered the race to be the

Conservative candidate for London mayor in next year's election. The Tories were taking so long trying to find someone suitable people were joking that they'd end up going with a golden retriever. And what do you know, they have ... Give me Boris over Ken any day, but what does the bloke stand for? Character is no substitute for policies. Will he understand the concerns of real Londoners? Will he address the congestion charge mess? Will he campaign for an English parliament? Absolutely not.

17 July I've been in Blackpool since Saturday. The weather has been glorious. Some folk blame it on global warming, but I suspect the real culprit is another scientific phenomenon – summer.

The heart of variety beats on in Blackpool. Here are the top five shows you have to see up here: 1) The Tower Circus, the best in Europe. The acts are genuinely breathtaking, and Mooky the clown is wonderful. 2) Buddy Lee – the best 'unknown' comedian in the country; he's warm, witty, down-to-earth and his act, a conversation with the audience, is never the same twice. 3) The Hot Ice show at the Pleasure Beach – sensational. 4) That endangered species, the traditional Northern comic thrives here: where else can you see Johnnie Casson, Cannon & Ball and mighty Mick Miller? 5) Tucker, the next Brian Conley, opens for Bernie Nolan on the North Pier. And of course, subject to availability, the legendary Joe Longthorne still performs at the Grand. This guy is the spirit of showbiz decanted into a tuxedo. Marvellous. (For a promising younger crooner, with a great

Bassey impression, check out Peter Anthony at the Queen's Hotel – the best place to stay on the Prom.)

19 July I haven't read the new Harry Potter book yet, but I understand that, at the end of it, Harry defeats evil Lord Voldemort with a secret herb he got from Jacquie Smith, the Home Secretary ... or Jackie Spliff as she's now known. As Gordon Brown says that cannabis should be reclassified as a class B drug, SEVEN cabinet ministers admitted smoking ganja when they were at college. That's what I call high office. The big clue came when they got together and appointed a Minister for Munchies. Is that all, though? Only seven? And only dope? Personally I reckon whoever came up with the idea for the Millennium Dome was on something a bit stronger than that. And as for the London Eye, imagine that planning meeting ... What we need is, like, this big ferris wheel that goes real slow, man. It seems you can't run a race if you've done drugs, but you can run a country...maybe we should have random dope-tests for MPs – it would certainly put an end to the rumour that several high-flying politicians are known privately as The Boys From the White Stuff. And while we're at it, let's dope-test the BBC's comedy department too, because only someone severely stoned could find something to laugh at in *Hyperdrive*.

24 July Is David Cameron nuts? What is he doing jetting off to Rwanda when his own constituency looks like a Wet & Wild water theme park? You don't desert your own people when they're in a crisis situation. We've got ten thousand homes flooded and many more people without power and water.

Cameron should have postponed his African publicity stunt and been on every TV and radio show asking tough questions. It was left to Ming Campbell to lay into the Government for not doing more to create proper flood defences. Cameron should have an affinity with water. He looks dead in it.

24 July Well, there's a turn-up. *EastEnders* has been in need of a couple of fit blondes for quite some time. Maybe the Mitchell Sisters could help find them some. Ronnie (Sam Janus) may have turned heads ten years ago but now, with her angular features, strangely taut skin and boomerang chin, she looks like a cartoon preying mantis. And hard-faced Roxy is as down to earth as the straw in her kennel. Bow Belles you say? Bow Locks. Yet Ronnie and Roxy - named, for a laugh, after the Kray Twins – are here to stay. This makes perfect sense. You're running a bar in Ibiza. You fly over to see a cousin you've never met get wed. You find chaos, death and hostile locals ... who wouldn't forget their business, renounce the sunshine and move in? The soap's logic is a wonky as Jonathan King's smile.

25 July Aren't these floods terrible? Ming Campbell's gone up to the Midlands to see if he can pick up any floating voters.

After I finish work tonight I'm going on a cruise...round the Home Counties.

The floods were so bad up my mate's way a flasher opened his raincoat and caught a trout. Adrian Walsh tells me: 'I saw a sign, it said: "When this sign is under water the road is closed". It's not easy going to Tesco in your snorkel and flippers. It's the first time I've done my shopping in a canoe.'

28 July Love this headline about drunk astronauts in the *Sun*: SLOSHED IN SPACE. The Gonads have a song about this already, 'Alconaut'! Seems NASA astronauts have been flying while smashed. So they must launch from the Ted Kennedy Space Center. Those new spaceman sayings in full 1) 'Take me to your lager' 2) 'One small shot for man, one giant barrel for mankind' 3) 'Fill me up, Scotty.'

28 July RIP Mike Reid. The legendary Cockney comic died today. As well as being Frank Butcher, Mike was one of the great gag-tellers and had a massive presence on stage. He honed his aggressive delivery playing tough East End pubs and clubs. He grabbed your attention and held you captive with his onslaught: 'Oi, winkle, wallop! Migraine!'

Mike shot to stardom as the first southern comic on *The Comedians* (series two; remember his skinhead jokes?) In *EastEnders* he added a bucket-load of authenticity. He was a real Cockney, and injected his own colourful lingo into the scripts, contributing memorable phrases such as 'Do you think I'm some kind of pilchard?' and 'What are you, some kind of double yoker?'

He was a great character on and off screen. His private life was hellish but he never gave less than his best. Britain is a greyer place for losing him. And British TV is greyer for operating a ban on gag-telling comedians. Don't miss the *Daily Star Sunday* today, I've got a spread of jokes from seaside comics in there. Here are a few tasters:

Frank Carson: I've got a pace-maker now. I leave the house in the morning and a little Nigerian runs in front of my car.

Mick Miller: I rang up Domino's Pizza today. The fella said, 'How can I help you?' I said, 'Have a guess.'

Dirty Rob: I like it when pop groups play together. I crossed the Sugababes with The Vibrators once and got Wet Wet Wet.

30 July Friends of new *EastEnders* star Rita Simons allege in *The People* that she has a history of drug use. Some friends! Apparently they realised she had a problem when she came fourth in the Tour De France.

12

Stop Global Whining

It's time to talk seriously about ecology. Today the world is facing the fall-out from insufferable levels of hot air and toxic noise pollution generated by yesterday's events around the world at the various Live Earth concerts. Live Earth was a global event best summed up by Madonna's quote: 'If you wanna save the planet, jump up and down.' Yes, that's it. That'll work.

It was a complete and utter waste of time, not to mention energy and resources. The organisers say they wanted to spread awareness of global warming. Is there anyone in the Western world who didn't already know about it? Was anyone anywhere actually thinking, Well I've heard what the United Nations, the Green Party and Zac Goldsmith have got to say, but I can't make my mind up about it until I know where Edith Bowman stands on the issue? Forget the boffins, let's hear from Terra Naomi!

The Earth's climate is changing, not for the first time. But Live Earth, like the eminent American windbag Al Gore, accepts without question the theory that human activity is the cause of it all. A significant number of leading scientists disagree. One of them, the US academic Steven Hayward has made a film to challenge Al Gore's An Inconvenient Truth. It's called An Inconvenient Truth Or Convenient Fiction and you can download it from the Internet. Other experts point out that it isn't just the Earth that is experiencing temperature fluctuations; every other planet in the solar system is also apparently experiencing a degree of warming, because, these experts say, temperature change is related to solar activity. It's the sun what done it.

Gore's film is full of unsubstantiated claims and errors. No polar bears have drowned looking for ice. No Pacific atolls have been evacuated. And you can bet your arse – even if it's as lardy as Al's – that sea levels will not 'rise by up to twenty feet' in our life-times.

Gore's hyped-up hypothesis has all the hallmarks of a great global scare like the Y2K bug, AIDS-will-kill-us-all or the 1970s theory that a new Ice Age was imminent. Every generation has to have an apocalyptic cause to fight for. In the fifties and sixties it was CND, who said unless Britain unilaterally got rid of Trident (leaving the Soviet Union's nuclear weapons conveniently intact) the world would blow itself to kingdom come. With the collapse of Communism, Green is the new Red, allowing another generation to echo the Soothsayer in *Up Pompeii* and tell us 'We're all doomed.'

But instead of challenging the hype, the BBC wheeled out renowned expert Alan Carr, the camp comedian, to talk about glaciers. We then got Geri Halliwell plugging her world tour, and a group of nitwits singing 'Que Sera Sera' ... 'what will be, will be.' Quite. Unless there's a thermostat on the sun, there may not be much we can do about any of it...

The only people questioning the official line were comedians like Dara O'Briain and David Baddiel. Wouldn't you rather have heard from a dissenting scientist? Or at least Jerry Sadowitz who might have pointed out that the effects of global warming could be countered by a quick burst of nuclear winter. I thought Hell would freeze over before we saw Les Dennis consulted for his views on climate change, but I guess global warming means that's now unlikely. At least the Pussycat Dolls were there, thank the Lord.

Yet even if you took Gore's doom-laden message at face value you might question the decision to spread his message via a set of mega concerts involving jet planes, limos, trucks, amplifiers, lighting rigs ... Sarah Brightman flew 5680 miles to get to Shanghai; Bon Jovi came by private jet – burning as much fuel in one hour as a family car burns in a year. The total number of air miles involved is estimated at close to 225,000.

Holding a massive rock concert to highlight global warming is like burning down a tower block to protest against arson...especially when the TV *audience averaged a paltry 900,000. The carbon footprint caused by yesterday's event is probably equal to what Luxembourg generates in a year.*

I'd have been more impressed if they'd played acoustically and arrived on pushbikes. People have short memories and little knowledge of Earth history. There has always been climate change – cycles of warming and cooling caused by the sun. The last ice age ended 10,000 years ago. Temperatures rose to the 'Holocene Maximus' five thousand years ago, when it was on average 3 degree Fahrenheit higher than now. They dropped again two thousand years ago, and went back up during Medieval Warming (between 600AD and 1100 AD) when there were vineyards in Kent and Greenland was a habitable Viking colony. 400 years ago, Britain enjoyed a mini Ice Age. It lasted into Victorian Times and people used to skate on the frozen Thames.

Green is the new religion. Most of its advocates are believers. They can't be dissuaded by mere logic any more than a devout Muslim could be. If you argue with them you're evil, you're a 'denier', a witch to be ducked. Some Western politicians and businessmen seem particularly keen to make sure China and India don't develop. Do they want to keep third world populations as a source of cheap labour?

Fossil fuels will run out eventually so nuclear power makes sense – although I note that that's not high on the Live Earth agenda. The biggest threat to the planet is human population growth and we don't hear them making a song and dance about that either.

I'm all for conservation. Mankind is dependent on the earth for our survival and should approach nature with respect, even humility. Greener living and recycling can only be a good thing. But useless, grasping politicians will use global warming as an excuse to bleed us dry. There will be green taxes to 'save the planet', green parking spaces (that cost you more), green rubbish collection policies (the dustmen turn up less often), and of course no end of 'guilt-free' green consumer goods that come with weasel labels like 'Earth smart' and 'eco-safe' or 'eco-friendly'. No fossil fuel was burned in the making of this mini-skirt.

TalkSPORT, 8 July, 2007

- I am taking this issue very seriously. The taxi that brought me to TalkSPORT tonight was one of those green cars. Yeah, it was a low emission vehicle, shame the same wasn't true of the driver.
- In *An Inconvenient Truth*, Al Gore asks Americans to cut electricity use. Shortly after, the Tennessee Centre for Policy Research had a butchers at Al's own energy. Turns out Al's twenty-room mansion uses double the energy per month that the average US householder uses in a year.
- Inconvenient facts: February 2008. Satellite data confirms that the Northern Hemisphere (except Western Europe) has been enjoying its coldest winter for decades. China, Afghanistan and the USA have seen epic

blizzards. California's unusual frost caused a billion dollar loss of crops. There has been more snow since any time since 1966, Damascus looked like a Christmas card and January's global temperatures were lower than their entire 20th century average. At the poles, Artic ice has risen back to where it was a year ago, Antarctic ice is increasing and getting colder, the polar bear numbers are on the rise. But, as usual, only heat waves and scare stories make the headlines.

Meanwhile it emerges that the 1930s had four of the warmest years of the past century – the hottest being 1934. These figures show a closer correlation to our star than to carbon emissions. With sunspot activity all but disappearing, we could well be about to enter a period of global cooling.

- Global warming is getting serious. Scientists say that in ten years time, Anne Robinson will be completely defrosted. The more extreme doom-mongers say the Earth could end up like Venus: 600 degree Fahrenheit and raining sulphuric acid. In other words, like Dagenham in August.

- Prince Charles has clambered on board the global warming bandwagon. Yes we can trust his judgement, can't we? This is the man who thinks Camilla is hot.

13

Three Men and a Goat

A while ago, Channel 4 introduced us to a happily married – but deeply misunderstood – American couple. They were Mark, who lived in a trailer in Missouri, and his lovely wife, Pixel, who was a pony.

Yes, you read that right. Mark had married his horse. And he wasn't the only one. *Animal Passions* trawled the States to unearth a parade of perverts who preferred to make the beast with two backs with a beast with four legs. Even by Channel 4 standards it was shocking. There were barking mad women who let their dogs give them a bone, and a creep with stallion love-bites on his shoulder-blades. (Just say neigh.) You were just relieved that Johnny Morris wasn't alive to see it; or indeed provide a commentary.

What made it worse was that these freaks could see nothing wrong with what they were doing. They called themselves 'zoophiles' although most could have walked straight out of The X-Files. And, cleverly, they used the language of gay rights activists to try and justify their unnatural lusts. To them, sex with animals is just the love that dare not bleat its name. By any standards they were profoundly disturbed and the show was nauseating. So why did C4 make it?

Ignore the old fanny they talk about breaking barriers; this was a purely cynical exercise to make the channel seem 'cutting edge' and wind up the general public. They want us to be outraged. And it worked. Well done. But should a responsible society allow this kind of demeaning programme to be broadcast? Object on old-fashioned grounds of morals or taste and you'll be labeled 'uncool', a dinosaur out of step with modern mores. So the temptation is to ignore it, or laugh it off. But shows like this don't exist in isolation. They have a drip-drip effect, poisoning our daily lives. The previous week, C4 screened footage of 'swingers' so explicit it would normally have been scrambled on a porn channel. (They also showed Jason from *Big Brother* pleasuring himself, proving he really is what he first appeared to be.) There have to be limits ...

Unchecked, the shocks will get bigger, the sick and freakish will slowly seem acceptable and before you can say 'Brace yourself Wellard' they'll have a zoo couple in Albert Square. Don't laugh; the soaps have already had incest, rape, and mass murder. What's a little horsing around among friends?

Three months after *Animal Passions*, Channel Five showed Rebecca Loos pleasuring a pig on their reality TV show *The Farm*. The only surprise was that the pig wasn't Stan Collymore! Producers say collecting boar semen this way is a standard farming practice. True enough. But by choosing Ms. Loos, a woman generally regarded as being loose, to go the whole hog in graphic close-up while broadcasting her sexual comments, Five were quite deliberately, and ham-fistedly, toying with bestiality.

This is unacceptable. But it's also the logical conclusion of the 'wannabe' trend that started on *The Word*: dimwits doing anything just to get on TV, TV producers being 'ironic' enough to broadcast their excesses, and us being nuts enough to watch. As for you Rebecca, get a grip! Not like that …

* * *

- EVEN *Emmerdale*'s Sam Dingle was shocked by *Animal Passions*. 'What?' he said. 'No sheep?' It certainly brought new meaning to saying 'My wife's a bit of a nag.' I blame the Byrds for popularising bestiality. Remember that Chestnut Mare who was just like a wife? What was that about? And as for Rolf tying kangaroos down … that's downright kinky.
- C4 missed the big story about Mark. Pixel the pony may have been his wife, but Daisy the cow was his udder woman.
- Jerry Springer once made a show on bestiality that was canned – quaintly it seems now - on grounds of taste. Can you imagine? I mean, what kind of sick animal makes love to a Jerry Springer guest?

Bushell on the Blog
August 2007

1 August A great white shark has been spotted off the coast of Cornwall, it was claimed by The *Sun* today. Although on closer inspection I understand it was just a lot of pollocks. A shark in Cornwall? It wouldn't last five minutes. Rick Stein would barbecue it. Besides, it'd be much more amazing if they'd seen some cod.

- Pete Doherty says life with Kate Moss was like the Vietnam War. Yes. The South was always welcoming but he got nothing but flack from the North. His big Tet offensive got off to a good start but ended in abrupt withdrawal.

2 August Go 74mph on a deserted motorway and you could soon find yourself placed on the DNA database for life. The police want sweeping powers to take our DNA samples for a whole range of trivial offences. If your old Nan accidentally drops a sweet wrapper in the street she could be forced to provide plod with a mouth swab. Her DNA would then be stored permanently along with rapists, killers and terrorists. Welcome to Big Brother Britain, 2007. This is nonsense, isn't it? Firstly, we don't need a DNA database to fight crime; we need fewer petty laws and tougher sentences for real crimes. Secondly, this is another step closer to a police state and who wants that? A universal database will allow a future government to classify our grandchildren by their genetic make-up. What if someone in authority decides that it would be socially beneficial to 'prune out' any of those who are genetically prone to cancer, obesity, congenital stupidity or red-hair? Their argument will sound very convincing, I'm sure. Maybe they'll delete individuals whose DNA suggests they are predisposed to become rebellious or inquisitive. These free-thinkers are such a burden on an ordered society ...

Labour control freaks are intent on curbing our freedoms and making us all servants of the State. You can't walk fifty yards from your home without being filmed, private mail is being intercepted, ID cards are looming. Pretty soon, you won't be able to get a passport without giving your fingerprints. We are losing our privacy and our freedoms at an alarming rate, something we have to resist. Individual liberty is the bedrock of a free society. The British people aren't servants of the state, the state should serve US. Instead, it pokes its big fat controlling hooter into every aspect of our lives: which school you can send your kids to, how you discipline them, where to smoke, what to eat and drink, what to think ... you can't film your child's nativity play, you can't be a passenger on a coach without wearing a seat-belt, you can't drive into London without paying through the nose. Some of these laws may make sense, but many don't. They're symptomatic of a Government mindset that wants to snoop, interfere and criminalise its citizens. If it were down to them, they'd wire-tap all our phones and have hidden cameras in every room of our houses and still the idiot chorus would chime: 'If you've done nothing wrong you've got nothing to worry about.'

Yet we know that the Government is neither squeaky clean

nor the fount of all knowledge. This Government is greedy and dishonest, it's far too big and often incredibly stupid. Government ministers have a track record of barefaced lying. Think very carefully before you allow this shower of creeps any more power over our lives. Or repeat after me: 'The future is unquestioning. The State knows best. You've got nothing to worry about. Bah, baaah.' Now hold still while they insert this micro-chip into your cranium.

3 August Chris Langham. Started on *Not The Nine O' Clock News*; finished on ITN, News 24, CNN...

Those Langham shows in full: Kiss Me Cock, Pervs Like Us, The Dick Of It, and Is It Legal? (NO!) He also directed Posh Nosh. Of course he did.

9 August If you're going on holiday abroad this month you're likely to suffer long delays, rude service and general inconvenience at our airports. So pretty much condition normal.

10 August Ken Livingstone says wannabe taxi drivers from ethnic backgrounds will be given a free motorbike to do the Knowledge. They'll get a bike, and waterproofs and schooling all for nothing, whereas white Knowledge candidates will still have to pay their own way. How on earth is this fair? The Knowledge is open to all, irrespective of colour. How can it be right to discriminate against candidates because of their ethnic background just to fit in with some insane PC quotas that exist only in Ken's head? This is reverse racism and its perverse, its unjust and its completely unjustifiable. Surely all candidates should be treated as equal regardless of their colour? Livingstone should either roll this scheme out to all

Knowledge entrants or leave things as they are. It gets worse. Some labour politicians want the Knowledge made easier so recent immigrants who aren't familiar with London streets can become taxi drivers. Yes that makes sense. That's what you want from a London cabbie: a lack of knowledge of London streets. Good luck getting to that important meeting while the nice Somalian driver tries to find the right page on his out-of-date second-hand A-Z ...

10 August It was the biggest *EastEnders* manhunt since Kat Slater's hen night.

Poor Patrick got coshed in the Minute Mart. He was left with a fractured skull and a small blood clot (pronounced 'claat'). He would have been more badly hurt except the wads of cash he keeps in his hat softened the blow. Immediately, Sean 'Psycho' Slater went on the run. Despite his head start and military training, Sean's idea of evading capture was to circle Albert Square without ever attempting to leave the area. Doh!

It was like the worst-ever episode of *The Fugitive*. He spent most of the time lurking by walls. Kevin crept up on him, Gus bumped in to him. The only people who couldn't find him were Walford plod, Keystone Division. They only stumbled on him when Ronnie realised Sean was holed up in the Queen Vic cellar. Well it was either there, the allotment sheds or the swings. Small tip mate, the best place to hide is BBC4 – nobody's watching that.

Sean is facing a GBH conviction. With any luck he'll also be charged with doing a piss-poor impersonation of Grant

Mitchell. The stare, the glare, the vest, the delivery, the crazed over-reactions ... all he needs to do is shave his head, find a red-faced hoarse-whispering brother and attempt a vaguely Cockney accent and he'll be there.

But is Sean guilty? Of course not. The clunking script was the worst case of misdirection since Sound TV's amateur magician night. We know Sean didn't do it, and that consequently Chelsea and Deano have committed perjury.

So whodunit? Who splat Pat?

Here are latest odds:

50/1 Eddie Booth, former neighbour with a long and sorry history of racial abuse.

40/1 Yolande Trueman, loving wife driven to breaking point by his constant lies and deceit.

15/1 Fat Pat AKA Lonely Loins, former lover, not been getting any for years (And for that small mercy, many thanks).

8/1 Victor Duke, the husband Yolande left in Trinidad.

10/1 on, Lucy's boyfriend Craig. Nut-job? Check. Motive? Check. Violent streak? Check. Yep, he'll be the one.

- SKA fan Patrick had a lucky escape. Better to come round to 'Hard Man Fe Dead' by Prince Buster, than go out to 'Long Shot Kick De Bucket'...

11 Aug Will *Celebrity Wife Swap* be affected by the row about TV faking? After all, it isn't technically a wife swap unless the couples sleep together. Not quite so keen on the idea now, eh Razor Ruddock?

15 Aug Is the world getting crazier? Suddenly Gordon Brown is 10% ahead of the Tories in the polls. Are you all nuts? How is

Brown getting away with it? He's broken Labour's election promise on a referendum on the EU constitution, he's making out he was nothing to do with the Iraq invasion, unemployment is running at 12 per cent, our pensions set-up is a disgrace – all down to Brown. Yet somehow, this twitching, shifty-looking, one-eyed, hair-dying, haggis-munching, nail-biting control freak seems unassailable. Why? They're saying Brown may call a snap election. It will be a snap election of course because all the main parties have identical policies ... Where do you stand on Europe? Snap! On Iraq? Snap! Or at least that was the case until this week. Dozy David Cameron has finally come out and said he will welcome cuts in taxation, red tape and regulations. Hallelujah. Now all he needs to do is advocate getting tough on crime, give the English a parliament, and tackle immigration and he might get somewhere.

- A shocking scene on Ann Widdecombe Versus tonight. Cops were pulling over and lecturing men for driving their cars alone in the 'wrong' part of Southampton. What a liberty. The criminalisation of the public continues apace. Still I suppose it's easier than catching criminals. Memo to Ann: there wouldn't be any street-walkers or kerb crawlers if prostitution was decriminalised.

    Of course the quickest way Ann could help stop prostitution would be to go on the game...

17 August The BBC has been caught out again, trying to stitch up John 'The Vulcan' Redwood by playing 14 year old footage of him in Wales mumbling along to Land of My Fathers, which is like showing Neil Kinnock falling over on Brighton beach every time he's in the news or constantly showing Gordon Brown biting his nails, sucking in his lower lip or promising your pension will be safe with Labour. Why is the BBC rattled? Because the Tories are finally talking sense on tax. They wanna cut stamp duty, slash corporation tax and reduce quangos. If they promised to scrap inheritance tax on family homes too, they'd really be cooking. The only thing with the whole Tory package is that they're talking about bring in green taxes at the same time. Why? Presumably to look hip. The idea that human activity is the main cause of climate change is unsubstantiated hysteria promoted by a government who can't wait to screw us with a new raft of taxation on the back of it. Which brings us neatly to these self-styled eco-warriors who are setting up camp at Heathrow. Mark my words they'll be the usual rent-a-mob of decrepit hippies, middle-class crusties dropping out to upset papa, tree-huggers, layabouts, freelance pikies and opportunist thugs. How much do you think it will cost to clean up all the junk left behind by the 'save the planet' rabble by the time they've finished? And will David Cameron resist the urge to get down there and hug a crustie? As Frankie Boyle said last night the best way to throw Heathrow into chaos is to book a flight.

We need an extra runway at Heathrow like a pile sufferer needs another haemorrhoid. What's wrong with building airports offshore instead of concreting over Middlesex?

19 August The Tories say they will slash tax but there's a 'but': they want to introduce a 'green tax' on flights. That's smart.

Who will this hurt apart from working-class families who enjoy one family holiday a year? Even if we accept the claimed human 'cause' of global warming (unproven), this tax won't work. All we need to do is take a train or ferry and fly from Paris, Belgium or Holland.

- Shockingly, knife crime has more than doubled in the last two years. Every day in 2006 there were, on average, 175 robberies at knifepoint in England and Wales. Why aren't the Government taking this more seriously? We need a Giuliani-style response: zero tolerance for kids who carry knives and proper punishment for those who get caught. And we need real cops on the streets to deal with it, instead of plastic cops – the Hobby Bobbies of the PCSO, who are nothing more than glorified traffic wardens. This week Thames Valley plod announced they have recruited two 16 year olds as PCSOs. Five other forces already employ 17 year olds to patrol the streets and protect the public. Does that make you feel safe? Thought not. You probably saw the picture in the week of uniformed cop Stephen Dean posing on a skateboard. There's a vision to terrify the Yardies – the cops are here and they're on heelies, we'd better turn it in. This is farcical. The Police Service has been eroded by political correctness, Home Office performance measurements, endless form filling, diversity seminars and senior officers who don't believe in anything except management and personal advancement. We have a police force that's forgotten what it's for and whose side it is on. Yes, there are bigger issues behind the gang violence, like family breakdown and loss of personal responsibility. It will take a generation to fix them. In the meantime, the Government must make our streets safe. Real cops, real sentences and real jail time is the only way to do it.

- I've got a great spread of gags from working-class southern comedians in the *Daily Star Sunday* today. Here are some of my favourites.

Rikki Jay: I just got back from a bad cruise. I told my Mum we had rain and snow. She said, 'You were lucky son, we had Hale and Pace.'

Ricky Grover: Kids have got everything these days. We never had paedophiles when I was a kid. We had to buy our own sweets.

Mick Pugh: The wife got a leaflet from a Harley Street clinic. She said, 'If there was anything you could change about me what would it be?' I said, 'Your surname.'

Jim Davidson: This Foot & Mouth disease is worrying. They've banned the movement of cows, so the Spice Girls reunion tour has been cancelled.

Dave Lee: It's not easy being fat. I tried computer dating once and they matched me up with Maidstone.

Ricky Grover: Bin Laden is a cheeky git. He keeps making these videos and next month he's teaming up with Lionel Richie to record a single: 'Halal...halal...is it me you're looking for?'

Jethro: I rang the newspaper to place an advert. They said, 'It's £1 an inch.' I said, 'Shit. I've got a 40 foot ladder for sale.'

20 August Ofcom has found me guilty of making a homophobic remark. The words I used, when taken out of context as they have been, appear completely different from my intention at the time. I have nothing against gay people and I grudgingly admire Peter Tatchell for much that he has done, not least for standing up to Mugabe. But I strongly disagree with Tatchell's on-record statement that he believes the age of consent should be lowered to fourteen. As far as I'm concerned, that is at the very least putting young people and children at risk of serious psychological damage from the attentions of sexual predators, whether they be gay or heterosexual. I wonder what the reaction would have been if on air I had called for the age of consent for heterosexual sex to be lowered to eleven years? I don't think it would have been Ofcom knocking on my door. More likely the Metropolitan police. Many gay people were also horrified by this demand. I would be happy for my views against the age of sexual consent being lowered to eleven, twelve, thirteen or fourteen years of age to be judged the London electorate. For the record, I couldn't give a monkey's what two consenting adults get up to in their own home. I hate bigotry. Far from being homophobic, I have actively championed great gay performers over the years, from Frankie Howerd to Paul O'Grady. I'm a huge fan of Alan Carr and Joe Keenan. I loved Freddie Mercury. Noel Coward and Kenneth Williams are comic immortals. Dale Winton is a family friend. I've lost count of the number of years I've campaigned to see more of Joe Longthorne on TV. I adored Barrymore before he was engulfed in scandal and worked with him on stage and on TV. Yes, I objected to Julian Clary's fisting remark, but as I said on his own show *All Rise With Julian Clary* that was because the joke was unsuitable for a live ITV show. Poor old Stan Boardman was banned from live TV for life for his much funnier Fokka gag. Why the double standards?

- Strange. You don't see many teenagers on marches demanding that the age of consent for gay sex is lowered. It's mostly old men...
- MEMO to The Hairy Bikers: next time you Ride Again it's probably best to avoid the M40.

21 August Don't let anybody think I'm not taking his homophobia allegation seriously. I genuinely regret causing offence. In fact, as a penance, I have agreed to write this week's column while wearing leather chaps, reading *Heat* and listening to Liza Minnelli. Just don't expect me to give *That Antony Cotton Show* a good review.

Clearly, the only way for this nonsense to end is for me to be pictured hard at it in a rampant homosexual orgy. So be it. Come on then Britney, your place or Shannon's?

22 August The great Chris Ellison has turned up on *EastEnders* as Len Harker. I would have loved to be a fly on the wall when he took that call from his agent.

'Great news, Chris, you've got a part in *EastEnders*.' 'Terrific, who am I playing?' 'You're on screen in August.' 'Great. What's the part?' 'You're breaking up.' 'Who-am-I-playing?' 'Fat Pat's love interest, must dash, meeting, laters.' 'Arghhhhh!'

Len's a quiet man with inner strength who makes rocking horses for a living. Brightly painted, garishly adorned, wooden...yes, you can see why he was attracted to Pat.

- A new study shows that people are still having sex into their eighties. The study was based on the love lives of just two people: Rupert Murdoch and Cher

23 August Every decent person in Britain is in mourning for Rhys Jones, 11, an innocent kid gunned down in a drive-by shooting in Liverpool. It was, we are told, an accidental by-product of a drugs-related gang feud that has been going on for years between two rival Merseyside estates. But what does it say about the uselessness of our courts and our cops that such a feud has been allowed to drag on like this? Children are killing children. Why has this sorry state of affairs been tolerated? The Home Office response has been predictably wet. Home Secretary Jackie Spliff went on TV and blinked away her tears but she parroted the usual Government lie that crime rates are falling and then claimed that Labour's ridiculous 'Acceptable Behaviour Contracts' could help. What bull. Our unelected Prime Minister Gordon Brown has promised a 'crackdown' and said 'where there is a need for more laws we will pass them'. I have news for you Gordon, old son: murder is already a crime! We don't need new laws we need the existing ones to be enforced vigorously and aggressively. Soundbites and spin are not enough. Politicians yap about longer sentences but our jails are already over-crowded. Will they build more prisons? How will they prevent the import of more guns from Eastern Europe if they can't control our borders? And will the Labour Party ever have the bottle to address the enormous social problems caused by 40 years of cultural liberalism?

We need the kind of aggressive zero-tolerance strategy that worked so well in New York under Giuliani: if you get caught with a weapon you will face jail time. When this approach was implemented in Hartlepool by DI Ray Mallon ten or so years ago, crime was cut by a third. For once, the Tories are right. Britain's high rate of family breakdown has left us a fractured society. Our welfare system has destroyed the work ethic; careless immigration and enforced multiculturalism has left us a distrustful, disorderly society. Too many of our streets have become a quagmire of dirt, fear and aggression. Too many of our people are voting with their feet and emigrating. But Cameron isn't honest enough to admit that much of the problem stems from the fact that we no longer make our own laws in this country – as the Chindamo case proves.

- Our prisons are over-crowded. One prison cell we could and should free up today is the one containing Ronald Arthur Biggs, now a sick old man who has suffered multiple strokes and is no risk to anyone. Keeping Ronnie banged up is vindictive and pointless.

- Funniest sight of the summer: those self-righteous 'eco-warriors' at Heathrow in anoraks getting soaked in the middle of August. Here's an inconvenient truth for you, Nasa just announced that the hottest year of the 20th century was 1934.

24 August Eviction night on *Big Brother*. Let's hope Tracey gets released back into the wild. I've heard enough of her feeble slogans to last a lifetime. 'Have it?' No-one wants it, love.

25 August Jeremy Paxman has upset luvvies by criticising the

BBC and the licence fee – welcome to my world. Paxo said rightly that the 'idea of a tax on the ownership of a television belongs in the 1950s.' He also said the corporation was in danger of forgetting its 'sole purpose' – making worthwhile programmes. Absolutely bang on. Instead of building an unwatched digital empire, the Beeb should concentrate on making great shows. Now watch how much crap Paxo will get from the tame media for telling the truth.

29 August A magnificent statue of Nelson Mandela was unveiled today in Parliament Square, but let's spare a thought for the Winnie Mandela statue. Separated from her ex-husband, and forgotten by the great and good, I understand the Winnie bronze stands neglected around the back of the Fraud Squad HQ with a 'necklace' in one hand and a box of matches in the other. Nelson is, of course, a lasting symbol of the universal struggle for liberty; but as a fine Mandela statue already stands on London's South Bank, this second one seems like overkill. Surely there's room for an imposing tribute to an English radical; Wat Tyler perhaps, Ned Ludd or Paul Foot who campaigned so tirelessly for the wrongly convicted. If we're going to honour South Africans, then what's wrong with the great Sid James? His screen persona was randy, hard-drinking and out for what he could get ... he'd fit in so well at Westminster.

31 August Yes! Brian Belo won *Big Brother* – just as I predicted weeks ago. His dimwit act bordered on genius. The Twins are for real, though and that's even scarier: their lips move, they speak, words come out that sound like English but

I can't follow any of it. It's incredible that these loveable, innocent, helium-squeaking nitwits have passed their A levels, amazing that they are university students, and mind-boggling that they are training to be social workers. Imagine them turning up at your door singing 'Jingle bell, jingle bell, jingle bell rock, we want your kids, like it or not...'

14

TORY! TORY! TORY!

Stop press! It's May 2008 and the Tories are back in business. Or so it seems. London has just witnessed the biggest blue surge since Dot Cotton flashed her varicose veins at Dr Legg. Boris Johnson, that bouncy Dulux Dog in a suit, has ousted Red Ken as Mayor, and across England and Wales the Labour vote has collapsed like house prices. Conservatives in the press see a blue moon rising; 2010 can't come soon enough.

But is the Tory Revival all it's cracked up to be?

Labour's decline is certainly for real. The people's party came third on 1 May 2008, losing 331 council seats. Third! Behind the Lib-Dims! 76 per cent of voters think they stink like a suburban back garden the night before the fortnightly rubbish collection. And that is amazing. It means that 24% think Gordon Brown has been doing a decent job. Who are these idiots? Labour has taxed the poor, nobbled the economy and buggered up the housing market. Social mobility has disintegrated. The gap between the richest and poorest has widened. The armed forces are under more strain than Prescott's waist-band. And yet one in four people still think Labour are worth voting for!

The rest of us can see that Gordon's credibility has been shot to pieces by a string of largely self-inflicted disasters: dithering over an election, dithering over Northern Rock, the 10p tax row, the climate-change tax scam, doubling road tax for family vehicles...

Battered and blooded, the glossy sheen of New Labour's confidence has finally evaporated. Emperor Brown stands naked before us, chewing his nails and trying to rearrange his Shrek-like features into something approximating a smile. It's not a pretty sight. The old pension raider is popping up on every TV chat show going, trying to prove he has the E factor (that's E for empathy, not effluvium or ectoplasm.) The bags under his eyes are now so heavy, even Terminal 5 couldn't lose them.

Looking listless and leaden, Gordon promises to 'listen and learn'. But if he did listen, he'd learn that we'd like him to leave. More than half of all *Labour* voters now want Brown to sling his caber back to Renfrewshire. He's like a bloke who's come round your house for a post-pub take-away who you can't get rid of. You didn't actually invite him, you asked his mate Tony, and Gordon just tagged along. But it's 2am, Tony's left and Brown won't take the hint. You can yawn and bang about all you like but the boring bastard just sits there droning on about 'long-term decisions' and 'feeling our pain'. He's hanging on like Robert Mugabe, but is marginally less popular.

TORY! TORY! TORY!

People are saying the only way Brown could frighten Cameron now is if he resigned. But who would take over the Labour reins? Ed Balls, a man smugger than a cat that's just eaten a canary? The android Miliband? They're done for. Finished.

* * *

IT HAS taken eleven years since Blair's first landslide for most people to realise that all that clever talk of aspiration, hope and prosperity was just that. Talk. Those easy promises of world-class hospitals and world class education sound like bad jokes now. That loud clucking noise heard between Tory cheers on 2 May 2008 was the sound of chickens coming home to roost. But does it mean David Cameron's Conservatives are the answer? They may well win in 2010, but then what? What do they stand for, and what should they stand for?

In the euphoria around Bo-Jo, no-one seems to have noticed that the Tories aren't actually doing that well. The Government is widely despised but only 35% of the electorate bothered to turn out on 1 May. Two-thirds of us couldn't even be arsed to vote. And the motivation behind many of those who did was anti-Labour rather than pro-Tory. Cameron's Conservatives don't mean a light in most of the major cities in the North of England. They have no councillors in Oxford, and only one in Cambridge. Why?

Surely the answer is that Cameron really stands for nothing at all. Or at least nothing different. Brown accuses Cameron of being a 'shallow salesman' and he's right. The problem for Gordon is that he can't even sell himself to his own party any more. His personal brand has all the allure of a postman's sock, while the slippery Cameron has successfully repackaged himself as the real heir to Blair, although it's unclear why that is in any way desirable.

On the surface, Dave has much in common with Phoney Tony: both are posh, polished and articulate. Both exude the sort of confidence that only the best public school education can buy. Both are as hard to nail down as jelly on a post. The big difference is, I suspect, that Blair was probably clinically insane. His self-belief was messianic and unsinkable. Whereas Cameron stands for nothing at all except turning himself into the Prime Minister and his old school chums into the Cabinet. Floreat Etona, indeed. It's hard to believe he means anything he says. He's as genuine as a £10 Rolex and as trustworthy as Wikipedia. ('Dave' is a triumph of style over substance.) He's not a leader, he's a PR stunt, with as much depth as a toddler's teacup.

In real terms, there is little difference between the parties, except that Brown is slightly to the right of Cameron. They might as well be rival soap brands: New Labour and Blue Labour, and that's tragic for Britain and for democracy. This has happened, largely, I think, because the media and the liberal Establishment have been allowed to create a fake political 'centre-ground'; a soggy consensus which is not shared by the public but which is broadly pro the European Union, pro-immigration, pro-taxation, pro-political correctness and anti anything resembling a decent education.

The Tories are all wets now, which is why the liberal news media feels comfortable bigging them up. They seem to take it as read that Brown did a good job as Chancellor.

But for all his talk of prudence, Brown's economic record is not great. He inherited a golden legacy from Ken Clarke and then squandered it. Brown was a tax and waste specialist. He chucked billions at the public services with no improvement in hospitals or schooling. The NHS is in chaos despite the valiant efforts of the workers. Literacy is getting worserer. Under Brown's watch, we have the worst fiscal deficit in Europe and six million people now work for the state – 10 per cent more (at a very conservative estimate) than there were in 1997. The Brown way will mean more regulation, more nannying and more fashionable nonsense.

Our tax pounds are squandered on transgender advisers, diversity managers and absurd health-and-safety snoopers. We have high taxes and poor services. A real Conservative Opposition would say loudly and clearly that this is wrong. They would say openly and proudly that their goal is to cut taxes and weed out waste, and then show us exactly where and how they would do it. (We don't know precisely where the Cameroons stand on tax but we suspect it's on Labour's shoulders.) Real Tories would argue passionately that state control and a command economy don't work, can't work and will never work.

Right across the board there are areas the Tories should be putting the boot into Labour and the *Guardian*-reading mafia of the muddle-headed and mundane. We've got five million Britons claiming benefits – generations who believe they have a right not to work. How can that be right? We've got the scandalous way fathers are treated by family courts. We've got social workers of staggering incompetence and some idiotic judges who should be locked in the stocks and pelted for their abject failure to do their jobs. Judge Julian Hall sticks in the mind. Last summer, Hall had a scumbag up before him who had raped a ten-year-old-girl twice. The Judge said the child had been 'dressed provocatively'. So she was asking for it, was she, your worship? Sickening. Hall called her 'a very young woman of ten'. This paedophile rapist was due to be free after just eight months – until the public kicked up a stink. Why weren't the Opposition up in arms? Why is their message as empty as Kerry Katona's head?

Because they are no longer Conservative in any meaningful sense. Traitor Tories tricked us in to the 'Common Market'. They helped tie up the cops with form-filling and dubious codes of practice. They brought in the Criminal Justice Act. Across the board, the Conservative Party has endorsed policies that are anti-family, anti-British, anti-punishment, anti-working class, amoral and pro-political correctness. Labour and the Tories are two sides of the same coin. They stand for the same liberal values and bloated state power. I recently joked on the radio that Cameron would be the first Tory PM since Tony Blair. But in reality the policy gaps between Major and Blair were minimal. And it seems likely that when Cameron does come to power most Labour policies and taxes will be left in place.

The Conservative Party used to stand for something. We might not have liked it but we knew what they were for. At its best, the Tories believed in self-improvement, self-reliance, education, the work ethic, deep family ties, and the notion of a community that helps itself. Real Tories would reclaim these core beliefs instead of aping Labour's multiple errors. They would advocate a state that meddles as little as possible in our lives, as opposed to one that spies on our every move. They would stress the fundamental principle that individuals rather than state officials are best equipped to make decisions that affect their future.

Real Tories would take less of our money by cutting taxes.

Real Tories would strive to reward hard work, reduce red tape, control immigration, clamp-down on crime, reinforce our sense of nationhood and encourage people to take responsibility for their own lives. They would reduce dependency on the State and make meritocracy their guiding principle. Real Tories would advocate the restoration of capital punishment, and bring our troops back from foreign wars that aren't in our national interest.

Above all, Real Tories would have the guts to tell the truth about our rulers, the EU, and let the people vote to throw this monkey off our backs.

As long as most of our laws are made by Brussels, domestic politicians can do little more than rearrange the deckchairs on the Titanic.

There may be Real Tories left in the Conservative Party, but they no longer control it, just as Real Socialists have no sway in the Labour Party. The closest Britain has to a free-thinking, cavalier party is UKIP. They were badly damaged by Kilroy-Silk and don't get much press. But the party has a solid leader in Nigel Farrage. They're still Britain's best hope of achieving independence. UKIP are the Real Tories now.

* * *

WHEN I gave Boris Johnson my second preference vote for London Mayor, it was to get Ken out rather than to put Boris in. But there's something likeable about the big buffoon. He's saying the right things about cutting waste and getting tough on crime. Can he deliver? I doubt it. Although in fairness, Boris promised to put more police on the streets and he's started that already. Brian Paddick is on the streets – looking for a job.

The Tory revival will at least increase our chances of a good sex scandal or two. Already we've seen Conservative donor Lord Irvine Laidlaw exposed for his spectacular Monte Carlo orgy involving three whores, a male gigolo, a trilingual bisexual, a dominatrix and a lesbian. That's what I call a commitment to diversity. The randy old goat has promised to try 'self-help'. You and I may have a different name for this.

* * *

I DON'T want to blow my own trumpet, but I was one of the first to see through Capability Brown's well-spun image of competence as this transcript of my Talk-SPORT rant from summer 2007 shows:

Suddenly, Gordon Brown is 10 per cent ahead of the Tories in the polls. Are you all nuts? How is Brown getting away with it? He's broken Labour's election promise on a referendum on the EU constitution, he's making out he had nothing to do with the Iraq invasion – oh really? Unemployment is running at 12 per cent, our pensions set-up is a disgrace – all down to Brown – and yet somehow this twitching, pouting, shifty-looking, one-eyed, hair-dying, haggis-munching, nail-biting control freak seems unassailable. Why?

The papers are saying Brown may call a snap election. It will be a snap election of course because all the main parties have identical policies....where do you stand on Europe? Snap! On Iraq? Snap! On education? Snap!

If Gordon does go to the polls it's odds-on he will win because he'll be up against the biggest, smuggest waste of space in Westminster, David Cameron, the Leader of Her Majesty's Opposition.

It is not over-stating the case to say that Cameron is as much use as a concrete parachute. He stumbles from one fiasco to another. He tried to persuade Greg Dyke, a life-long Labour man, to stand for London Mayor. He attempted to win over Polly Toynbee, a woman so wet that if you blew on her she'd ripple. He got himself into a completely unnecessary row about grammar schools, in the process betraying the bright children of the poor who are the ones who benefit most from selective education.

What is he thinking? As it happens, not a lot. Repackaging oneself as the real Heir to Blair, is hardly a desirable state of affairs. Tony Blair's decade in power was disastrous for Britain. His name is now a by-word for cynicism and spin, hypocrisy and evasion. Blair vowed to change the face of the country and he did. It's just a shame the country he changed was Iraq. The Government sent our forces into battle ill-equipped and with no clearly defined objective. We had five wars in five years, WMD lies and a dead scientist in the woods. Under Blair, taxation rocketed, the economy was wrecked, education was in crisis, immigration surged, the honest citizen criminalised while real crime is unpunished, and yet more of our sovereignty has been surrendered to Brussels. New Labour gave us the Dome, the Cash for Coronets scandal and a health-and-safety obsessed nanny state. Why on earth would you want to emulate that?

*　　*　　*

I'M still baffled by the cult of Tony Blair. I met him a couple of times and he's charming, but the man's like a snake oil salesman. He'll tell you anything you want to hear. When I had dinner with the then Prime Minister eight years ago, I asked him what would happen about the BBC licence fee. 'Oh that,' he said with a smile. 'That's going.' It's now in place until 2012, when of course it will be extended again. Blair would make a great footballer, he can take any position.

Still, the good news is that Tony is expected to earn £10million over the next year or so. So at least he'll be able to buy himself a peerage.

Five reasons why Maggie wasn't as great as she was made out to be:

1. She betrayed our fishermen and farmers.
2. She wrecked Britain's manufacturing backbone. Good-bye coal and steel, hello quangos.

3. She pushed the Single European Act through Parliament, taking us deeper into Europe.
4. She cut the armed forces, tied up the cops with paperwork and gave social workers more powers.
5. She signed the Anglo-Irish agreement, the first stage in selling out to terrorism.

But she had principles and she had a spine. Thatcher was one of the few modern politicians who could command your respect. Even if you hated her.

15

An Uncommon Market

Our rulers, the European Union, say that selling goods using imperial measures is not an offence. That's big of them. Commissioner Gunther Verheugen even had a pop at the British press for 'repeatedly and erroneously printing stories' about 'people having to buy their food from markets in kilograms rather than pounds'. Not true, said Gunther. Brussels no longer wishes to force us to go exclusively metric. 'Pounds and ounces are in no way under threat from Brussels and never will be,' he said.

The news made all the papers, and it was trumpeted as a triumph for our Metric Martyrs. Days later, Hackney Council seized non-metric scales being used by Colin Hunt, one of the original Martyrs, in Ridley Road market. Two cops and two council officials told him that, under EU directive 80/181, measuring fruit and veg in pounds and ounces was still a criminal offence. Colin Hunt then faced his third prosecution for this 'crime'. This news was not reported, except by Christopher Booker in his *Sunday Telegraph* column.

Just before Christmas, the stallholder Janet Devers received papers from Hackney Council charging her with thirteen criminal offences, including the use of imperial scales. She was then faced with a bill for the council's costs and a hefty fine. Do you suppose Gunther will have a whip-round for her? Don't hold your breath.

They're only minor incidents in the great scheme of things, but they're telling ones. Pretty much everything we are told about the European Union is a lie. The 'project' has been built on betrayal and baked in deception since day one. Edward Heath, the quisling Tory leader who took us into Europe in 1972, promised voters that the Common Market was just that – an economic trading block. Heath had known since 1960 that the end-game was a federal superstate, but he chose not to disclose that knowledge to the British people. At the rigged, dishonest referendum of 1975, shameless politicians persisted with the pretence.

Roy Hattersley later acknowledged that the referendum arguments had dealt superficially with what the new Europe involved. The EU agenda is, and always has been, complete political union; the plan is to become a single European nation (the old Mosley dream) run by the bureaucratic institutions of Brussels, with a Europe-wide police force and a Euro Army.

National institutions like Parliament have been left in place merely to maintain the illusion that we still govern ourselves. In reality, more and more of our laws (70 per cent at the last count) originate in Brussels.

Smoke and mirrors, deceit and lies have been the hallmarks of the EU from the start. Just over sixty years ago, an Italian former Communist, Altiero Spinelli, who was one of new Europe's key architects, wrote that politicians should quietly set up all the ingredients for the new superstate and only declare its true purpose when they were in place by unveiling a Constitution. Another founder, Paul-Henri Spaak, advised that the only way the project could be achieved was to make out that it was only a Common Market. And that's precisely how it happened; we were repeatedly lied to.

The process looked unstoppable until 2005 when the peoples of France and the Netherlands were given the chance to vote on the Constitution. The unthinkable happened – both countries rejected it decisively.

British voters were told there was no point us voting, too, as the Constitution was dead, and that should have been the end of it. But you can't stop a juggernaut that easily. First José Manuel Barroso, President of the European Commission (and a former Maoist), insisted on BBC2's *Newsnight* that the project wasn't all over. Then Peter Mandelson, the EU Trade Commissioner (and a former Young Communist), suggested that the Constitution should be revisited. And, lo and behold, in 2007, like a zombie rising from the grave, the Constitution returned under the guise of the European Treaty.

Labour, who had promised the British our chance to vote on the Constitution, once again resorted to deception. Gordon Brown told us there was no need to keep its referendum pledge because 'the Constitution has been abandoned'. It hadn't been. The new Treaty and the old Constitution are 96 per cent identical. It gives the EU a permanent president, foreign minister and cabinet. All of us are now citizens of the European Union. The Treaty gives Brussels more powers to dictate laws, and it hastens the Common Defence Policy, which will mesh all of the armed forces together. That will be followed swiftly by the Europe-wide *gendarmerie*. Nothing significant about the rejected Constitution has been abandoned, except the name. They'd just dropped the references to EU flags, anthems, mottos and the special Europe Day.

Given the chance, our rulers know that voters would kill the Treaty stone dead. French President Nicolas Sarkozy warned that Brussels was out of touch with its citizens. Sarko tore himself away from the cleavage of Carla Bruni long enough to warn of another cleavage 'between people and governments'. He said, 'There will be no Treaty if we have a referendum in France.' A referendum, he went on, 'would bring Europe into danger'. In other words, we're being stitched up again. The Euro-élite know we'd reject their plan, so we won't get the chance to vote. That democracy thing… so last century, don'tcha think?

Britain is now part of a vast one-party State, ruled by a Euro-Government that we can't unseat. We've suffered a back-door coup d'état; we've been taken over by stealth.

We learn nothing from history; having faced down the Soviet bloc, the EU bureaucrats are busy creating something that closely resembles it. The EU is cumbersome, meddlesome, slow, bureaucratic, inefficient and corrupt. It is contemptuous of democracy and is governed in secret by an unaccountable cabinet. Like the USSR, it is doomed to end in tears.

For anyone who's interested in a comprehensive explanation of the thinking behind the EU and how it came into being, I heartily recommend *The Great Deception* by Christopher Booker and Richard North.

Bushell on the Blog
September 2007

3 September JOB DONE screams the headline in today's *Sun* as our boys pulled out of Basra. What despicable duplicity. The *Sun*'s claim rings as true as George Bush saying 'Mission accomplished' in 2003. Job done? Iraq is in chaos, with Iran stoking the flames of civil war. No-one questions the guts, skill and grit of our fighting forces. But they were sent into Iraq without a strategy and they've paid a heavy price for the folly of politicians. The blood of 168 of our brave fighting men and women is on the hands of the British Cabinet. 'Withdrawal' means retreat from a war we should never have been part of. What a sorry end to Bush and Blair's knee-jerk adventurism. The *Sun* does our people no favours by persisting with their pathetic lies.

5 September Gordon Brown says he admires Margaret Thatcher. This is getting confusing. Now we've got Cameron as the new Blair, Brown as the new Maggie and Ming presumably as the new Methuselah. Sadly for all of us, George W is still the old George W.

7 September The words 'Livingstone is a c***' have been sprayed on top of a London bus. This insult to the London Mayor is being taken very seriously. The Met are determined to find the vandal responsible. Seven million Londoners will be taken in for questioning.

- Are we really meant to believe Kate McCann killed her own daughter? This latest sick twist in the Madeleine case looks more like the Portuguese plod desperately covering their own backs to protect the tourist trade than a significant development. Algarve cops have notched up a shocking catalogue of blunders. Do they now add insult to injury? How could Kate have killed Maddie, removed her body and hidden it in such a short space of time with her husband and friends just yards away? How would she have disposed of the corpse under the gaze of her family, TV news crews and the world's press? It beggars belief.

- RIP Ronald Magill. The actor who played the wonderfully grumpy Woolpack landlord Amos Brearly died yesterday. Amos was one of *Emmerdale Farm*'s finest creations, a real character who will be remembered as much for his double act with Henry Wilks as for his luxuriant mutton-chop sideburns. Will we see his likes in *Emmerdale* again? Nay, nay, Mr Wilks, nay, nay. We're lucky these days if we even see a sheep.

11 September ITV booked Jim Davidson for *Hell's Kitchen* because he's an outrageous comic with non-PC views. They then kicked him out for expressing views which were felt to be non-PC and outrageous ... it's like booking Bob Crow and acting surprised when he unionises the kitchen and calls a strike (one out, both out please, Adele). Isn't it odd how telly bosses panic whenever any actual reality threatens to invade reality TV?

It seems to me as if ITV is running scared of Ofcom, a ludicrous body whose function seems to be to curb free speech and enforce reverse racism. According to these pillocks it's OK to call someone a fat white bastard, but shameful to describe a car as 'ginger beer.' You can mock anything English, American or Israeli, upset Royalists and Christians, and ridicule working-class people week in, week out, as long as the sacred cows of 'diversity' aren't challenged. No-one was less likely to negotiate this perverse minefield of modern manners unscathed than Jim Davidson, although incredibly he did manage to last longer here than in his third marriage.

While Adele burnt the brioches, Jim burnt his bridges. Brian Dowling accused him of homophobia. Jim confessed to Brianophobia. I believe him. Vain, self-centred, immature, talentless, Brian is someone every gay man I know wants to slap. The crunch point came when he squawked: 'I'm equal to you Jim, in everything we've ever done.'

Really? Jim may be a mixed-up, complex bloke; but he's also the funniest stand-up of his generation. How would Brian entertain an audience? Surely the demand for piss-poor Spice Girl imitators has been cornered by the Sugababes. In Jim's day, you needed talent to become a TV star. Now it's enough to be camp and emotionally incontinent. Granted, Jim was inconsiderate. But so what? Since when has not being touchy-feely been a crime? Janet Street-Porter has been trampling over people's feelings for thirty years.

Without Jim, the show was just amateur cooks coping badly, Marco being magnificent and the occasional sharp line from Deayton's writers. Like the Shilpa incident (bullying, not racism) this row leaves a nasty taste on the mouth because it reminds us that 'thought crime' is now part of our TV culture.

Viewers don't need the State to tell us what's right, we're capable of making up our own minds.

- I'm swinging behind Barry McGuigan now – but expect Adele to win. By the way, Deayton is a humourless git off-camera. How he's got the nerve to sneer at other celebs after what he got up to is anyone's guess.

12 September There's an article in today's *Sun* about Jim Davidson's sexual encounter with a man. This is taken from an interview I did with the comedian – kicked out of *Hell's Kitchen* on Monday for a derogatory remark. The full quotes are much funnier: 'I was out on the town with my bodyguard in Berlin,' Jim said. 'And we pulled a couple of girls in a bar. One was really pretty. So I said to my bodyguard, right she's mine – perks of the job and all that. But the pretty one went straight for him and I was left with the minger. She was a dodgy-looking, short-haired Oriental thing, a bit lumpy. But I was drunk and I didn't care. She couldn't speak English but she obviously wanted to get friendly. So we slipped out and she gave me a good old Gillian Taylforth out the back. Afterwards we slipped back into the bar and my minder asked me if I'd noticed anything funny about her. I said, 'Big feet'. He said, 'Adam's apple too...' It was a fella! He spoke to her in Thai and she ran off screaming. He said, 'Yeah, that's definitely a bloke.' I wasn't too bothered though. It only upset me later – no card, no letter, no phone calls.... I should have guessed as soon as I saw it, cos she was reading the *Angling Times...*'

13 September Days after Madonna was described by Malawi

adoption officials as being 'as perfect as Mary Poppins' she was spotted leaving a restaurant carrying a Purple Penetrator strap-on in a see-through carrier bag. She's Mary Pops-it-in! Blimey, if Mary used that on Bert it would certainly explain his irritable vowels syndrome. 'Luv a duck, Mary Pawpins, next time use more grease...' It was a masterful PR stunt but it raised some perplexing questions, like: was the Purple Penetrator modelled on Ian Gillan or Ritchie Blackmore? Is it best used on a strange kinda woman? And was Mary really such a perfect nanny? As I recall she stuffed those kids full of sugar, took them racing and dumped 'em as soon as the wind changed.

14 September Book News: two London authors, John King and Martin Knight, have formed their own publishing company to reissue vintage London fiction. London Books launches its classics range next month with two neglected novels written in the 1930s: *Night and The City* by Gerald Kersh and *The Gilt Kid* by James Curtis. Both books are set in the seedy underbelly of Soho and the West End and cost £11.99. Next year, they will re-publish Alan Sillitoe's *A Start In Life* too. London Books is a labour of love devoted to finding a voice for literature by and about real, everyday Londoners. It's a welcome antidote to the head-up-its-arse world elitist world of modern publishing and the cynical sausage factory of true-crime garbage. John King, who wrote *The Football Factory*, *England Away* and *Human Punk* among other authentic novels, says, 'The marginalised fiction of the past can be as relevant and exciting today as when it was first published.' Here, here. London Books will also be publishing a new novel from Pete Haynes, former drummer with the Lurkers. More details at www.london-books.co.uk.

16 September The ghost of Cindy Beale haunts Albert Square. Ian thinks he can smell her perfume, a heady blend of gin and other men. Will it be ectoplasm next? If he starts finding mysterious damp patches around the house, it won't be the first time.

Please note: Jane Beale's perfume wasn't tested on animals ... until that night she got off with Grunt Mitchell

- THE Beeb should launch a range of soap scents: SLAG! by Grant, Dogging by Phil. And Ooh I Say by Dorothy Cotton, the distinctive aroma of sanctimonious hypocrisy and Grandad Jim's pants.

23 September I spoke at a dinner in honour of Laila 'Big Mo' Morse, today, despite the fact that seven years ago I launched the Mo Must Go campaign in The *Sun*. Days after Laila joined *EastEnders*, I dubbed her a Big Daddy lookalike and said 'the last time we saw a face this hard on TV it was in a documentary on Mount Everest.'

'Laila,' I added, 'delivers every line like she's reading it off an idiot board.'

I stand by it all, but what a difference a few years makes. Since then, Mo has become one of our favourites: a rare ray of sunshine in an increasingly bizarre soap world. And that's something even her TV alter ego Madam Zora couldn't have predicted.

24 September Gordon Brown's keynote speech to the Labour

Party conference was cripplingly dull, but it did prove one thing: Brown is as vain, deluded and power-mad as Blair ever was. A boastful phoney; a slippery chancer hiding behind a veneer of substance. The speech was full of vacuous waffle aimed at *Daily Mail* readers, meaningless phrases as divorced from reality as a Hobbit reading a Harry Potter book in an episode of *Heroes*. But mostly it was all about him. 'This is who I am,' he boomed. Although who he really is remains a mystery to all of us; even, you suspect, his nearest and dearest. At one stage Gordon starting interviewing himself (surely Jonathan Ross's dearest fantasy). Yet none of what he said made much sense. He spoke of guaranteeing British jobs for British workers, without mentioning that EU membership has guaranteed that British jobs will continue to go to East European workers. 'Education is my passion,' he said, an odd boast from the leader of a party that has done its level best to destroy the pursuit of excellence. Shamefully, he barely mentioned Iraq and Afghanistan. Of Scottish devolution and the imbalance of power caused by devolution there was not a word. But he did beat his chest about the NHS. An ill-informed outsider listening in might have been surprised to learn that the Labour Party has been in office for the last ten years, with Brown pulling the strings, and that much of the mess that the country is in – from the NHS to street-crime and insane immigration – is down to him. It beggars belief that this grim, socially awkward, repressed control freak looks a better bet to win a snap general election than the wretched Tory-lite Conservatives.

- Oona King says listening to Gordon Brown is 'better than sex'. Oona, love, you're not doing it right.

- High drama on *Coronation Street* tonight as Christian slapped Hayley Cropper. Be fair, he had to hit her – he couldn't exactly kick her in the balls. Christian blacked her eye and made her nose bleed...all from one slap. Never mind Corrie – this kid should be on *The Contender*.

- Farms are now at risk from bluetongue, a rare but dangerous virus that can be caught either from working with Gordon Ramsay or French kissing Ann Widdecombe.

28 September Boris Johnson was feeble on Radio 4's *Today* programme this morning: unbriefed and unbothered, with no thought-through policies for London. It appears his strategy is just to waffle and bluff his way through the Mayoral campaign. It won't wash. Boris is an amiable enough bloke, but he's not a serious contender for the job. What a great choice for Londoners: Ken or Ken Lite.

- Boris has had seven push bikes stolen in London. What kind of an idiot has seven bikes nicked and doesn't invest in a padlock?

- Billie Piper enjoyed two shags, three blow-jobs and some light spanking in half an hour on *Secret Diary Of A Call-Girl*. Or as Paris Hilton calls it, a first date. It's fair to say Billie hasn't been stretched by the role...but then she's yet to meet a punter built like Paul Ross. I wonder if it's true what they say about *Dr Who*'s women: no matter how small they look from the outside, once you get inside them they're oh so much bigger. Billie saddled one guy and rode him like a horse while whipping him with a riding crop. If that was a game of charades, I'm pretty sure the answer is 'Rawhide'.

- Billie playing a prostitute...does that make Rose Tyler the original good time traveller had by all? Even more puzzling, why does she have sex with her knickers on?

29 September Culture Secretary James Purnell's picture was digitally inserted to make it look like he had been present with other Manchester MPs to celebrate a hospital redevelopment project. This same guy had the gall to lecture the media about trust! Gordon Brown's spin-free Labour Party! You've got to love 'em. In reality, Brown spins like a whirling dervish. Here's Gord in a blue tie, here's Gord with Maggie, cos he's a one-nation Tory, honest. In a related story, Tony Blair was digitally removed from last week's Labour Conference. Expect the next 'straight' MP caught up in a gay scandal to be digitally inserted in bed next to Oona King.

- No sign of Ian Beale in *EastEnders* at all this week. That's worrying. There's a very real chance he may still be alive

30 September The best of the month. Top TV show: *The Black Donnellys* (ITV2). Book: *Soldier* by Mike Jackson. Film: *The Brave One*. Album: *Magic* – Bruce Springsteen. (Album of next month: *Kings Of Street Punk* – Various Artists; available now from GandR London). Top ad: the Phil Collins gorilla. Surprise joy: Grumbleboat's version of the Chas & Dave classic 'Gertcha'.

16

Vindaloony

I worked for The *Sun* on and off for 16 years. I'd like to think some of my articles had journalistic merit. I opposed the EU, for example; supported the Smithfield meat porters in their fight to keep their market open; and I campaigned to prove the innocence of the UDR Four. So why is it that, for many years, nine out of ten *Sun* readers who stopped me in the street would ask the same question: 'Oi, Gal, how hot was that curry you had to eat?'

The year was 1993, and Abdul Latif, *Viz* comic's favourite chef, had just added a new dish to the menu of his renowned Rupali restaurant in Newcastle: The Curry Hell.

'Clear your plate,' he'd promised, 'and you eat for free.'

The *Sun* ran the story and Kelvin MacKenzie, then the paper's Editor and a great loss to polite society, had a brainwave.

''Ere, Bushell' he said. 'You like a ruby. Get your arse up to Geordieland and polish off one of these ****ing things.

Show them ****ing Northern shirt-lifters what Londoners are made of.'

And of course I responded in the only way any self-respecting person ever did to the mouthy, Millwall-supporting incubus. I rose to my feet, looked him straight in the eye and defiantly muttered the words: 'Yes, boss.'

It didn't sound like much of a challenge. I prided myself on my cast-iron guts. I'd eaten curries from Dehli to Dagenham. Vindaloos, Tindaloos and Phals. To this day, my favourite Spice Girl is Madhur Jaffrey. I'd even survived the legendary Wrath of Khan that they served with a topping of malicious chilli peppers in Margate – and eaten the leftovers for breakfast.

But nothing prepared me for The Curry Hell.

The ingredients were a trade secret but chef Abdul confided that they included five tablespoons of the hottest chilli powder known to man. The rest of it was probably a mixture of sulphuric acid and Victor Meldrew's bile juice.

'Twenty-five people have tried this dish since the *Sun* wrote about it,' he told me. 'Only two of them managed it. I haven't seen either of them since.'

He put his hands theatrically in imitation of prayer. I stayed poker-faced. The rascal was trying to psych me out. I would ignore him. But I couldn't ignore the audience. The place was packed with *Sun* readers all keen to witness my do-or-die attempt. None of them was eating the Curry Hell.

I downed a couple of pre-match lagers, chose a table close to the gents and prayed.

Not hard enough. The curry was so hot you could hear it coming – crackling and spitting. My confidence started to wobble. It dissolved entirely as soon as the dish arrived; the food was the colour of molten tar. Same texture too. It looked evil, I swear it had a pulse. And it smelled like something you'd scoop out of a cesspit.

'Are you sure about this, Mr Garry?' asked Abdul. Yes, I nodded. Show no fear. Nan but the brave...

I pushed in my fork, not entirely convinced it would come out again in one piece, and took a bite. How best to convey the experience, gentle reader? Imagine French-kissing a flame-thrower. After three forkfuls, my eyes started to water. My nose stung. Five mouthfuls in, my face was as red as Fergie's freckles. Sweat poured freely. There were, and I apologise in advance for this, tears on my pilau.

'Nice?' asked my tormentor.

'Blinding,' I rasped. Every eye in the restaurant was on me.

I ate some more. Now my mouth, lips and tongue were ablaze. This must be what they serve up in Hades to people Old Nick doesn't like. My throat felt like someone was strangling it from the inside.

'Would you like another lager?' asked Abdul.

'Just pass the fire extinguisher,' I said.

I was not sitting comfortably.

After ten more forkfuls I was convinced the muck had scorched the lining off my tongue. My mouth was numb. It would cost me £6.50 if I didn't finish it. Just £6.50? I would have paid £650 just to end the pain. What was at stake? Only my job and my reputation. I'd have bucketloads of scorn from MacKenzie, but was it that big a deal? I was too young to die.

'After a few spoonfuls people change language,' said Abdul.

'A*%$***!' I replied.

'I hope you're praying to the right God,' smirked Abdul who seemed to be turning red and sprouting horns.

I muttered the magic words 'Salman Rushdie' under my breath and offered him a forkful.

'Get that ruddy stuff away from me,' he said. I knew how he felt. At that moment I hated him. He was a genius. He could make a mint marketing meals for masochists. I was feeling more knackered than Jim Davidson's best man. But I knew victory could be had – as long as I had the will. And a side-order of chilled Savlon.

'I hope you're not intending to get into bed with your wife tonight,' Abdul quipped.

I'm not a racist person but right then I would cheerfully have booted him back to Bangladesh. The only thing getting shagged tonight was my insides. His poison, having torched my throat, had now started to burn holes through the lining of my stomach.

But there were just five mouthfuls left. Just five. I was sweating like Heather Mills on a lie detector. Slowly, surely, I cleared the plate. I'd done it. I'd won. With a smile plastered on my face, I backed out of the Rupali, waved gleefully and then dashed off to stick my head in the Tyne.

My triumph was short-lived. On my three-hour rail journey back to London, I spent two and a half hours out of my seat. I prayed the train didn't stock Izel. This time at least my prayers were answered.

Abdul hadn't told me the Curry Hell is ten times hotter on

the way out ... If anyone had struck a match in that cubicle after I'd left the consequences would have been devastating.

The pleasure of achievement was off-set by the agony of the experience. Abdul's dish was vinda-lousy. It was like eating a distress flare. You'd need an asbestos palate and a metallic stomach to even contemplate it.

But Abdul had swelled with pride when I told him it was the hottest curry in the country, if not the world.

'Yes,' he beamed. 'It's not just hell, it's bloody Hell.'

Did he eat it himself? I asked.

'You're joking,' he said. 'I'd rather have fish and chips.'

• Scientists say that eating curry improves the memory. Really? If that's the case, how come when you get the bill in an Indian restaurant someone always says: 'I don't remember ordering that...'?

17

Bashing the Bishop

'Muslims do not need British values. We believe that Islam is superior; we believe Islam will be implemented one day.'
Anjem Choudary, 2006

How do we solve a problem like Shariah? How do you hold a moon beam in your hand... if someone's hacked it off? How do you find a word to suit Dr Rowan Williams? A flibbertijibbit? A will-o'-the-wisp? A clown?

The head of our national church is an acute embarrassment, as woolly of mind as he is woolly of beard. He's started a storm with his ill-judged comments about Shariah, saying that it 'seems unavoidable' that some aspects of Islamic religious law will be adopted in Britain. Well, stone me!

Williams mused, 'An approach to law which simply said, "There is one law for everybody and that is all there is to be said... " I think that is a bit of a danger.'

Really? Wouldn't most people think quite the opposite? That there should be one law for everybody, and that the biggest danger arising from this row is that some people might take the Grand Mufti of Canterbury seriously. Rowan Atkinson has more moral authority, and at least he's supposed to be funny.

Dr Williams's argument is an abject surrender to multi-cultural madness; it is also morally suspect and cowardly. Even someone as unworldly as the Mufti must know that many people are rightly concerned about the idea of 'no-go' areas for non-Muslims in this country. Basic rights for women are denied under several forms of Shariah; much of Islam is diametrically opposed to good old British traditions like tolerance and equality before the law. And if the head of our established Church won't fight for our values, who will?

Yet, despite the weakness of his case, I'm glad Williams said what he did, because when you think about it, the authorities are quietly bending over backwards to accommodate Muslims anyway. They're already treating them differently from other faiths. Bigamy, for example, is against UK law. But recently it came to light that husbands with multiple wives in this country can now get benefit payments for each of them! Try and get away with that if your name's Billy Smith from Walthamstow.

All over the country, informal, unofficial 'courts' of Muslim elders sit and pass judgment on members of their own faith who have broken Shariah law; and no one blinks an eye. Fines and punishments are dished out in what is emerging as a parallel legal system. Canon Guy Wilkinson recently noted that, in areas like marriage and divorce, 'there is evidence that there is no proper connection with the civil courts, and that women in particular are suffering'. And of course the cops have turned a blind eye to 'travellers' law' for years.

The real reason the Archbishop's speech caused such an uproar is because he's let the cat out of the bag. British society is already being quietly Islamicised, with the covert approval of this shower of a Government. Gordon Brown has said he wants Britain to become the centre of global Islamic banking; we have Shariah-compliant mortgages; the Saudis are buying up Western companies ...

Where does this madness end? Will we tolerate people who have their own children mutilated because it's their culture? Should we allow Muslims to stone adulterers in their communities and cut off the hands of thieves, or do we decide that our values actually are more civilised and more just, and are worth making a stand for? You can't allow different communities to decide which bits of the law they want to adhere to.

Williams says that Muslims shouldn't have to choose between the 'the stark alternatives of cultural loyalty or state loyalty'. I'm afraid they should and must, and they should know that, when they do something that breaks English law, they will be prosecuted.

This Welshman is an embarrassment to the Church of England. Under his guidance, the schisms in the Anglican Church have deepened. He has been weak over gay clergy and divisive on the subject of women bishops. Worldwide, as he runs up the white flag on Islam, the Church is on the verge of a fundamental, perhaps irreversible split.

More Catholics now attend Sunday worship in Britain

than Anglicans precisely because the Church of England is wet, weak and has lost its way.

Wouldn't it be for the best if, at this year's Lambeth Conference, he did the Lambeth Walk? Anglicans need a leader who is smarter, more effective and more attuned to public opinion; someone who treasures British values and is prepared to fight for our way of life.

- Today's Bible reading: 'Hold fast that which is good': 1 Thessalonians 5:21.
- Fed up with the C of E? Why not try the Church of Gal? We allow smoking and drinking in our churches, which are known in the faith community as 'public-houses.' Our motto is 'beer is living proof that God loves us and wants us to be happy' (Benjamin Franklin). We permit free exchange of off-colour jokes and open debate (the ancient rite known as 'freedom-of-speech'). We have no dress code, but our vergers (never virgins) or 'barmaids' can expect to receive more rewards (drinks) from the lay brethren if they adhere to the traditional ceremonial attire (low-cut tops; skirts the size of weightlifters' belts) and smile coquettishly at the holy words 'Mine's a large one.' Especially if they know it's not true.
- It's ridiculous that people are getting Rowan Atkinson mixed up with the Archbishop of Canterbury. One is a bumbling clown that no-one takes seriously, and the other one played Mr. Bean on the telly.

February 2008

*   *   *

War of the Worlds

'*We now know that there is, in the East of London, a foreign city with 200,000 alien inhabitants. The question is whether we want them at all and whether their presence in our densely populated State is not cause of vast economic mischief and of profound danger to the future of our race.*'

Not my words but those of the *Daily Mail* published nearly 100 years ago. Back in 1911, the peace of British streets was threatened by an undesirable alien of a different kind, the Jewish anarchist, who bombed, killed, maimed and plotted ceaselessly against the status quo.

Some would argue that there is a direct parallel to the hostility expressed towards militant Muslims today, to the kind of anti-Semitism that was openly expressed back then. Like today's Islamists, the new Jewish settlers segregated themselves from British society; they spoke a strange foreign language and dressed differently. With their odd black clothes, hats and heavy beards they looked sinister; unutterably out of place.

So, today's Left argue, just as public opinion was wrong to demonise the Jews, then those who oppose Fundamentalist Islamists are equally misguided; they're nothing better than damn racists who are also destined to be proved wrong by the passage of time.

There will be some turmoil, a few more bombs, but give it a few decades and we'll all be getting along like a Tube train on fire.

Sounds great. But it's not quite right, is it? First off, the anarchists and, later, the Bolsheviks, were arguing for a working-class uprising, not for the creation of a dictatorial Muslim state which would curb free speech, stamp out feminism and re-criminalise homosexuality. They were motivated by the (misguided) politics of human liberation, not by regressive religious faith.

2. Globally, Judaism was not engaged in a war with the West.

3. The radical Islamist has no desire to integrate.

4. His separateness is enshrined in and perpetuated by the bonkers creed of multi-culturalism.

5. His long-term goal is not to assimilate but to take over, and impose Shariah law in Britain.

6. The numbers are vastly different. It's true that only a minority of British Muslims follow the Fundamentalists, just as only a portion of the Jewish refugees supported the anarchists. But there are officially 1.6 million Muslims (unofficially more than 2 million) in the UK and 10 per cent of them make a significant fifth column.

7. The relationship between Christianity and Islam is also now very different from that of Christianity and Judaism; we have been at war for centuries.

8. Overseas adventurism in the Persian Gulf has fanned the flame of domestic terrorism, spurred on the bombers, and made a bad situation worse.

So how should we deal with the rise of Islam here? Should we oppose it and seek to repatriate all Muslims, like the far Right, or embrace it, and turn intellectual somersaults to apologise for its reactionary attitudes and anti-Semitism, like the far Left? Or is there a smarter, more considered response?

Bashing the Bishop

To argue about Islam, we first have to understand it. So let's start by saying what's good about it. Islam is a simple religion which has just five central pillars; it comes from the same roots as Christianity but teaches that Jesus was a prophet, not a son of God. Mohammed wanted two things: submission to Allah, and the moral improvement of his people. Christian thinkers see it either as a heresy or a reformation. The Muslims I've met and spoken to have all put a strong emphasis on their families, they treat the old with respect, they're polite and are open to debate. But there again, I don't bump into the likes of Mohammed Hamid ('Osama bin London') or old Sinj Majeep, the terrorist doctor who tried to set Glasgow airport ablaze.

Crazy people say Muslim hostility towards the West began with the Crusades, conveniently forgetting that the Holy Land was Christian before the birth of Islam in the 7th century AD; it has always been a religion of conquest. On his deathbed, the prophet Mohammed is said to have instructed his followers, 'Let there not be two religions in Arabia.' This town ain't big enough for the both of us. Or, in this case, the three of us.

The battle to kick all Christians and Jews out of Western Arabia kicked off. Islam's forces seemed unstoppable; 100 years after Mohammed popped his clogs, they'd taken Persia, Palestine, Syria, North Africa, Egypt, Portugal and Spain. France would have fallen, too, if Charles Mantel, the Hammer of the Franks, hadn't turned the tide decisively at the battle of Poitiers in 732.

But the Islamic offensive continued; they took Sardinia, Corsica and Sicily and, in 846, they sailed up the Tiber and sacked Rome. The Muslim armies called it on, and got their payback. In 1095, Pope Urban II advocated the First Crusade to liberate Jerusalem. 'Deus vult,' he said. 'God wills it.' Four years later, led by Godfrey of Bouillon and Raymond of Toulouse, the Crusaders triumphed. They massacred Muslims – just as the Christian knights and their families would be slaughtered at Acre Castle. Historian Warren Carroll wrote, 'Before 1095, all the aggression had been Muslim.' Later Crusades were less successful. Our own Richard the Lionheart failed to retake Jerusalem after it fell to Saladin in 1187.

The fanatical Ottoman Turks spearheaded the next wave of Muslim aggression. They overran the Balkans and, in 1389, they battered the Serbs at Kosovo. The Ottoman Turks demanded a blood tax from the Christians they conquered; one boy of every five was taken from his family and raised as a Muslim. Christians also had to pay a kind of prayer tax, too, to practise their faith. In 1453, Mehmet the Conqueror captured Constantinople (now Istanbul). In 1521, Suleiman the Magnificent took Belgrade; eight years later he laid siege to Vienna.

But Muslim forces didn't have it all their own way. In 1492, Ferdinand drove the Moors out of Spain. Sea battles raged in the Med between the fleets of Suleiman and Charles I, the Holy Roman Emperor. In 1570, Suleiman captured Cyprus and Pope Pius V called for a last crusade to liberate the island and keep Malta and Crete free. A mighty 'infidel' fleet, led by Don Juan of Austria, sank or smashed 273 Ottoman ships at the battle of Lepanto. The Med was won, but the battle for Europe went on.

Bashing the Bishop

The forces of the Ottoman Empire reached Vienna again in 1683 and were decisively mullared by King John of Poland. Pope Innocent II formed a Holy League that drove the Turks back, and so the tide of history had turned again. Islam was now on the retreat everywhere; Egypt fell to Napoleon and then Britain.

It took the British and French to save the Ottoman Empire from Russia. The French took Algeria; Italy defeated the Turks, then the Balkan League defeated them, and the First World War finished them off as a world power, their last great victory being Gallipoli.

In 1917, the British Army liberated Jerusalem and Lawrence led the Arab revolt to kick the Ottoman Empire out of Arabia. Sadly, Allied treachery soured the victory. The rest of 20th-century history is well known. After the Second World War, the Arabic and the Islamic peoples of the Middle East demanded independence, and the West pissed them off mightily by creating the state of Israel.

A new Islam arose from the chaos; using terror as a weapon, they fought back against the oppressor everywhere from Algeria to Somalia. The Afghan rebels – including Bin Laden – defeated Soviet forces. Hezbollah kicked Israel out of Lebanon, and the fight-back climaxed with the destruction of New York's World Trade Center in 2001.

After 9/11, a Chinese friend invited me to his birthday party. Some of the guests were Muslims, all of them were moderate and all of them agreed that the Yanks had it coming. I was shocked. How could the slaughter of 2,974 innocent office workers be justified? The answer was simple – they despise America. They see it as evil and corrupt; they

237

hate the Yanks for preaching democracy while propping up corrupt, oppressive regimes, for supporting Israel and for invading Iraq. They abhor degenerate American popular culture – drugs, porn, booze and rock. Above all, they object to the presence of US troops on Saudi soil (the leadership of al-Qaeda are all Saudis); they are particularly offended by the female soldiers.

From the Muslim point of view, the US and their allies – principally Great Britain – have defiled the Middle East, insulted Islam and carved up their territory for decades. We are the enemy – culturally, militarily, historically and permanently. No wonder Islamism is such a powerful pull for disaffected Muslim youth across Europe.

A combination of insane immigration, naïve liberalism and destructive multi-culturalism has encouraged a fifth column to blossom in the UK; they simply want to destroy our way of life. Many Islamic terrorists are British born and educated. We appease Jew-hating extremist groups, offering them sanctuary – it's 'Londonistan' now. MI5 reckons up to 400,000 people here sympathise with the global 'jihad' and that as many as 1,200 could be involved in terrorist networks. And it is Saudi money that has spread the most aggressive forms of Islamic faith.

Many Muslims are loyal UK citizens, of course, but even they are ambivalent in their attitude to terror. We have to stop pretending that Islam is a peace-loving religion – it never has been.

Writing in 1899, Winston Churchill said something that would probably get you arrested for hate crime today. He wrote, 'Far from being moribund, Mohammedanism is a militant and proselytising faith. It has already spread throughout Central Africa, raising fearless warriors at every step; and were it not that Christianity is sheltered in the strong arms of science – the science against which it had vainly struggled – the civilisation of modern Europe might fall, as fell the civilisation of ancient Rome.'

Yes, the might of Rome did fall, not to a mightier opponent but to a relatively weak but morally certain belief system – Christianity. Now the West is wealthy and militarily strong, but mentally and morally weak. Radical Islam is the opposite, militarily weak but morally certain, which makes them stronger in the long-term than we are. They don't need to defeat our armies in pitched battles to win; they've already seen how quickly we capitulated to the IRA.

Britain has a problem on its hands which will take generations to solve, and it doesn't help that the West is crippled with self-doubt. We're Godless, decadent, unsure of who we are or why our values are worth fighting for; we can't even reproduce ourselves.

By handing so much power to the State, we have allowed successive generations of British people to drop out of any notion of personal responsibility. We have no real social contract, no sense of history, civic pride or duty. As a society, we're cheapened by rampant materialism and permissiveness. No one commands the moral authority to demand an alternative to the rising tide of unhappiness, marriage breakdown, abortion and sexual diseases.

In our 'anything goes' society, the thing mostly likely to go is our society itself.

What are our kids going to fight for? Gay bars, Gordon

Brown's right to tax us 'til our balls ache, and the gormless
Archbishop of Canterbury? I think not.

If Western civilisation is to survive this new war of the
world, we need to rediscover our faith. How can we fight
for the hearts and minds of disaffected youth if we don't
believe in ourselves? As Victor Hugo said, 'You can resist
an invading army... you can't resist an idea whose time
has come.'

* * *

Call Me, Call Me Any Time, Call Me

Oxford's new mega-mosque opens later this year, and the
local Imam wants to call the faithful to prayer using a
loudspeaker. Already it is suggested that any objections
would be 'racist', except that most of the people who live
near the mosque aren't Muslims. These poor sods will
never be able to have a lay-in again.

Imagine the first Saturday morning – you're dead to the
world after a Friday night skinful when suddenly you're
rudely awakened by two minutes of amplified
gobbledegook. With your head pounding from the effects
of last night's ale, you'd be forgiven for assuming that your
daft mates had spirited you off overnight and dumped you
in Marrakesh. But these two-minute broadcasts will only
happen three times a day, a spokesman claims (it's
normally five times a day in Muslim countries.) Isn't it
unreasonable to object? After all, Oxford's churches ring
their bells. The Bishop of Oxford, John Pritchard, thinks
so. 'Relax,' he says, 'enjoy community diversity.'

That might be easier to do if any Muslim country allowed

church bells to ring once a week, or if there was any tradition of using loudspeakers in the Muslim world, or if the first line of the muezzin's call to prayer wasn't 'I bear witness that there is no divinity but Allah'. Surely the best way to keep the peace in Oxford would be for the Muslim minority to respect the feelings of their neighbours and put a sock in it? Sikhs and Hindus manage to coexist unobtrusively. Why can't they? Oxford may now be home to many faiths, but it is not a Muslim city. Not yet, at any rate.

Being unobtrusive is not high on the list of priorities – as witnessed by the massive Sunni mosque designed to accommodate 70,000 worshippers planned for the East End with Red Ken's blessing. And clearly, many of Britain's Muslims have no wish to coexist. Recently, the Asian Bishop of Rochester, Michael Nazir-Ali, soberly expressed his concerns about the lack of integration into British society of some Muslim communities. Islamic extremists had, he said, created no-go areas where non-Muslims are subjected to hostility and intimidation. The knee-jerk reaction was entirely predictable.

The Bish was immediately bashed by Hazel Blears and William Hague; he also received some touchingly traditional death threats from a few Muslim nut-jobs. This seems absurd – I mean, it's not like he'd done something really offensive like publishing a cartoon. That he is right, and that fundamentalist ghettoes exist, is beyond dispute, and if Blears really doesn't recognise the Bishop's description of some of our inner cities, I'd suggest she calls her old Cabinet chum John Reid. When the old Stalinist bruiser asked a Muslim audience in East London to stand up to extremists in their midst and not let their children be groomed to become suicide bombers, the message did not meet with universal approval. Reid, then Labour's Home Secretary, was shouted down by a furious Abu Izzadeen, who spat, 'How dare you come to a Muslim area?' That's right – how dare a British Home Secretary venture into a youth centre in London's Leytonstone... which, last time I looked, was still on British soil.

Fourteen months earlier, London's public transport system had been the target of a co-ordinated attack. At 8.50am three bombs exploded within 50 seconds of each other on three separate Tube trains. Fifty-seven minutes later, a fourth bomb went off on a London bus in Tavistock Square. Fifty-two innocent commuters were killed, around seven hundred others were injured. Abu Izzadeen described the four suicide bombers responsible as 'martyrs' and 'completely praiseworthy'.

Fundamentalist Muslims don't do integration, or tolerance, but they are given endless leeway by the liberal Establishment. Muslim women are beaten, bullied, married off against their will and sometimes even murdered by their families in the name of religion and traditional values. Generally the authorities turn a blind eye in the name of 'cultural relativism.' When C4 exposed fanatics operating inside English mosques, the West Midlands police investigated the programme makers. This attitude goes beyond moral ambiguity; it's political cowardice. Cultural suicide.

*   *   *

A STORY based on the *Three Little Pigs*, has been rejected by a government quango in case it offends Muslims. Becta, the education technology agency, attacked the digital remake of the harmless children's classic because 'the use of pigs raises cultural issues'.

Why is the *Three Little Pigs* offensive to Muslims? Muslims are forbidden to eat pigs, which they see as unclean animals. But in the most popular version of the story, no pig is eaten. And in the other version, two of the pigs are eaten only by a wolf. As there is no suggestion that the wolf is a Muslim, we can only assume some viewers might theoretically assume the cartoonists were saying wolves can't be Muslim and take offence from that.

In reality, no Muslims were offended. This was another case of nit-wit white liberals taking offence on their behalf. 24th January 2008

* * *

TV'S The Great Asian Invasion went in to a lot of detail about curries, and not quite enough on the irreconcilable differences between Muslim fundamentalism and Western values. But on the burning subject of Bangladesh cuisine: does it ever worry you when they just have 'meat curry' on the menu and don't specify where it came from?

I mention this cos one of the waiters in my favourite East London eatery died and the chicken hasn't tasted the same since.

- There's a new Muslim doll on the market. There is a talking version but no-one's had the guts to pull the string – Frank Skinner.
- STOP PRESS. 28 February 2008. Islamic scholars in Turkey are to review the Hadith (the sayings of the

Prophet). In a move likened to the Protestant reformation, they say that Muslim teachings will be made more relevant for the 21st century, resulting no doubt in a new kind of Iman: the Mullah Lite.

Bushell On The Blog
October 2007

1 October That's more like it. William Hague put the boot in to Gordon Brown yesterday, dissecting his double-think bullshit and telling it like it is. Hague said Brown's £100 billion raid on pension funds made Robert Maxwell 'look like an amateur.' He detailed the 100-plus stealth taxes Brown has foisted on us and mocked his pledge to restore trust when he can't even be trusted to stand by Labour's promise on an EU referendum. With pin-point accuracy, Hague rained blow after blow on the whole slick Brown myth. If only he was the contender and not the corner man...

2 October Well, what a coincidence. Two days in to the Tory Conference Gordon Brown suddenly finds time to fly to Iraq to grab a few headlines. Brown announced that 1,000 troops would be home by Christmas. Now it turns out that half of these have been announced before: 270 are already back here and 500 aren't even in Iraq. Cynical? Not spin-free Gordon surely? It's worth remembering how little time Brown gave the Armed Forces in his own conference speech last week. Many good men and women have died in the pursuit of New Labour's overseas adventurism. It is despicable that their ill-equipped comrades are now being used in a shameless and transparent PR stunt. The whole trip stinks like a Basra outhouse.

- At last the Tories are talking tax cuts. Reducing stamp duty and raising the threshold for inheritance tax is a good start. But it's still nowhere near enough. It's time someone questioned the Government's right to tax our income and squander it how they please. They take far too much and piddle it up the wall on paper-shuffling bureaucrats, incontinent welfarism, unelected bodies and their own pension schemes. Shouldn't the boot be on the other foot? Shouldn't MPs have to justify every brass farthing they take from us? And shouldn't Tory MPs have the guts to argue for slashing state spending? The whole tax system is baffling, complex and designed to pull the wool over our eyes.

7 October *Bruce On Vegas* stank like a Mob graveyard. Unable to interview stars of today like Danny Gans and Jerry Seinfeld, Bruce was largely reduced to chatting to relatives and friends of dead greats. Except, being Bruce, the show was all about him.

Toes all over Britain must have curled up like Aladdin's slippers as Bruce tap-danced on Elvis's stage, tinkled Liberace's ivories, and sang like a wounded bison in a restaurant full of bemused Yanks. Underpinning it all was Forsyth's seeming belief that he is our equivalent of showbiz gods like Sammy Davis. It's a belief no-one shares. Bruce was a terrific game-show host, but his every attempt to cut it as an all-round entertainer or comic actor bombed like Arthur Harris. Those who survived Slinger's Day are still traumatised by the memory. I think Forsyth thinks he's a superstar. He's not. Even his stature as national TV treasure is compromised by that elephantine ego. He's a tap-dancing, crap-talking, big-headed, wig-headed bore. The poor old befuddled soul can't even host *Strictly Come Dancing* properly. He's strictly gone gaga.

8 October This blog, along with its author, are disappearing until November. All the Diana cobblers is too much to take. Through the miracle of slingback and the information super-highway, *Bushell On The Box* will continue to appear in the *Daily Star Sunday* throughout October. See ya!

12 October Happy Anniversary, *Emmerdale*. Lord knows they need it. Unusually for a farming community, their only crops are shock and disaster in heavy rotation. They've had the plane disaster, the storm disaster, Noreen's permanent wig disaster. Drive down the country lanes here and the only sign you'll spot is 'Pick Your Own Calamity.'

18 October There's a new Terry Wogan show out: point on view. Did you see him in those moleskin trousers? It looked like the mole was still in them!

25 October I'm in the US checking out the latest TV shows. Sad to report Michelle Ryan is pretty ropey as the new Bionic Woman. The former Zoe Slater is leaden, sullen and about as lively as the Queen Vic bust. It's hard to see why anyone, even an unaccountable shadowy government agency, would have invested $59million in this dull bird. And viewing figures are dropping like Marie Osmond on the dance floor.

Michelle's shoulders may be as square as her jaw, but she's outclassed and out-acted by her rogue rival Sarah (Katee Sackhoff). Sadly this mucks up the chances of other *EastEnders* being recruited to play comic book heroes.

If Zoe had cut it as a bionic babe, then why not Charlie as the Blob, Anthony Trueman as Doctor Strange or Peggy as the Incredible Shrinking Woman? Blushing Bradley would have made a terrific Human Torch. Fat Pat IS The Thing. And think what chaos Little Mo could have caused with a red hot Iron Man...

- *Katie & Peter Unleashed* is the worst chat show ITV has ever produced, which when you consider they made *The Sharon Osbourne Show* is quite an achievement. The only way this show would work is if during an interview Katie whipped out her breasts and started slapping her guest around the face with them. Unleash those beasts and we're talking business...

31 October People often ask me if I live anywhere near *EastEnders*. Not really, but late at night if you listen carefully, you can hear the screams ... I'm a Londoner born and bred. The family home was in Charlton, just over the river from Silvertown and Custom House, the hardest part of the East End. No-one ever really missed Custom House. Except the Luftwaffe. But no matter how tough life was growing up around here there was always laughter and song, and there was a richness of spirit that you find in poor urban communities everywhere ... except on BBC1. The pubs had comics, the clubs had turns, and bookies were packed. There were card schools, Derby Day beanos, rock bands. And there were always characters, the sort of chancers you'd see on shows like *Minder*: diamond geezers, slippery toe-rags, duckers, divers, street-corner skivers and takers of diabolical liberties. Sadly, one or two of 'em ended up in the Thames, wearing the type of boots you can't buy in Clark's. Things changed of course. Jobs went, tower blocks came, and the white working class got demonised by liberal opinion. But you can still find the old culture and community spirit in pocket. And just as Ray Davies dreamed of preserving England's village greens, I'd love to keep alive the spirit of working class London:

We are the Cockney preservation society
God bless stag comics, Madness and variety
Pearly kings, pie and mash, and lack of sobriety.
We are a rhyming slang and back-slang fraternity
God save the noble art and notoriety
Hooky goods, Stinky Turner, and variety.
We are the VAT avoidance society
God save Arthur Daley and prosperity
And long may we puncture pomposity.

18

Gay-Per-View

Television today is so relentlessly gay, it's a wonder the *Radio Times* doesn't come with a pink Versace wrap and a free glass of Muscadet.

Mainstream TV entertainment is as pink as a Barbie play tent, but it's not the sexuality of the presenters and shows that irritates, so much as their overwhelming lack of talent and suitability.

Kenny Everett, Frankie Howerd, the iconic Kenneth Williams… these men were gay and they were comedy giants. Compare and contrast them with many of today's equivalents. Graham Norton is a quick-witted fellow who worked and rated well late-night on Channel 4 with a substantial lead-in from *Big Brother*. At the time, nothing about Norton's jokes or the content of his show – including an exotic dancer firing ping-pong balls from her nether regions – suggested that he was suitable for a family audience. But at the end of 2003, BBC1 hired him anyway for £6 million.

It's fair to say his Saturday night BBC1 performances have been underwhelming. Stripped of his trademark filth, Norton turned into a gurning grotesque straining to fake an interest in a series of insipid, light entertainment formats. As his tribute-act vehicle *The One and Only* demonstrates, he has no empathy with the contestants and can't be arsed to pretend otherwise.

The only time he comes alive is on his BBC2 chat show *The Graham Norton Show*, which is pretty much his old Channel 4 show with slightly less filth. The BBC has spent millions of our money to establish what any producer with half a brain would have realised from the start – that Graham Norton works best late at night with as few editorial controls as possible.

ITV is just as bad. After losing the brilliant (and gay) Paul O'Grady's 5.00pm chat show, they decided they could replace him with the hammy soap actor Antony Cotton from *Coronation Street*. Incredibly, ITV announced that he was 'the new Paul O'Grady', failing to realise that O'Grady is a brilliant comedian, naturally funny with impeccable timing, while Cotton is just a naff buffoon in love with his own cheesy reflection. He made his chat show début in August 2007 singing 'Copacabana'. He was as camp as a crêpe suzette and just as flat. It rapidly became clear that Cotton couldn't sing, deliver gags or interview – he made Richard Arnold seem like Dimbleby, and he resented every moment the spotlight was off him. When comics were on getting laughs, Cotton looked mortified.

It was a cast-iron disaster; even his guests looked embarrassed to be there, and rightly. Viewing figures nosedived faster than the FTSE and the show was cancelled after one series.

Cotton, to no one's surprise, turned out to be just like his *Corrie* character, Sean Tully, but with a bigger ego and no wit in his script. Being gay is not a problem if you're a talent. Simon Amstell is a lightning-witted genius who adds much to the joy of the nation; Alan Carr is a funny guy who plays equally well with pensioners and students; Dale Winton is a cherished game-lord and housewife's favourite. But simply being gay should not be enough to justify a career in television, let alone your own show.

* * *

Not All Right At the Back

Gay people have existed since the dawn of time, and there's no reason why they shouldn't be on TV. Two things niggle:

1. TV's insistence that gay characters must always be righteous and noble. As a rule, TV gays are young, handsome and blameless, nice guys portrayed in the best possible light, like goody-goody Derek on *EastEnders*. *Coronation Street*'s Sean Tully can be selfish and bitchy, but no soap has included a gay equivalent of *Corrie*'s predatory, middle-aged pervert Bobby Ockton. They're not there to 'reflect reality', but to glamourise a lifestyle choice prevalent in broadcasting. Homo-obsessive TV bosses aren't 'confronting prejudice', they're glamourising their own lifestyles.

2. Today's gay culture is irredeemably shallow – drag queens, neat freaks, Liza Minnelli, pretty boy bands, endless Kylie documentaries and anorexic, flat-chested

models. They're all becoming increasingly tired, unsurprising and unrewarding. Gay culture was far more creative when it was repressed and an in-joke. *Round the Horne*, for example, was so much cleverer and funnier than Julian Clary's tired old schtick. Contrast Kenneth Williams' ('We've got a criminal practice that takes up much of our time') with Julian's fisting jokes and anal fixation.

I see Clary as a vain and shallow creature, who has built a career on his looks and one joke – sodomy. TV executives have been trying and failing to turn him mainstream since *Trick or Treat* in the 1980s, while deliberately blocking the careers of more obvious Saturday night entertainers. It took a sideways move into soaps to reinvent Shane Richie and Bradley Walsh as TV treasures, and a trip to the jungle to do the same for Joe Pasquale.

In 1993, Julian Clary made his infamous remark – 'I've been fisting Norman Lamont... ' – live on ITV's Comedy Awards. On Channel 4, he'd have got away with it, but this was ITV. Kelvin MacKenzie was furious. At his behest, I wrote an article calling for Clary to be banned from live ITV events as his judgement couldn't be trusted. It still strikes me as unfair that Stan Boardman was never forgiven for his much funnier Fokker Wolf gag, or that the TV careers of certain household names were abruptly derailed for making 'homophobic remarks' in private off-camera.

Far more leniency is shown to gay entertainers who cross the line. Take the extreme case of Michael Barrymore, once Britain's favourite Saturday night star, once a friend and someone I enthused about for years. Michael was special; he took John Cleese's manic Basil Fawlty character and reinvented it as a stage act, adding buckets of warmth and humility. Britain loved him because he seemed to be one of us, a man of the people, and we forgave him much.

It was well-known in TV circles that Barrymore was gay, but viewers didn't know and it was a shock when he came out. The man was so loved that the public stood by him, though, and they kept coming to his live shows after he owned up to alcoholism and drug binges, too. I went to his post-rehab, comeback performance in Blackpool and you could have grilled toast on the warmth of that seaside crowd.

The mysterious death of Stuart Lubbock changed all that. In March 2001, Lubbock, a 31-year-old butcher and father-of-two, ended up dead in Barrymore's pool following a party at the entertainer's house. There was a significant level of alcohol and drugs in his system and he had suffered serious anal injuries. Essex cops said that he was so badly injured that, had he lived, it was unlikely he would have ever walked again.

This didn't stop ITV from trying to resurrect Barrymore's career. ITV commissioned a Martin Bashir interview and a top ITV executive masterminded the opening sequence of footage in what turned out to be a cynical PR exercise. Bashir, famous for his Diana interview, gave Barrymore a soft ride. Neighbours had heard Stuart Lubbock's screams an hour before the police were called, yet Bashir let Barrymore claim it had been a peaceful party with no sex. The case remains open and it still looks like a messy tragedy.

No one is suggesting that Barrymore was directly involved in Stuart Lubbock's death, but the fact that it happened on his property with his friends puts him beyond the pale.

Did ITV really believe his career matters more than a young man's life? Apparently so. Viewers, however, largely sided with Lubbock's widow, who had been left to bring up two children without a father. We have yet to see their story on screen.

* * *

ANYONE with a less than ecstatic view of the 'gaying' of British culture is automatically denounced as 'homophobic'. But the real problem isn't straight society's fear, or dislike, of homosexuality, but influential gay people's infatuation with themselves. The love that once 'dare not speak its name' can now rarely shut up about it.

In television, this homo-obsession means that every kind of genre must feature characters who are out, proud and, of course, all-round nice folk, designed to show homosexuals at all times in the best possible light. This 'positive discrimination' sometimes spills over into propaganda, but is more likely to produce tedium and falling ratings.

It was brave and certainly original when US soap *Dynasty* gave the world Steven Carrington, a bright, thoughtful gay man eager to build bridges with his bigot father, the ruthless tycoon and wife-rapist Blake. Admittedly, they later bottled out and had Steve come back to bat for the straight team. But the novelty wore off years ago, along with any semblance of reality.

Brookside followed *Dynasty* in the 1980s with Gordon Collins, then *EastEnders* gave us the short-lived pairing of barrow-boy Barry and elder graphic designer Colin – the relationship that sparked the *Sun*'s 'EASTBENDERS' headline.

The soap was less convincing when it tackled AIDS. Straight fruit and veg stall-holder Mark Fowler was the only man in medical history to be HIV-positive for more than a decade and put on weight, although some of that may have been down to his extra-heavy mono-brow. Mark had contracted the virus from his wife, but how she'd caught it was anybody's guess. That vagueness was consistent with the hysterical line churned out by the AIDS lobby that 'everybody is at risk' and we would 'die of ignorance'. It was around this time that thousands of startled spinsters received Government leaflets from Norman Fowler in the 1980s advising them about the dangers of vigorous anal sex.

The lesbian sisterhood had its turn in the spotlight at Christmas 1993, with Beth and Margaret sharing the first televised Sapphic kiss on *Brookside*. *Emmerdale* quickly took over and became a haven for lipstick lesbians, led by glamorous serial seductress Zoe Tate, whose girlfriends included a butch lorry-driver (the van dyke).

Coronation Street has long been our campest soap opera; its foundation stones have been strong women and weak men. *Corrie* was the first soap to feature a male-female transsexual character – Harold/Hayley Cropper (played by an actress who hilariously became pregnant in real life, forcing the director to shoot her from the neck up; I'm no expert on the sex-change procedure, but it seemed obvious that Hayley had been overdosing on the oestrogen).

The *Street* was the last to have an openly gay inhabitant, though. That changed in 2003, when TV suits put pressure on *Corrie* producers to fall in line. Nitwitted knicker-stitcher Sean Tully (Antony Cotton) became a *Street* regular, and *Corrie* recruited Jonathan Harvey (the over-rated gay writer responsible for the screamingly unfunny BBC2 camp-com *Gimme Gimme Gimme*) to oversee the new storylines.

Odd Todd Grimshaw, who'd been merrily dating Sarah-Lou, the hottest girl in the *Street*, suddenly came out of the closet. Sarah's adoptive dad Martin Platt went nuts and decked Todd's boyfriend, fellow male nurse Karl Foster.

At the insistence of ITV bosses, and after more behind-the-scenes rows, Karl was brought back a few months later to get his own back. He hadn't even attempted to hold his fists up when Martin had gone for him the first time but, for his brief return, Karl suddenly became handier than Amir Kahn. He battered Mart and left triumphantly. Platt? Splat!

By August 2004, we had gay lib in the Rovers and Jack Duckworth in drag.

Poor old Jack was dressed up in a party frock to play bowls. Why? He was made to wear a G-string. Why? In fact, Jack looked so rough, it's understood that Wayne Rooney fancied him. Bill Tarmey is a marvellous actor, of course, and he had some terrific lines, but it was all ridiculously contrived.

In another scene reminiscent of *EastEnders* at its worst, Rovers regulars turned on Les Battersby for being bigoted. It might have gone down well with Network Centre and *Attitude* magazine, but it was completely out of sync with the rhythm of the soap. Would the locals really have been so understanding so soon after Todd had broken Sarah-Lou's heart?

Suddenly, we had Stonewall in the public bar, a she-male running the caff and our favourite character poncing about like Mrs. Gout-fire. Or Jack Duckie-worth. I was just glad Albert Tatlock wasn't there to see it. Ena Sharples would have been blowing steam out of her ears. What next, I wondered? Would Betty run off with a Ukrainian woman shot-putter? Would Newton and Ridley be caught cottaging?

No, Sean got Violet pregnant. Or rather, having failed to rise to the occasion, Tully provided his seed for Violet to 'shovel in'. (We can't be sure what with; possibly Eileen Grimshaw's icing piper. Let's hope she cleaned it out first or Vi could be giving birth to an 8lb French fancy.) The humour was largely accidental as Violet warned Sean, 'It could get messy,' adding later, 'I'm filling up.'

Jonathan Harvey had a dreary agenda to push. Sean said he had seen a bloke 'paying more attention to his can of beer than his child... how come you have more of a right to a child than me?'

Which raises the question – do gay men not drink? But hang about – a child isn't a right, it's a responsibility. Here we have a single woman with no prospects having a baby on a whim in the full knowledge that society – i.e. you and me – will pick up the tab. Once, when *Corrie* had a sense of morality, someone would have pointed out how selfish Violet was being, and someone else might have reminded her she could have frozen her eggs 'til the right bloke came along, rather than depriving her kid of a full-time dad.

Flouncing cliché Sean is the weakest stitch in the *Street*'s rich tapestry of humour. Yet ITV are so proud of the character, they put him up for Best Newcomer at the Soap Awards two years on the trot.

Coronation Street's strengths have always resided in small joys – warmth, believable characters and witty dialogue. They're still here, but they're increasingly buried under an avalanche of storylines you don't give a flying duck about.

TV's gay advance continues apace across all light dramas and soaps. *Emmerdale* is now so over-populated with male homosexuals you wouldn't be surprised if auditions for the stage musical version of *Brokeback Mountain* were held in the Woolpack. Even sci-fi has been given a sparkly gay makeover thanks to Russell T Davies, the man who resurrected *Dr Who* and dreamt-up its *Torchwood* spin-off.

Swansea-born Davies, a bright, articulate man, admits that 'being gay helped me to become a writer… when I used to send in scripts, being gay gave me an edge.' But why should it? Davies came to prominence with the multi-award-winning *Queer As Folk*, a drama series about three gay men – the cock-sure predator Stuart, his wishy-washy pal Vince, and the under-age schoolboy Nathan, whom Stuart initiates into graphic man-boy loving. Although praised for its realistic depiction of gay promiscuity, the series finished as pure wish-fulfilment with Stuart and Vince in Arizona, and Stuart pulling a gun on a stereotypical fat redneck who called them 'faggots'. A fairytale indeed.

The show established Davies as a substantial dramatist – at least in the eyes of TV commissioning editors. His subsequent gay-tinted ITV drama series *Bob and Rose* flopped and *Mine All Mine* did little better.

His biggest and best delivered idea for the network was *The Second Coming* – a powerful two-parter shown over consecutive evenings about the new Messiah walking among us. No, not Kevin Keegan. It was praised in some quarters as thought-provoking, although the only thought it provoked in this viewer was that Russ must have been studying the *Life of Brian*. Chris Ecclestone had a divine revelation while snogging Lesley Sharp (blessed are the big noses). He spent his first night as the Son of God setting off car alarms (he's not the Messiah, he's a very naughty boy). He finally topped himself with poisoned pasta, killing God, Lucifer and all religion. But how? Davies never explained this divine domino effect.

His conclusion was that, freed from the shackles of faith, mankind would 'grow up' and find happiness. It would have been an original thought if Marx and Nietzsche hadn't had it already – and look where they got us.

The new Christ proved his divinity by filling Man City's stadium with night-time sunshine – the first miracle at Maine Road since the glory days of Denis Law. Sadly, the holy glow couldn't hide the holes in the plot.

Davies then turned his hand to *Casanova* for the BBC, although it wasn't a patch on Dennis Potter's version. Give him his due, though, it was Russell T's idea to revive the *Dr Who* franchise with Ecclestone as a dour northern Time Lord and it proved a huge commercial success for

BBC1, especially when David Tennant became the Doctor in Series Two.

So maybe it's churlish to point out that his sci-fi sucks like a turbo-charged Dyson. Russell's plotting is frequently thinner than his freakish cosmetic surgery creation Cassandra. His episodes are a mess of cribbed visual ideas, camp theatrics and feeble aliens like the Slitheen (cue childish fart jokes), and he displays a lazy reliance on the Doctor's sonic screwdriver as a magic wand. In one episode, the Tardis gave Rose the power to evaporate Daleks made from dead humans, and to bring corpses back to life. If the time-travelling police box is that all-powerful, there wouldn't be an alien threat in the universe big enough to worry about. The hottest single episodes of the new *Who* ('Blink' with its genuinely creepy statues; the solo Dalek; the Victorian gas creatures) were all written by other contributors.

The spin-off *Torchwood* is more 'adult' – in other words, rampantly sexual. Its generally a mess of gay lust, bisexual banter and poor sci-fi. Series Two began with Captain Jack snogging and fighting his former partner ('in every way') Captain John, while both men lusted over Gwen and Ianto.

Someone at BBC Wales had clearly watched Series One and concluded that what *Torchwood* needed most wasn't better stories but more gayness. But as straight males are the main audience for sci-fi, you have to wonder if they'd really thought this through.

Straight men don't figure much on TV's radar any more, though. BBC1 axed the successful comedy-sports panel game *They Think It's All Over...* for being 'too laddish', and straight men have a walk-on part in reality shows as foils for smart alec gays.

Queer Eye for a Straight Guy works on the premise that gay men are intrinsically cooler and more fashion conscious than straights. This premise can instantly be disproved with four names: Elton John, Ron Davies, Boy George and Peter Tatchell.

Sky One's *There's Something about Miriam* gave six straight guys the chance to romance a sultry Mexican model Miriam Nago, who, unbeknown to them, was a pre-operative transsexual. Laugh? I did when the men sued, and Sky had to stump up an out-of-court settlement before the show went to air.

The daftest gay-themed TV show was Bravo's *Manhunt*, featuring hunky male models being dropped out of a plane wearing nothing but their pants. For the first time in history, it was about to start raining men.

Here's the problem – gay TV execs are on a mission to change us. Most people accept that what two consenting adults do in the privacy of their own homes is entirely a matter for them. But at the same time, we can live without overt sexuality – gay or otherwise – at tea-time, and thereby introducing our kids to concepts that needn't concern them. Tolerance is not enough for the gay lobby however. They want to be accepted, loved and needed; they also want to us to laugh along with jokes about felching, fisting and the rest. They want to be in our face but, if we react with anything less than delight, they want to be able to denounce us as bigots.

So what has TV got for blokes (straight and gay) who prefer a pint, a pie and a football match to a shopping trip and a Judy Garland-inspired makeover? Not much, is the answer. Straight men in ITV dramas are generally effeminate or emasculated. Two-fisted geezers like Terry McCann, Jack Regan and Richard Sharpe are a forgotten breed. It's all drippy new men, rapists and 'metrosexual' soccer players now, with walk-on parts for Richard Arnold. We get a choice between hysterical melodrama and tall tales of hen-pecked yuppies in thrall to plain but decisive every-woman types usually played by Caroline Quentin.

When a show comes along like *Life on Mars*, full of blokeish blokes, it becomes an overnight hit. Gene Hunt, the two-fisted, no-nonsense 1970s cop – an obvious homage to Jack Regan and the show's supposed anti-hero – became a cult sensation. Yet still TV bosses don't get it.

Only Fools and Horses, the biggest sitcom success of our times, hasn't spawned a single copycat show. Indeed, if you went to any TV company and pitched for a series about three heterosexual men, one a pensioner, living off their wits on a south London council estate, you'd be out the door faster than you can say, 'Lovely jubbly.' Unfortunately, the people who run TV don't live on the same planet as the viewers.

In 2007, *Hell's Kitchen* brought together the disparate world views of Jim Davidson, the right-wing, working-class comic, and Brian Dowling, reality show winner and darling of the *Heat* set. Their inevitable clashes were put down to Jim's attitude; he was roundly condemned as a homophobic dinosaur and asked to leave the show.

But there was more to their clash of worlds than this.

Jim is a self-made success story; a brilliant teller of gags and anecdotes; he earned his fame through years of TV shows and live performances.

Brian's special skill is that he's a bit camp. The former air-steward triumphed on the 2001 *Big Brother* series and has eked out a living on late-night TV through his amazing ability to read an autocue. His talent, I guess, is being a little bit 'fabulous'. And that's it.

Throughout his confrontations with Davidson, Brian wore his gayness on his sleeve; he defined himself by his sexuality because that's all he's got, and that's all that makes him interesting. At least Alan Carr is funny.

Jim, who has no problem with gay people, defended himself saying 'I'm not homophobic... I'm Brianophobic,' but that truth didn't suit ITV.

So where next for the millions of TV viewers who are also, mildly, Brianophobic and who resent these ego-driven nonentities being propelled beyond their abilities? I'm not advocating repression – live and let live, me – but some measure of meritocracy and equal opportunity might be nice. And maybe a period of quiet introspection from TV's tireless gay lobby would be beneficial for all. Let's try promoting performers, actors, producers, directors and, crucially, writers on the basis of their talents rather than their age, class, sexual orientation or colour.

* * *

More Equal Than Others
In October 2007, four firefighters in Bristol were reprimanded and heavily fined after being accused of

homophobia. Their 'crime' was to have disturbed an outdoor gay orgy in a public park. The four-man team had heard noises and shone their torches at the bushes where these nature-lovers were hard at it. They were doing in public what they really should have been doing in privet.

One of the outraged witnesses to the 'dogging' rang the friendly neighbourhood Terence Higgins Trust, who advised him to make a formal complaint to the Avon Fire Service. The firemen were suspended while a three-month public inquiry, paid for by the taxpayer, of course, looked into the matter. The disciplinary committee concluded that the fire crew was guilty of this heinous thought crime. Two men were fined a grand apiece, one was demoted, and the fourth received a written warning; all were then transferred to other fire stations.

So, in summary, four heroes – four men who regularly put their own lives on the line to protect and serve the public and had 26 years of service between them – were punished, while a bunch of selfish prats with hurt feelings won the day. Topsy-turvy isn't the word. The last time I looked, having sex in public was an offence; and if a heterosexual couple had been caught committing an act that is 'lewd, obscene or disgusting in a public place', they would fully expect to be charged with outraging public decency.

And so the divide widens between permissive law-makers and the public, the vast majority of whom would have cheered on the firemen if they'd hosed the dirty buggers down. A combination of political correctness and self-interest is making gay people more equal than others.

This trend reached a head in October 2007 when the

Labour Government announced that it is going to introduce a new law that will make 'homophobic' comments a criminal offence, punishable by up to seven years in prison. The Justice Secretary Jack Straw promised that the law would only be used against those who incite a culture of intolerance. But: 1. We already have laws to stop incitement to hatred and violence. 2. We can't believe him. We've already seen an Oxford student slung in the cells for joking that a copper's horse was gay. We've seen writer Lynette Burrows interrogated by cops for expressing her considered disapproval of gay adoption on the radio; and Stephen Green of *Christian Voice* was arrested by officers from the city's élite Minority Support Unit for handing out leaflets quoting the Bible in a Cardiff park. The law will be used to stifle free speech and suppress debate. It's another goose-step forward into the era of thought crime.

A few years ago, Tony Blair's Government tried to legalise cottaging – sex in public toilets. Mercifully, this was thrown out by the Lords. The late Gerry Fitt, a socialist peer and the son of a labourer, said rightly, that any father taking his son into a public bog would be 'absolutely disgusted' at what was going on in the cubicle, adding, 'There will be some fathers who feel as I would have if I were 20 years younger that they could see themselves taking physical action.' In other words, try something like that in Basildon, pal, and you'd be lucky not to get clumped. Even if you are George Michael.

If someone was to repeat Lord Fitt's words now in public, they would almost certainly get a visit from the pink Plod.

The defence seems to be: this is our lifestyle choice and, if you question it, you're a bigot. But if my lifestyle choice involved receiving blow-jobs from naked blondes in town centre doorways, I would fully expect to be up before the beak if somebody caught us at it.

These people are brazen though. Take Mark Oaten the Liberal Democrat MP, a married father of two, who in 2006 was revealed to have been enjoying 'acts too disgusting to describe' with a couple of rent boys, one of whom he had been paying for sex regularly. He duly resigned as the Lib Dem home affairs spokesman. In the eyes of some voters, he's a snake and a hypocrite – the year before he had condemned a judge for cavorting with rent boys. Once this would have meant the end of his career. But no. Oaten continues to pop up as bold as brass on *Newsnight* and *Question Time* as if nothing had ever happened. The BBC don't wish to be seen as 'judgmental' you see; and, like George Michael, Oaten sees himself as the victim of homophobic hysteria. So the man takes the piss in more ways than one. He has no sense of shame.

Peter Tatchell of Outrage says that the Lib Dems were 'the most closeted party', adding 'Mark Oaten is not the only Liberal Democrat MP who has sex with men.' But all parties have MPs who prefer to remain in the closet. Think of Ron 'Dogger' Davies, Peter Mandelson and Nick Brown, to name but three prominent Labour men. While Lord Tebbit, Tatchell's ideological opposite, caused headlines when he said of secretly gay Tories: 'Don't kid me that there are only one or two.' When witty Tory Alan Duncan outed himself in 2002, Tebbit wrote 'Britain is a very tolerant country. The great mass of us have no desire to emulate Mr Duncan's activities under his duvet ... we do not wish to join in; we just wish profoundly that he would not bore us with his sexual problems.' To which a great many of us would mutter 'Here, here.'

So does it matter? People have a right to privacy, of course. But if you are a gay MP who is conning the public by claiming to be what you are not then it should matter. If you secretly lust after adolescent boys and vote to lower the age of consent for example, then it's right and proper that the people who elect you should know about your predilections in advance.

If Peter Tatchell hadn't been outed in 1983, he would have been Labour MP for Bermondsey.

Many now see Tatchell as a brave man standing up for gays. He is usually referred to as a human rights activist. His courage is beyond question; his morality less so. The one-time Maoist activist at the Polytechnic of North London had the balls to take on Mugabe's thugs as well as Russian cops. But just ten years ago Tatchell managed to alienate a lot of people, gay and straight, by attempting to justify adult sex with those below the age of consent.

Being a clever guy, though, he didn't refer to it as paedophilia but as 'intergenerational sex.' In a letter to the *Guardian*, Tatchell applauded the self-serving 'experts' cited in the book *Dare To Speak*. He called them distinguished. The editor of the volume, one Joseph Geraci, also edited Paidika, a Dutch paedo rag. Featured in both the book and the magazine was one Ralph Underwager, co-founder and leading light of the False Memory movement, who coined the term as a legal defence for those accused of child molestation. Tatchell wrote that 'intergenerational sex is considered normal, beneficial and enjoyable' in some societies, failing to add that so are female circumcision and public stoning. Tatchell said that not all sex involving children is harmful and that it is 'an initiation to the adult world.' No doubt the same arguments were advanced by the career paedophiles 'caring' for children in scandal-blitzed Islington and North Wales, or those allowed to foster children by New Labour 'progressives'.

Don't worry about that old perv propositioning your fourteen year old son. He only wants to initiate him into the adult world. He might even be your MP.

19

Northern Crock

Northern Rock was going down like the *Belgrano* until Gordon Brown and Alistair Darling decided to bail it out – with £55 billion of our money.

That figure isn't a misprint – £55 *billion* pounds. That's more than the annual defence budget, and it's twice the total council tax bill. Even Jonathan Ross thinks that's a lot of dough.

Horrified by scenes of grannies queuing outside the bank, Chancellor Darling stepped in to guarantee savers' deposits. It was a short-term fix to shore up confidence but, as the billions continue to pour in, there's less and less chance of Darling getting our money back.

State subsidies are the financial equivalent of heroin; the wretched junkie always craves another fix and, as the weeks roll on, the Northern Rock pit is looking as bottomless as an anorexic supermodel.

The McChuckle Brothers, Brown and Darling, are in

the dock here. It is one thing to protect the funds of the depositors, and quite another to bail out shareholders and underwrite the losses of incompetent speculators. We are being robbed, and the Government is driving the get-away car.

It has cost you, me and every other tax-payer an estimated £1,800 a pop to prop up the investments of people we don't know. We – the public – are subsidising private profit. Why? No investment is cast iron. My brother Tel invests his money unwisely nearly every day – in various three-legged gee-gees – but it's never been suggested that the State should make good his losses. What makes Northern Rock any different?

The 'Northern' in the name is the first clue. If this former building society was called Southern Rock and based in Sevenoaks, the Government wouldn't give a tuppenny damn about it. They wouldn't have lifted a finger for Coutts, but Newcastle-based Northern Rock has more than 100,000 small shareholders, most of them living in the north-east of England. It's a Labour heartland, with seven MPs in the area, and if its 6,000 jobs go to the wall, you can bet your bottom dollar that thousands more Labour votes will go with them.

So Joe Public has to shell out again, but we didn't wreck the Rock. Its boss, Adam J Applegarth, did. The recently-departed, £760,000-a-year Chief Executive and his dingbat management team ran the company into the ground. They borrowed too much from the money markets and lent out too much to home-buyers. More precisely, they borrowed short from the wholesale market to lend long to retail customers. And when the world financial system conked out in August thanks to the US sub-prime crisis, the bank's risky strategy was left more exposed than Paris Hilton's privates. They had no room to manoeuvre.

They had dumbly believed the flow of easy money to be risk-free. They were wrong. The result was 'a liquidity problem'. They ran out of cash. Private-sector money decided that the Rock wasn't worth saving and the company would have gone tits-up if the McChuckle Brothers hadn't come riding to the rescue with a horn of plenty stuffed full of our tax pounds.

Many gullible folk assumed that the Government knew what it was doing. After all, Brown has a reputation for prudence, hasn't he, and Darling must surely be a safe pair of hands; Brown is his puppet master after all. Gordon appointed him and continues to pull his strings. The underlying message was that this man is as safe as he is dull. Up until the Northern Rock crisis, the only interesting thing about Darling were his *Thunderbird* eyebrows.

But it's becoming increasingly clear that the pair of them don't know what they're doing. The Government's intervention was a knee-jerk reaction with no thought-out policy, for which the technical term is 'panic buying'.

Right now, Darling looks less like a Grey Man and more like a cross between rogue trader Nick Leeson and Mr Macawber, putting off decisions until tomorrow while hoping against hope that his luck would change.

They're squandering not just our cash but also whatever reputation Brown had for financial competence – much of it undeserved, by the way, as Brown neither likes nor understands free markets. Basically, they've fleeced us; they've stolen our money and there's no sign that we'll ever get it back.

Darling named Virgin Money as the preferred bidder for Northern Rock and Branson's brilliant PR machine immediately kicked into action. He took out ads in national newspapers talking about 'our new and exciting bank', addressing Rock shareholders as if he was already in the driving seat. But no contract had been signed, no money had changed hands. The message? We're Batman, Robin and the X-Men rolled into one. We're the only ones you can trust to get it right, so what are you waiting for?

If Branson had acquired the bank he would have been in a win-win situation. If he'd succeeded he would have made a huge percentage of the bank's profit. If he'd failed, the Treasury would have lost most. Nice work if you can get it. In the event, it didn't happen.

While he was Chancellor, Mr Prudent changed the traditional way this kind of banking crisis was dealt with and brought in a 'tripartite system' involving the Bank of England, the Financial Services Authority (the City watchdog) and the Treasury. The system was tested by Northern Rock and found seriously wanting. Yet the fault lines in this tripartite bank supervision system were exposed in 2006 during a simulated Whitehall 'crisis exercise' when Ed Balls – Brown's closest confidant – was a Treasury Minister. It's inconceivable that Brown wouldn't have known. So why hadn't the Treasury taken remedial action before Northern Rock ended up in the Newcastle Brown-stuff?

When Brown insists this mess is nothing to do with the Government, he is telling porky pies. Massive reforms are needed urgently to prevent this kind of cock-up happening again.

The most frustrating thing is that this all could have been avoided. Lloyds TSB wanted to take over the Rock back in August 2007, but they were blocked. Even when the bank went belly up, Brown could have told the Treasury to put them into administration, bought all the assets and liabilities from the receiver for a quid, and then run the Rock down in an orderly fashion. Instead, they are on course to settle for the worst possible course of action, which Vince Cable summed up as 'the nationalisation of risks and losses, combined with privatisation of gains'.

As we tick off the mistakes, let's spare a thought for the beleaguered former Chief Exec, Adam Applegarth. When Rock shares were riding high, Applegarth flogged £2.6 million worth. He has not had to repay his bonus; he has no 'liquidity' problem. Mr Applegarth resigned from the bank after its collapse last autumn, but stayed on in a caretaker role until December, when he walked away with a payoff of £380,000. That's a goodbye 'drink' worth half of his annual salary for wrecking the company. Cheers!

- If Brown could stump up £55billion for a small Newcastle bank, why didn't he rescue MG-Rover, or Leyland or GEC-Marconi? Or the mines, come to that.
- The Northern Rock crisis has had a knock-on effect on Japan's banking system. I understand that Tokyo's

Origami Bank has folded. Kamikaze Bank shares are plummeting, and the Sumo Bank has gone belly up.

- STOP PRESS. Feb 18 2008. Shares in Northern Rock were suspended after the Government's decision yesterday to nationalise the stricken bank.

Many Labour MPs celebrated by singing The Red Flag. They saw nationalisation as a Socialist measure creating a 'People's Bank.' As usual they have got their heads up their arses. The Government who dithered and delayed for half a year are now madly promising 'business as usual.' Instead they face a new set of headaches, including the threat of legal action from shareholders whose holdings are likely to become worthless. And nearly half the workforce is likely to be laid off. It seems that taxpayer liabilities could be as high as £110billion. Nationalisation only makes sense as a stepping stone to liquidation that should have happened last September. There is no word on how temporary nationalisation is going to be – or how soon taxpayers can expect all or any of our money back.

Bushell on the Blog
November 2007

1 November Sad to hear that Paul Fox of the Ruts died while I was away. He was one of the finest guitarists to come out of punk, and an all-round nice guy. Paul had been diagnosed with inoperable lung cancer earlier this year. He died at home in Uxbridge on 21 October. That makes three great punk guitarists in as many years (JJ Bedsore of The Blood, Nidge Miller of Blitz, now Foxy). Memo to Mickey Geggus, get yourself down to BUPA, son. I'd hate to lose you too.

7 November Nigel Hastilow has quit as a Tory candidate after saying that John Enoch Powell was right about immigration. Our thoughts on Powell are for the moment irrelevant. What matters is how pointless the Tories have become. A Conservative mentioning Enoch makes as much sense as a Labour MP invoking the spirit of Nye Bevan. Labour aren't Socialist and the Tories won't discuss immigration sensibly. More importantly, even if they were elected they wouldn't do anything about it. If Hastilow wants to clamp down on mass immigration, he's in the wrong party.

- Sir Paul McCartney has been pictured kissing Nancy Shevell. My mate rang Macca up and asked if he'd be going down on one knee again soon. 'No,' said Paul 'I told ya – I'm divorcing that mad bitch.' (Nancy kissed him in the Hamptons. If it was on the hampton that'd be some picture ...)

- Heather Mills' GMTV meltdown was the true horror of Halloween. Let's hope ITV respond responsibly and book her for the jungle immediately. Heather says she won't have pelvic surgery cos 'I can't spend four months on my back.' I dunno. Why break the habit of a lifetime?

11 November The quiet dignity of today's Cenotaph ceremony is an enduring testimony to all that is good about Great Britain. It's right and proper that we remember the terrible carnage of the two World Wars. It's right and proper that we recall the heroism and suffering of generations who were braver, tougher and more loyal than our own. And it's right and proper that we never, ever forget the supreme sacrifices they made. But it sticks in the craw to see those craven politicians there, hypocrites who have sold our sovereignty down the river and sent our under-funded, ill-equipped forces to die in the doomed follies of Iraq and Afghanistan. What do all those proud ex-servicemen really think of Blair, Brown and Cameron? You could bet your life their views would make Prince Philip blush. Today, as we honour the memory of those who fell so that Britain might live, let's also remember our armed forces today and send out the message loud for all to hear: bring the boys home.

13 November A man has been convicted for having sex with a bicycle. Apparently the bike said the experience wasn't all that, but the chain did come off once. Many mysteries arise from this. How do you have sex with a bike? Why is it an offence? And why would you do it? Clearly the man is either a bikesexual or a pedalphile. Unless it was just one big misunderstanding; he'd asked in the pub where he could get laid, and the barman suggested the village bike...

14 November Security Minister Admiral Lord Alan West of

Spithead made an about turn today. On Radio 4's *Today* programme, war hero West was asked for his views on Government plans to extend the amount of time a terror suspect can be held without charge. His answer was clear. 'I want to have absolute evidence that we actually need longer than 28 days,' he said. 'I want to be totally convinced because I am not going to go and push for something that actually affects the liberty of the individual unless there is a real necessity for it. I still need to be fully convinced that we absolutely need more than 28 days and I also need to be convinced what is the best way of doing that.' Here, here. After coming off air, he was humiliatingly summoned to Downing Street. After a half-hour meeting with a furious Gordon Brown, the former First Sea Lord executed a perfect U-turn at maximum speed. His views had been 'clarified' by the Prime Minister. Or rather he'd been persuaded to submerge his true opinions under a foamy spray of political expediency. Lord West told reporters that he is now 'personally convinced' that there is a need to change the law. He said: 'And what is very difficult, I believe, because we have to balance civil liberties, is how we actually move forward to achieve it. And that's where the real difficulty's going to be. I personally absolutely believe that within the next two, three years, we will require more than that for one of these complex plots. So I am convinced that's the case.' What a farce. The Admiral proved his bravery during the Falklands conflict, when he won the Distinguished Service Cross for commanding the frigate Ardent. As a 34-year-old he remained at the helm of the vessel when it had been hit by Argie bombs in San Carlos Water. He saw 22 of his men die on board and only ordered the ship to be abandoned when the steering failed. How can a man with such proven guts lose his bottle in the face of a monstering from Gordon? In the Falklands, Admiral Lord West was fighting for British freedom. This hard-earned freedom includes habeas corpus, which the Prime Minister seeks to scrap. He would have served his country better if Lord West had stuck to his guns, and resigned from Government, rather than parrot the party line. England expects no less.

15 November *The Mighty Boosh* is back for a third series and it's brilliant. I love this show, it's weird, it's silly, it's more off the wall than a ten-year-old squash ball and, crucially, it's very funny. If Spike Milligan, Syd Barrett and Salvador Dali were all young and writing comedy while ingesting magic mushrooms it would probably end up like this. Highlights of episode one included that psychotic Dickensian Cockney villain threatening Howard with his eels, the cosmic stag trip and Howard getting used and abused by a sex-mad widow who pounded him 'like yesterday's beef.' Vince should go on *Dragon's Den* with that celebrity radar kit. (Especially if it means Deborah Meaden then gets sucked into a psychotic Cockney's hat.) All together: We are super magic men, we stay up till 5am...

17 November Kate Garraway is useless *on Strictly Come Dancing*. If she were a topless dancer she'd have two left tits.

18 November Stephen Fry has won an international Emmy for his documentary on depression. If that doesn't cheer the bastard up, nothing will.

19 November Gordon Brown offered GMTV's Fiona Phillips a ministerial job. It gets worse. Gordon only approached Fiona after Lorraine Kelly turned him down! 'Brulliant.' Is this the same Brown who pledged in June that his government wouldn't be obsessed with worthless celebrity culture?

- Her Majesty the Queen and Prince Philip are celebrating 60 years of happy marriage, although according to a new documentary from RDF they divorced in 1992.

20 November Two computer discs jam-packed with info about children and their parenthood have been lost...and that's just the Ulrika Jonsson file.

21 November Scientists at the UN have finally admitted they overstated the threat of a global AIDS epidemic. Political correctness has corrupted AIDS projections since the 1980s. Billions were spent telling us we were all at risk. We weren't. In Britain, the groups at risk were gay men, junkies, immigrants from sub-Saharan Africa and people who had sex with them. When I pointed this out in the early 1990s I was vilified. I'm glad to be proved right but disgusted by the millions of pounds that were squandered.

- What a pile of crap England were tonight. England's first-half performance was the most miserable 45 minutes of telly since the last Dawn French special. The difference between us and Lewis Hamilton? He'll still have a McLaren in the morning. Already the texts are coming through: 'Steve McLaren is going to the England Xmas party as a pumpkin, he's hoping someone will turn him into a ****ing coach', 'England to change their shirts, the three lions to be replaced by three tampons to signify the worst period we've ever been through', and best of the lot: 'McLaren has stated that tonight's result won't come as a shock. Everyone knows you can always get a group of blokes from Eastern Europe to work much harder for a lot less money...' Here's what is not funny, though - the buckets of dosh McLaren will get paid for being an even bigger failure than Sven. Talk about rubbing our noses in it.

- Identity theft is all the rage, but what if someone steals your identity and your family and friends like him better than you?

- Some good news for Steve Mclaren: no-one wants to steal his identity...

22 November *I'm A Celebrity* needs Janice Dickinson like Lynne Franks needs stomach staples. She's gold-dust. Yes she's hateful, self-centred and cosmetically terrifying – Janice has Steve Tyler's face and the body of a zombie Iggy Pop. Even kangaroo balls shrivel in her presence. But she's kicking life into a series that's been badly miscast. (Anna, Jason, John...they're like a Who's Who of Why Them?) So far, Janice has revealed that Malcolm McLaren 'smells of dirty farts', branded John Burton Rice 'gay' for eating a crocodile's penis and called Lynne 'a shrew'. Her one-liners are a joy. Especially 'I'm a supermodel, I haven't eaten for years' and 'I can't eat croc dick, are you insane?' Oh man! She doesn't wear a bra, she said: 'Why should I? I paid good money for these puppies.'

Best of all, Janice clashes constantly with Lynne Franks, a rancorous old cow who could suck the joy out of a Cup Final.

Dreary Lynne is one of those women who feel duty bound to lecture anyone who disagrees with her. She herds up the gullible for absurd chanting sessions ('Why can't she keep her chanting to herself?' asked Janice reasonably.) Her dance moves make Garraway look good. She 'needs space.' Lynne is full of more crap than a blocked up sewer pipe. All that mystic mumbo-jumbo...Zeus save us! Mercifully, even the combined power of Mother Earth, the universe, Zen Buddhism, the Navaho Indians and her own 'higher self' won't save Lynne from getting the boot soon.

In this company, latecomer Chris Biggins seems like a showbiz giant. The other blokes aren't much cop. There's John: obscure TV chef, looks like a slightly younger Victor Meldrew. Marc: soap dimwit; doesn't seem to realise that flirting with Cerys Matthews might wind up his girlfriend. (We know he's not acting, we saw him in *EastEnders*) Jason J Bland: got his wimpy arse wupped by Cerys. Rodney Marsh: part Peter Pan, part Billy Liar, all arse. Anyone remember him taking 'a penalty at Wembley in front of 100,000 people'? Thought not. Most of the women are dull too. Gemma works better in 2D. And as for Anna Ryder Richardson, Anna Why's-she-here? Richardson more like. She's only gone to Australia to see her career go down the plug-hole in the opposite direction. Katie's good value, but since when does not winning a BBC2 reality show make you a celebrity?

25 November. Paulo Hewitt is in the *Mail On Sunday* today revealing the devastating truth about his ex-friend Paul Weller. One night it seems Paul gave Paulo money to get a round in and then demanded his change. Wow. What a rotter. Oh and he nearly hurt himself with a cup. What stories! What insight! What cobblers.

26 November Dogging, swinging, sex in public, web-cam sex…everything agony aunts were moaning about on *Sex In The Noughties* has been done by *EastEnders* cast members in real life. It must be like the Hellfire Club up at Elstree. They're not just actors, they're pioneers on the wilder shores of sexuality. Which certainly makes you look at old Dot in a different light.

27 November On *Spooks* tonight, a *Question Time*-type show was taken over by right-wing gunmen. Ridiculous. Nothing interesting happens on *Question Time*.

20

Battling for Benny

Benny Hill was Britain's biggest ever comedy export, shown in more than 100 countries and adored the world over; especially in the USA. Benny's comedy was marinated in the honest vulgarity of English popular humour. This shy, modest man was genuinely a people's comic, loved by millions but strangely detested by the likes of Ben Elton and other chattering class snipers. To them, Benny was 'sexist'.

The sanctimonious Elton denounced him as 'a dirty old man.' 'Women are getting raped,' he ranted, 'and there's Benny Hill tearing the clothes off nubile girls while chasing them round a park.'

Had Ben actually bothered to watch Benny's shows he might have noticed that the girls always ended up chasing HIM. If anything Benny's jokes were anti-men. It was the blokes who walked into lamp-posts. The blokes were always the losers. Especially if they were small, bald and slappable. Women on Benny's shows fared far better than say Carol

Cleveland on Monty Python who tended to be wheeled on in stockings and suspenders as a fetching bit of eye-candy.

So why was Benny shunned while the Pythons are still revered? Simple. It's all about class. The Pythons, who I adored, were from the right Oxbridge background. University boys. Benny went to a bog standard secondary modern in Hampshire. His bawdy down-to-earth humour was never likely to play well with hectoring professor's son Ben Elton.

Of course there was far more to Hill's comedy than mild seaside postcard smut (not that there's anything wrong with that). He was the first comedian of the television age, and the first to use the medium as a target. A typical Benny Hill show mixed parodies of TV hits with visual comedy, clever mime work, comic songs and character comedy. Lisping Fred Scuttle, Ernie the Milkman and Chow Mein the Chinaman are remembered with affection to this day.

And, OK, it may be that he was past his prime. But Benny still brought in millions of viewers. None of that seemed to matter, though. Benny Hill was old school and so he had to go, because one of the odd thing about po-faced eighties 'alternative' comics and their TV executive groupies is that they couldn't abide any alternative to their brand of PC student union humour.

In 1989 the gutless trendies at ITV shamefully caved in to the joyless prudes who you suspect had never even watched the show to begin with. Benny Hill was summoned to Thames TV and sacked in a humiliating ten-minute meeting. He had generated millions of pounds for the company and yet they treated him like a cloakroom attendant who'd been caught with his hand in someone's jacket pocket.

The great man was devastated and there is little doubt that Benny's sacking hastened his death in 1991.

Since then, not one of the fashionable comedians who TV has invested millions in have had a quarter of Hill's success, although *Little Britain*, whose stars cite Benny and Dick Emery as influences, has done best – and has run out of charm much faster. If Elton thought Benny was anti-women, Lord knows what he makes of the way elderly Dorises are portrayed by David Walliams and Matt Lucas as puking, incontinent grotesques. While Mitchell and Webb's comedy sketches, that involve punching and killing women, have been broadcast without a voice raised in protest.

Throughout the Nineties, the dead hand of political correctness, coupled with the desire to be seen as hip and to make commissions inspired by the phoney god of demographics, managed to drive all the laughs out of prime-time television. Harry Hill's inspired TV Burp is now the only comedy show on ITV that transmits between 6pm and 9pm. A whole generation of working class British comedians has been denied access to the medium that would and should have made them household names.

Ironically, Benny Hill's show remains a ratings smash wherever it is broadcast. It was number one on BBC America in 2005, but so far the Beeb has shied away from repeating the shows here. Apparently there is too much 'stigma' attached to his name. They seem to have forgotten that the PC prudes had it in for the *Carry On* films in the eighties too – for the same feeble-minded reasons (alleged 'sexism').

The *Carry On*s which were also once banned from our screens are now rightfully cherished and shown on Channel 4 and the BBC. Even *Carry On Henry* where Sid James as the monarch does go looking for a wench to rape...Yet, bizarrely, Benny Hill is still seen as beyond the pale.

Abroad, the prejudice doesn't exist. Benny Hill enthusiasts range from Barry Humphries to Tom Wolfe via Greta Garbo, Clint Eastwood and Snoop Dog. Every big US act seems to love our Benny. Even the Black-eyed Peas are fans. At Christmas 2006, Objective Productions made a documentary for C4 where they tested Benny's humour on a young British audience. To nobody's surprise but theirs he went down a treat.

- It is a national scandal that Hill's legacy is unrecognised in his own country. Which is why I'm leading a campaign for a statue to be raised to honour his memory. We have the backing of the Heritage Foundation, Graeme Ibbeson (who sculpted the excellent Eric Morecambe bronze at Morecambe) has the design and a platoon of stars are ready to drum up the cash. We even have various councils fighting for the statue to be located in their town.

  Stump up some of the cost, chaps, and he's yours...

  Anyone donating £100 or more to the Benny Hill statue will have their name permanently linked to Benny's splendid erection. Please make cheques out to the Arts & Entertainment Charitable Trust (registered charity 1031027) and post c/o the Heritage Foundation, Green Acres, 3 Birchwood Chase, Great Kingshill, Bucks HP15 6EH . Payments can be accepted under Gift Aid. All Benny fans can now buy a handsome 11-inch cold-cast bronze version. They cost £95 (plus £10 p&p) – and money from each sale goes towards the statue's construction. Buy online at http://www.morecambe.co.uk/bennyhill.

*　　*　　*

IT'S been fun to watch the backlash against Ben Elton gaining momentum on the stand-up scene. Mark Steel put him in Room 101. Stewart Lee reckoned he is more despised than Bin Laden who 'at least lived his life according to a consistent set of ethical principles.' Toby Young put it best, saying Ben Elton 'started out as an alternative comedian railing against Thatcherism and now earns a fortune writing librettos for truly awful West End musicals. His name has become a by-word for shameless hackery. He's the biggest sell-out of his generation.'

21

Power to the People

When I was sixteen, I marched to Aldermaston with the CND. My fellow demonstrators were a strange mix: young and old, Communists and peaceniks, Methodists and hippies dropping 'Mandies' (Mandrax, a downer); not my kind of drug or my kind of people but it felt grown-up to take part. One game old girl with a megaphone kept up a continual barrage of slogans, imploring bemused commuters to: 'Get off the bus and march with us!' in a voice more suited to Radio 4's *Woman's Hour* than the rough-and-tumble of a political demonstration. It was surreal. Looking back, the best thing about that CND experience was seeing space rock legends Hawkwind play at the end, with dancer Stacia, a heavy-breasted, six-foot-tall woman who performed wearing nothing but luminous paint. When people complain that political meetings were like watching paint dry, they had clearly never seen it do so on a very bouncy, naked woman.

Like the other marchers, I assumed that rock and left-wing politics were natural bed-fellows. Rock, like youth cults, had to be on the side of the angels. The suits were Tory; the kids were Labour and that was that. We just had to try and forget that a Labour government had recently banned pirate radio. And that Tony Benn, latterly the revered face of the Socialist Labour Left, was the Postmaster General who declared broadcasting pioneers 'a menace' for the crime of opening up the airwaves to pop.

It was Benn, then known by his rather grander birth name of Anthony Wedgewood Benn, who drove the pirates underground. Labour's 1967 Marine Broadcasting Offences Act made it an offence to advertise or supply an offshore radio station from the UK, forcing Radio Caroline to relocate to Holland. There were even plans for MI5 to knock out the off-shore broadcasters – even though they were outside British waters. Only the pirates' huge popularity among the young convinced the authorities to back off. The stations were forced off air eventually – Caroline was fatally nobbled by falling advertising revenue – but their bold enterprise changed the face of radio forever, liberating the airwaves and forcing the BBC to launch Radio One (Britain's state-run radio station) as a Caroline clone.

Comrade Benn's heavy-handed approach did little to loosen the Left's grip on pop, however. Many of our most cherished rock icons make Hugo Chávez look like a dithering wet. Pete Townshend is a former Young Communist; John Lennon, a multi-talented millionaire Marxist revolutionary; then there was big-hearted Joe Strummer whose brand of rose-tinted Stalinism counterbalanced punk's in-built nihilism. From Dylan to Billy Bragg, from the MC5 to Tom Robinson, the left-wing tradition in popular music is pretty much the accepted orthodoxy. Dissenting voices were few and far between. Think of Steve Harley's Cockney Rebel song 'Red Is A Mean, Mean Colour'; chortle in solidarity with the Strawbs' send-up of the abuse of trade union power 'Union Man'; and goose-step gingerly around Alex Harvey's over-enthusiastic rendition of the Hitler Youth toe-tapper 'Tomorrow Belongs To Me.'

The 'revolution' didn't wash for everyone. David Bowie caught the mood of the post-'68 generation when he wrote 'All the Young Dudes': his older brother was in his bedroom, listening to the Beatles and the Rolling Stones singing about insurrection. But young David and his mates were never impressed. Revolution was a drag, he sighed – there were too many snags. In the USA, the presumed unity of the anti-war movement was shattered forever when those untamed right-wing barbarians, the Hell's Angels of California, laid in to student protestors at Berkeley in the Autumn of 1965 and then offered to fight the Viet Cong. Sonny Barger wrote to President Johnson:

Dear Mr. President,
On behalf of myself and my associates I volunteer a
group of loyal Americans for behind-the-line duty in
Vietnam. We feel that a crack troop of trained
gorrillas [sic] would demoralize the Viet Cong and
advance the cause of freedom. We are available for
training and duty immediately.

Elvis, the King of Rock 'n' Roll himself, famously offered his services to Richard Nixon in the battle against narcotics, subversion and 'the hippy element.' Elvis wrote to the President in 1970 asking to be made a Federal agent at large in rock 'n' roll circles. They met shortly afterwards, but the King never got his badge, so there was never a legion of Ted Feds actively banging up jailhouse rockers. Which is, on balance, a shame.

In 1970s Britain, most pop stars who voted Conservative kept quiet about it. Imagine being seen to share opinions with Ted Heath. But things changed later that decade: punk happened under a Labour government. In 1977, petty-minded Labour council dullards were banning punk bands from council-owned venues. Sham 69 responded with a song called 'Red London' that argued that London streets were turning Red and there was no democracy 'Free yourself from this,' Jimmy Pursey pleaded, 'Individuals rule.'

The history of pop politics is a catalogue of blunders and embarrassments. Left or right, politicised rock has been largely cringe-worthy. Consider:

1 The Woodstock Festival, August 1969

This hippy hiatus came dripping with dippy idealism. Woodstock Nation was supposed to be youth culture's great stand against The Man; the zenith of flower-power achievement. A quarter of a million largely stoned or tripping enthusiasts turned up to a field in New York State. But no one had given much though to the catering: and shortages were threatening to spark chaos until President Johnson stepped in.

Power to the People

The authorities didn't send in the National Guard, they dropped food parcels. Local women's groups made sandwiches and farmers donated grub, but irony of ironies, it was the US Air Force that kept the hippy nation from going tits up.

Woodstock was a con, with the Altamont Speedway Free Festival that December its tragic punch-line. Even as the myth was being recycled in print, on film and on record, the reality of the hippy dream was looking increasingly bleak. Haight-Ashbury, once seen as the ultimate advert for Californian sun-soaked love-and-peacenik living, degenerated into a festering sore of smack abuse, prostitution and mugging.

Similarly, the Black Power movement, passionately espoused by white middle-class urban radicals, degenerated tragically into black racism.

However you slice it, the Hippies were a disaster. They contributed to a short spell of political liberalism which rebounded with the Reagan administration and the Moral Majority. The creed of free love (aka no morals) backfired with rising rates of herpes, AIDS and family break-down. Drug culture (tune in, turn on, cop out) led to smack and crack ravishing the ghettoes, sapping the will to fight back. And America's retreat from Indochina led to the rise of butcher Pol Pot who submitted Cambodia to a new and terrible genocide.

Well done, everyone.

The hippies themselves just cut their hair and moved into business, the media, law and politics – their rightful place as mature bourgeois adults.

It was much the same in Britain, except here the hippies were far more influenced by traditional left-wing politics and the Marxist- (and post-Marxist-) inspired 1968 student uprising in Paris. The long-term result was a major influx of the careerist middle class into the Labour Party and local government, which accelerated Labour's decline among working class voters, and lead to a corresponding rise of Essex Man and Thatcherism. Yet hippy thinking proved tenacious and continues to pox education, family life and the law. For me, the image that best sums up the hypocrisy of the era is one of John Lennon crooning at us to imagine that we have no possessions while renting a whole apartment in Manhattan just to store his wife's furs. It says a lot for the common sense of working-class kids at the time that the majority of us paid no attention and got stuck into Desmond Dekker instead.

2 The Protest Singer

Bob Dylan was a folk musician who broke through to rock audiences. His early songs were radical, bleak and extremely whiny. He sang 'A Hard Rain's A-Gonna Fall', painting an apocalyptic future of a nuclear winter that never happened. The pessimism caught on. Barry McGuire had a hit the following year with 'Eve of Destruction' while Zager and Evans echoed the downer mood, asking if mankind would survive to reach the year 2525. If only *Dad's Army*'s Private Frasier had recorded a novelty single based on his 'We're all doomed' catchphrase he'd have made a mint.

3 The Rolling Stones

'On our side' said the Left, largely because of their student union bar favourite, 'Street Fighting Man' But the Stones' right-on credibility wilts like Clark Kent in a Kryptonite Jacuzzi when you consider 'Brown Sugar', a song celebrating the fun to be had flogging black slave girls. Like some hideous old perv in a flasher's mac, Jagger sings about what a scarred old slave owner could do with a feast of female flesh – whipping the women and generally revelling in the taste of sweet black slave girls. No KKK disco should be without it.

In December 1969, while the cops were rounding up members of Charles Manson's 'family' in California's Death Valley, Michael Phillip Jagger was tied up in a meeting with business adviser Prince Rupert Lowenstein working out how to avoid paying tax to the Labour government. Years later, Mick admitted, 'My heart's socialist, my head is Conservative.'

4 John Lennon

The Bolshy Beatle, John, went from the raw brilliance of 'Working Class Hero' to the pious pits of 'Imagine', a ridiculous dirge marinated in utopian dopiness and written on a piano that later sold for more than two million bucks. 'Imagine no possessions' indeed. John's politics went ga-ga from the moment he and Yoko relocated to New York in 1971 and started hanging out with middle-class Yippie leaders Abbie Hoffman and Jerry Rubin. His judgement was already suspect: Lennon gave money to Michael de Freitas, better known as the murderer Michael X. But in

Manhattan, John lost his old class consciousness and started churning out songs that were little more than agit-prop slogans. Take the doggerel-cursed double album *Some Time In New York City* on which Lennon espouses feminism ('Woman Is The Nigger Of The World'), Attica prison rioters and Irish nationalism. On 'Sunday Bloody Sunday', he sings about 'Anglo pigs and Scotties' and declares 'Repatriate to England all of those who call it home', while 'The Luck Of The Irish' is utterly twee old cobblers, right down to the lyrics about leprechauns. Yoko's screeching avant-garde offerings, 'Sisters O Sisters' and 'We're All Water' are particularly dire and the album died on its arse. It was all a far cry from the never-released joke version of 'Get Back' allegedly recorded by the Beatles, pirate copies of which have long been circulated in rock circles. It features John Lennon singing 'Don't dig no Pakistanis taking all the people's job... get back to where you once belonged.'

5 David Bowie

Flirting with homosexuality was one thing, but no one had expected super-cool Bowie to flirt with fascism. The Thin White Duke was later to plead temporary insanity caused by substance abuse for his actions in 1976. Returning from Berlin after the European leg of his 'Station To Station' tour on 2 May, Dave cheerfully sieg-heiled fans and photographers at Victoria Station. Some fans returned the gesture. It was no isolated moment. In an interview published in that September's *Playboy*, Bowie referred to Hitler as 'the first rock star' and praised his stage presence.

He also stated that Britain was 'ready for a fascist leader' (a thin, white Duce?).

His lyrics show that a fascination with the Third Reich had long haunted the Brixton-born star. Bowie's song 'Quicksand' on the 1971 album *Hunky Dory* runs the gamut from Aleister Crowley to Golden Dawn occultists, SS chief Heinrich Himmler, the after-life and Nietzsche's belief in the coming superman. Himmler of course was a lean, mean anti-Semite machine. The man who put genocide into practice. The man who sold the earth? Later, a calmer chameleon blamed excessive cocaine consumption for his springtime for the Führer flirtations. By the end of the year, Bowie was laughing it all off. In 1977, he denied it vociferously.

6 The Clash

The band that turned the heads of thousands of teenage socialists, me included. We over-romanticised them to a ridiculous extent because the Clash gave punk's anger a purpose. This was rock played with a clenched fist. The Clash claimed to be working class yout' from under the shadow of the West Way and we, like mugs, believed them. But they were never what they seemed. Mick Jones and Paul Simonon were middle class art students while Joe Strummer's standing as the Wolfie Smith of punk was slightly dented when it eventually emerged some time later that his father was a British diplomat. Our Joe was born John Graham Mellor and had been educated at the City of London Freemen's School at Ashtead, a private boarding school, and then at art college. He was an all-round good guy, but he was faking it. At the time Strummer wrote

'White Riot' he was living in a white mansion. Still, to a left-leaning music press, understandably concerned about punk's negativity and its casual flirtation with Nazi imagery, the explicit socialist stance of the Clash came as a breath of fresh air. Writing in *Socialist Worker* at the time, I seized on them to defend punk from crustier comrades. Joe was a stale old Stalinist at heart, but back then it didn't seem like it. Anti-dole, anti-bureaucracy, anti-the-music-establishment, The Clash appeared to stand for a socialist alternative to Rotten's barbed nihilism. How were we to know that beneath the angry words they were just another Rolling Stones struggling to get to the very USA they claimed to be so bored with...

7 Rock Against Racism

Roger Huddle, a likeable printer at the Socialist Workers Party's print works, and Red Saunders, a talented Trot Theatre performer, had been kicking about the idea of organising a Rock Against Racism concert ever since Bowie's Victoria Station shenanigans in 1976. Eric Clapton's drunken outburst at a gig in Birmingham that August spurred them in to action. Clapton, a brilliant blues guitarist whose third solo hit had been a cover of Bob Marley's 'I Shot The Sheriff', told his audience that Britain was becoming over-crowded and urged them to vote for Enoch Powell to prevent the country becoming 'a black colony'. Later, Clapton defended his position, saying that it wasn't racist to be concerned about unfettered immigration; he also admitted that he'd been drunk and pissed off because an Arab had goosed his wife.

Huddle and Saunders wrote to the music press opposing Clapton's comments and asking for support for a Rock Against Racism campaign. Hundreds replied. They came up with the slogans, 'Reggae, Soul, Rock 'n' Roll, Jazz, Funk, Punk – Our Music' (cruelly snubbing the UK folk, country and blues scenes) and 'NF = No Fun'. The first issue of the RAR fanzine 'Temporary Hoarding' heavily featured the Clash. Both Huddle and Saunders were SWP members and local branches helped organise shows. Carol Grimes from Vinegar Joe was a frequent performer, but the RAR network of gigs helped to build and break bands as diverse as the excellent Ruts and Steel Pulse (RAR roller-coasted alongside punk, the rehashed hippy ideas of its leading members being balanced at first by punk's fury and energy).

1977 had seen the launch of the Anti-Nazi League; unlike Rock Against Racism which had been a roots-up development, the ANL (or Anal, to its detractors) had been formed by the SWP Central committee specifically as a front organisation. Leader Tony Cliff liked to refer to the SWP as 'the cog within a cog' of the broader-based ANL and Right To Work Campaign, drawing in less committed folk to activity that helped to win them over to the full-blooded Bolshevism of the party. Punks, soul boys and soccer yobs rallied to the cause, uniting with young blacks and the usual mobs of mouldy hippies and middle-class professionals to stop the NF marching through Lewisham in the August of 1977. When we were fighting with the police at the bottom of Belmont Hill, the Clash's 'White Riot' was running through my brain (until I got hit on the head by half a house brick chucked by my own side).

It is of course the greatest irony in modern politics that the National Front became associated in the public mind with street violence when they were never directly responsible for it. Whenever NF activities were subject to intense scrutiny by leading judges and senior cops, as happened after the Battle of Red Lion Square in 1974 (Lord Scarman's Report) and The Battle of Lewisham (Scotland Yard's Commander Helm in a *Jewish Chronicle* interview) three years later, they affirmed that the NF were 'not the instigators' – or indeed the participants – in the disorders; that the Front's demonstrations were lawful and that they were 'at all times responsive to requests from the police.' A lot of good it did them though. We attacked them, or we made a lot of racket and fought the cops. And the authorities responded by banning NF marches because of the probability that they would be attacked by far-left boot-boys. It wasn't until the rise of the odious British Movement that the boot was on the other foot and left-wing events were attacked with relish by the bully-boys of the Right.

The Tom Robinson Band was *the* RAR band. Cambridge-born ex-choir boy Tom was a decent enough bloke, but unworldly. Never a punk, he'd been in a folky, acoustic trio called Café Society whose only single was 'The Whitby Two-Step'. TRB formed in January 1977 and were a pretty average pub rock band. Their rapid growth, and signing that same year, was more to do with their politics than their music; although the apolitical 'Motorway' was a fine stomp-along anthem. Robinson epitomised the trendy rent-a-cause mentality of student Leftism and consequently won massive support from the media. His lyrics were right-on and naff. Tom worked through every fashionable cause going. There was 'Right On Sister', 'Sing if You're Glad to be Gay' (cringe if you're not) and 'Martin' (patronising piffle delivered in puke-worthy Mockney accent). It sure lacked the punch and certainty of the Clash's political anthems like the revolutionary 'Remote Control'.

'Who needs Parliament?' asked Joe Strummer, denouncing MPs as 'fat and old, queueing for the House of Lords.'

Back in the real world, Tory opposition leader Maggie Thatcher gave a speech reflecting Clapton-ian fears of being 'swamped by an alien culture' and, in April 1979, was duly elected prime minister. The NF was beaten, not by the Left, but by a radical of the free-enterprise right. Demoralised, the Front lost momentum, split into three rival factions and has never looked dangerous since. Not too surprisingly, RAR, which had been formed by self-confessed hippies, drifted in to soggy politics. They launched the ludicrous Rock Against Sexism while continuing to book and patronise Rastafarians, the most misogynist grouping of people in Britain this side of the Sid The Sexist Fan Club. The ANL went the same way, sprouting laughable sub-sections along Vegetarians Against The Nazis lines. But what really scuppered the campaigners was the defection of leading rock performers who were profoundly pissed off with the way the SWP was using them and Anal to recruit and convert their fans.

Back in 1979, the 2-Tone bands took up the RAR message and out-did it. They didn't have to preach, they physically embodied its spirit.

8 Rock Against Communism

Nazis could never hope to exploit rock as well as Reds. For starters, rock and pop's traditions are clearly entangled in sinewy black roots. Slack-jawed bigots have been opposing that devilish 'nigra music' since the 'concerned white citizens' of Alabama first set out their stall in the 1950s. And serious Neo-Nazis have always hated it. Their literature makes it quite clear that they consider rock 'n' roll to be a 'Jewish/Bolshevik conspiracy' to corrupt clean-living white youth who'd all be a damn sight better off learning to waltz. Only the recent popularity of *Strictly Come Dancing* gives them any sort of hope.

The populist far Right were shrewder. At the beginning of 1979, the Young National Front attempted to reverse their flagging fortunes by fighting the Left at their own game, launching their own umbrella alternative to RAR: Rock Against Communism. Not a success. Very few groups were willing to commit themselves to RAC's self-styled crusade to 'kick out the Reds, Pakis, blacks and Jews' and the ones that did were uniformly dire. Leeds bands The Dentists and The Ventz were the most notorious. Others involved included Tragic Minds, White Boss, Column 44 and the piss-poor Afflicted (who never played outside of one doss-hole of a pub in Deptford, South London). It was unfortunate for the YNF that their leaders undermined their recruitment drive. Chairman of the National Front John Kingsley Read condemned football hooligans stating that they should be 'whipped until the skin falls off their back'. John Rotten was also slagged off in NF publications, described as being 'no better than a white nigger'. The only music that met with tacit racial-nationalist approval was the electronic sounds that gained popularity at the start of this decade, post-Kraftwerk.

The real Nazi band was Skrewdriver. In the 1970s, singer Ian Stuart (born Ian Stuart Donaldson, the son of a Lancashire factory gaffer) was torn between his true beliefs and his imaginary career. Skrewdriver split at the end of 1979, reforming in 1982 before coming out as Nazis in '83. Tired of keeping the shrinking NF afloat, Stuart created and spearheaded the Blood & Honour 'White Power' movement so beloved by Hollywood. In movies, they seem like the Strasser brothers. In reality they were more like the Chuckle Brothers. Stuart once took to the stage of the 100 Club wearing a Nazi helmet. It was too big for him, so to keep it on his head he stuffed a plastic bag into the back of it. A couple of numbers in, the bag fell out and the helmet dropped down obscuring most of his face and improving the view dramatically. Master-race, my arse.

9 Gay Rights

The cause celeb of the late '80s and '90's was gay rights. The first band to be denounced were Guns 'N ' Roses, whose song 'One in a Million' made decidedly un-PC references to 'immigrants and faggots.' Many rap and reggae artists were enthusiastically anti-gay, causing much confusion on the Left. Which minority to support? Gay activists won the day and albums by artists such as reggae stars Buju Banton, Beenie Man, Elephant Man, TOK, Vybz Kartel and Bounty Killer were denounced and a campaign was launched to ban their music. Brighton was the first place to forbid sales of 'homophobic' albums in music stores. 'Freedom of speech... ceases to be valid when you are talking about incitement to murder,' said Brighton and Hove councillor Simon Williams. Although to date no action has been taken against Tom Jones for 'Delilah', Twisted Sister for their Falklands song 'Shoot 'Em Down' or ditties glorifying Stalin, Che, the IRA or Osama Bin Laden. Some murderers are more equal than others.

Jamaican academic Dr Lez Henry argued that if the gay activists' claims were true, then the genre would be inciting violence against everyone. He said: 'In reggae dancehall culture everything is the recipient of violence. From the sound systems to the person who plays the set, to the unfaithful baby mother, to the person who looks at you wrong. It's not just gays.' Jamaican professor Carolyn Cooper agreed: 'A parent will say to their child, "me a go kill you wid licks today," and the parent doesn't intend to actually kill the child. It is a statement to suggest the seriousness of the offence that the child has committed. It's not meant to be literal – it's a metaphor. We come from a culture in which verbal power is very important so that people who do not even have guns will be singing "boom bye bye in a batty bwoy head." What they are doing is asserting their sense of displeasure with homosexuality.'

The extreme AIDS misinformation campaign of the '80s may have triggered the anti-gay backlash. In the UK even the Conservative government were bamboozled by the 'we're all at risk' line, issuing leaflets that informed shocked spinster pensioners of the dangers of over-enthusiastic anal sex.

When the great Freddie Mercury died of an AIDS-related illness, Cockney comic Jimmy Jones remarked: 'Ashes to ashes/Dust to dust/If you'd stuck with fanny/You'd still be with us.'

10 Beyond politics

Post 9/11, the old certainties of pop politics seem increasingly distant. Charity singles and, as a by-product, televised charity concerts have boomed since Band Aid and Live Aid, replacing mass political protest as the conscience of pop; attracting the usual mob of earnest, ethical and tedious egotists. In 2007, we had Live Earth as the music biz embraced the great 'man-made global warning' con. Live Earth: from the people who cured African famine and made poverty history... just don't mention all the planes, trains, private jets, limos, trucks and tour buses that it required.

The biggest trend in modern pop is conservative. TV talent shows *X-Factor* and *American Idol* have proved enormously successful, largely because Joe Public has always liked laughing at useless wannabes. Simon Cowell, the brains behind them, has become an international star because of the brutal honesty of his opinions. He's a household name in the States. Like Saddam Hussein and Osama Bin Laden. The Yanks call him 'Judge Dreadful' and quake at his bluntness. He insults them and they love it, the slags. He makes stars – well, in the States at any rate. Before Leona Lewis, *X-Factor* winners have tended to be one-hit wonders. Yet Cowell's vision of pop is as narrow as one of Chris Stein's skinny ties. His autobiography makes it clear that he hated punk, most rock, even Dylan. He likes safe, sanitised MOR pop. A discreet veil has been drawn over his own musical history. This is understandable, for Cowell is responsible for more criminal records than Cops. He gave us hits by Bob the Builder, The Teletubbies and worst of all, Sonia. He's released singles by Will Young, Gareth Gates, even Zig and Zag. He has worked with puppets; imbecilic blithering puppets! And, as I said, Zig and Zag too. Every time he makes a fine-sounding claim about pop music, remember that this is the chump who turned down Take That and signed up Robson and Jerome.

Cards on the table, I like him. He's on the level. But what can Cowell ever give us? Another Will Young, or if we're really unlucky, another Cheeky Girls. If you write your own songs, if you're too young or too old or you don't look like a model, Cowell doesn't want to know. He wants pretty karaoke singers who do what they're told.

At heart these shows represent everything that is wrong with modern pop. The UK music business is stale and manufactured again; run by burnt-out users who see artists as disposable products to be hyped rather than creative talent to be nurtured. *X-Factor* is the new orthodoxy. The dull limits of its vision are what the next wave of real rebel bands has to confront and overthrow. If they've got any sense, they'll give party politics a berth as wide as Beth Ditto. Because the lessons of the last four decades make it clear that pop revolutionaries change nothing. The only message that means a light is the punk one: Do It Yourself.

Power to the People

Postscript

What of Oi! I hear you ask. Weren't the Oi! bands an outrageous right-wing conspiracy? The line taken by people who would have rather gargled horse manure than go to an Oi! gig was that Oi! was for skinheads and all skinheads were racist or worst. This was cobblers, and I should know: I compiled the first four Oi! albums, and managed two of the leading bands at a time when I still considered myself to be a Trotskyite. Oi! was working-class punk, full-stop. The Oi! message was unity between 'skins, punks and herberts' (terrace hooligans), and the bands attempted to bring working-class youth together to fight against common enemies like unemployment, low wages and police oppression. Besides, skinhead culture is steeped in West Indian influences; a true skinhead could no more be a racist than a real Mod could. I tell the full story of Oi! at garry-bushell.co.uk. The only problem at the early gigs was football hooliganism. After the 1981 Southall riot, Oi!'s true message was drowned out by a hysterical tabloid reaction informed by that beacon of sanity the *Daily Mail*. But look back at the sleeve notes and lyrics. The controversial *Strength Thru Oi!* album was dedicated to Jesse Owens, the grandson of a slave whose stunning victories at the Berlin Olympics took the shine off the dream of Aryan supremacy. Oi! songs included 'National Employers' Blacklist', 'Jobs Not Jails', 'Hey Little Rich Boy', 'Working-Class Kids', 'The Murder Of Liddle Towers', 'Last Night Another Soldier', 'The Real Enemy' and 'I Still Believe In Anarchy'.

The Oi! bands were obsessed with class – and football

309

violence. Stinky Turner put it succinctly when he said, 'Oi! is working-class and if you ain't working class you'll get a kick in the bollocks.' Not much of a manifesto, admittedly, but a bloody long way from Der Stürmer.

The bands were either old-school leftwing or they were anti-politics. That was understood around the world. Outside of England, Oi! lit a fuse that still burns today. Oi! bands can be found everywhere from Red China to Argentina. In the Philippines, the manager of an Oi! band was pulled up by fans angered by their message of 'black and white unite and fight.' 'What about the brown and yellow people?' asked one indignantly.

Oi! was reborn in the USA as Streetpunk, inspiring a new wave of hard-hitting bands like the Bouncing Souls, Maninblack and the Dropkick Murphys. Agnostic Front covered Cock Sparrer songs, and the excellent Rancid, America's answer to the Clash, recorded their own Oi! anthem, 'Avenues & Alleyways'. A huge fan of the early Oi! bands, Rancid's half-Danish guitarist Lars Frederiksen has recently produced the new album by the Masons, a group formed by guitarist Steve Whale of The Business. Bands from Blink 182 to The Briggs cite the Cockney Rejects as a major influence. This year, the Dropkicks were joined on stage by singer Liberty Hayes, the teenage daughter of East End Badoes vocalist Terry Hayes. The Oi! influence in Streetpunk is unmistakable. The latest album by the Street Dogs shows the Boston band wearing Fred Perry shirts, flat caps and drinking stout. They've recorded a cover of 'There's A Power in a Union'. It could have been us in the White Lion in 1980.

Power to the People

- Latest Rolling Stones set list: 'Hey, you, Get Off of My Lawn'; 'Wild Hearses'; '19th Prostrate Breakdown'; 'I Can't Get No Large Print Fiction'.

Bushell On The Blog
December 2007

1 December Tony Holland, the co-creator of *EastEnders* has died aged 67. Tony came up with the idea of the soap set in a Victorian square and based the characters on his own family, which is why the show had a sense of realism back then. We all knew a Lou Beale and an Angie Watts. And we knew men like Den were to be avoided at all costs. The characters and the relationships rang true. Compare that to the depressing schizophrenic mess that the soap has become, as slowly, madly and dully, it lurches towards its traditional Christmas of Tears. In the coming weeks, Kevin Wicks will die; while Max and Bradley's marriages will go belly up, an emotional catastrophe that's been more signposted than the O2 stadium. This week Vinnie Monks used Pat to make Shirley jealous. That's Fat Pat, a 65 year-old, 18-stone, hard-faced pensioner; a woman so frightful her first husband died on purpose. It was as baffling as a) Vinnie fancying Shirl while he was sober and b) Vinnie then turning the tipsy Terrahawk down when she wanted him...

Meanwhile, Uneven Steven has been smashing up his own stall for no convincing reason. Deano is being bashed about by a prison bully. And Billy Mitchell, the soap's perpetual whipping boy, was sacked from Fat Barry's old part-time joke job as a Christmas elf. Ho-ho-bloody hopeless. Billy ended up rolling home as pissed as Shirley's mattress to the disgust of Honey, his simpleton missus, but worse is yet to come. They'll be homeless soon. Keep punching Billy, son, you'll get knocked out soon enough. Meanwhile the writers have made Phil crooked – he never was to start with. When he first appeared on screen he was just hard. Now he's the only villain you know who dresses like a tramp, lives with his Mum and habitually grasses. The week's big story was Kevin stealing and torching a knocked-off motor which Phil had supplied and which he'd accidentally flogged to a copper. Although why he didn't just change the plates and flog it again escapes me. Oh and they've re-opened the e20, AKA Scarlet's, the Cobra Club, Angie's Den and now the R 'n' R... Whatever they call it, it's the only nightclub that opens in daylight. It's such an economic disaster even Branson wouldn't bail it out. The good news? Dawn Swann is working there and appears to have the Mitchell Brothers down her top. The bad news? The Mitchell Sisters are in charge. Poxy fancies herself as a DJ; she also fancies every bloke in Walford. And Ronnie is being stand-offish with Jack, so they'll be an item in the New Year (ditto, Tania and Sean.) But it's not all joyless, predictable garbage, honest. Heather did a wacky dance and Phil half-inched two of Ronnie's fuses. Laugh? I nearly head-butted a Samaritan. Today's *EastEnders* is a pale, joyless shadow of the soap it once was. The noise you'll hear in the background next week is Tony Holland turning in his grave.

6 December Angry cops may demand the right to strike after the Government decided to undercut a recommended pay deal. A police strike, that would be a turn-up for the books. The only thing is, how would we tell? Our local station is empty most of the time. Car break-ins are never investigated. All you get is a crime number for insurance claims. You never see a proper cop on foot patrol. In fact, the only time we see a cop is when he's hiding behind the bushes with a speed gun.

11 December Bob Spink asked a question in the House about the European Gendarmerie Force today. He asked the Foreign Secretary to give an undertaking that the EGF would never be allowed to operate on British soil. Milliband's answer was: '...but I am happy to reassure him that a nation must give its consent before any operation can be held in it.' In other words ... no. Armed foreign cops will be allowed to operate here.

12 December Alan Davies has bitten a tramp's lug-hole. It brings whole new meaning to Q.I. – Quite Inedible. Alan's a vegetarian. Maybe he thought the dosser had cauliflower ears. I reckon someone told him it was fun to bite a bum and he got the wrong end of the stick.

- God bless Joan Rivers. The woman has more bite than Alan Davies in a Cardboard City feeding frenzy. I've just watched her on the Royal Variety show. Shameless Joan stormed on stage like an animated corpse, denouncing the other acts and shaking up this annual snooze-fest. 'Fatso sang my opera,' she said of Paul Potts. 'The other one played my piano. And they've told me I'm not allowed to swear, so good night and thank you.' But Joan stayed and churned out a cavalcade of near-the-knuckle chuckles: 'It's my daughter's birthday,' she said. '34 years ago tonight in New York City I was going 'Get this thing out of me!' And 34 years ago plus nine months, I was saying the same thing.' Attack, performance, stagecraft – she has it all. But Joan got her biggest cheer by introducing 'the most amazing balancing act since Heather Mills got her new leg.' Liverpool takes a dim view of unhinged, parasitical nuisances.

This was a much better Royal show than last year's miscast disaster, but the hosts stank. What have Kate Thornton and Philip Schofield got to do with entertainment? Thornton is an average-looking boiler who isn't funny, interesting or opinionated. Schofield is a smug git who talks about women's periods on day-time TV, which isn't any kind of a job for a man at all. Lumbered with a leaden, laugh-free script, it felt like they were lecturing us, rather than moving the proceedings up a gear as a proper compere – like Bradley Walsh or Brian Conley – would have done. Paul Potts deserved his big moment, but he was off-key. Have his new gnashers nobbled him? ITV's comedy bookings remain as baffling as Malkovich's accent in Beowulf. Stephen K. Amos struggled. What was he doing so high on the bill? The tokenism was transparent, and insulting. Al Murray's Incy-Wincy Spider didn't work. Nor did Big Howard Little Howard. As for Russell Brand ... he may be a delightful rascal, but ITV had to crank up the canned laughter to make him sound like a smash. The visual response didn't match what we were hearing.

Wouldn't it be better to book hot bands and proven comics rather than the other way round? Not Tarby, though. The audience loved him, but Jimmy's gags made Joan Rivers seem youthful.

17 December Nuts TV sex expert Lou Prior suggested couples make love in a supermarket trolley this week. Dear Lord, is she sure? It brings new meaning to 'Clean up in aisle nine.' Probably best to do it in Safeway's. The queue is quicker for eight inches or less.

21 December Tony Blair has been accepted into the Catholic Church by the Cardinal Archbishop of Westminster. It's no secret that our former Prime Minister has been a closet Catholic for thirty years. But why would the Pope want this high-profile celebrity sinner on his books? Apart from the small business of an illegal war (judicial murder), Blair's voting record contradicts every Catholic doctrine going. He has consistently supported abortion, and opposed reducing the time limits for terminations. He gave legal status to civil partnerships, and indulged in some mystical 're-birthing' New Age mumbo-jumbo. If Blair has changed his mind about abortion, now would be a good time to tell us. If he hasn't, then shame on the Catholic Church. Given his history of broken promises, perhaps Tone will teach the faithful something new: the sign of the double cross. The C of E should be celebrating that such a man has gone over to the other side. Now, if the Anglican faith could find its backbone, we'd be laughing.

23 December Has he gone yet? Parkinson I mean. No disrespect, he's a TV institution and all that. But Parky is taking longer to leave ITV than our troops did getting out of Basra. And they didn't have to suffer Judi Dench singing. It's not like it's the first time he's retired either. So why did ITV make such a song and dance about it? We've had a month of back-slapping nostalgia and more old flannel than a pyjama warehouse. Billy Connolly, Michael Caine and David Attenborough turned out for him; a stellar line-up which Peter Kay likened accurately to *Cocoon*.

Last night, more vintage footage – Burton, Lennon, Orson Welles, Connolly again, and of course the Emu. And because you can't get mugged down Memory Lane it was terrific telly. It also reminded us that Parky's heyday was the 1970s on BBC1.

So what must Des O'Connor make of all this? Des, older readers will recall, was ITV's own chat show king, regularly delivering thirteen million viewers a week. Des had just as many magic moments as Parky, most involving Freddie Starr, Stan Boardman and Fokker Wolf planes. But ITV axed his hit show, replacing him disastrously with Brian Conley, and shunted Des to early afternoons where he doubled their viewing figures. So they moved him again and cut his budget, before replacing him disastrously with Sharon Osbourne. And that was it. There were no tributes, no farewell specials, no rosy-tinted look-backs. Nothing. And OK, Parky was a more substantial interviewer. At his best he was inquisitive, knowledgeable and he asked difficult questions.

But the Parkinson who sparred verbally with the great Mohammad Ali became a different beast on ITV, asking the likes of Tamzin Outhwaite such searching questions as: 'Have you always been gorgeous?'

Chat shows have changed, and so has the nature of celebrity. The hosts have got funnier as the stars got smaller.

And Parky? He just felt out of time.

Jonathan Ross is the score to beat now. ITV need someone just as bright, cheeky and informed to take him on. Danny Baker or Nick Ferrari could do it. But on past form, they'll probably give their next chat show to Kerry Katona.

22

What's What: A Guide To Modern Cobblers

Aliens

There aren't any. At least none we're ever likely to meet. Think about it rationally. The nearest star to our sun is Alpha Centuri, four light years away. Our fastest vessel would take 70,000 years to get there. UFO nuts think aliens are coming here from even further away. So these creatures are so advanced they can defy the laws of physics, bend time and traverse space at speeds we can't even comprehend, yet when they finally arrive here all they want to do is stick a probe up a yokel's backside. This doesn't just beggar belief, it buggers it sideways with an inter-galactic flashlight.

The first people who claimed to have been abducted were Betty and Barney Hills from Portsmouth, New Hampshire in 1961. After a UFO sighting, Betty later 'remembered' her abduction via a series of nightmares. In other words she dreamt it. Barney's description of the space critter they encountered exactly matched the aliens shown on sci-fi TV show The Outer Limits nine days before. Of all the millions of abductees since, not one of them had the forethought to take a credible picture, press 'record' on an audio cassette or video the experience on their mobiles...Why? Because they're either frauds or fantasists or they're suffering from sleep paralysis (mild brain seizures) or they're mentally ill.

God

God does not exist. Richard Dawkins has proved this beyond question. Cliff Richard and Bobby Ball disagree, but you'd put money on Dawkins to get a damn sight further they than would on *The Weakest Link* (if not *Don't Forget The Lyrics*).

However, our brains are clearly hard-wired to believe in the supernatural. And if all gods are imaginary, this gives us carte blanche to believe in whatever religion we choose. Nitwits have embraced everything from dodgy Eastern gurus to Angels via transparent made-up tripe like scientology. You or I might privately be drawn to Buddhism or paganism, with their respect for nature and the circle of life, but frankly even this won't do. We live in dangerous days. Britain needs to bring back the tough, unbending gods who saw us through darker times. Forget Ganesh and Siva, Thor and Tiwas are proper divinities. They'd inspire fear and devotion. They could kick the arse of any Arabic upstart god in a fist-fight. And if the weak, self-doubting West doesn't get behind them, then we will all burn in Hell.

Dawkins

The atheist Richard Dawkins, known to God as the leader of the Opposition, recently turned his guns on various New Age nitwits. The words sledgehammer and nut come to mind. What will Dawky do next? Picket chain-store grottos, heckling the children with stirring cries of 'There is no Santa'? Or run through primary schools rubbishing nursery rhymes and fairy stories? The problem with Dawkins is that he comes over as unbending as any evangelical nutcase. He is a fundamentalist atheist; a no-hellfire preacher. He won't be happy until only his views prevail. Which is why the TV show *Balls Of Steel* should set him up with a ouija board, a burst of flame and a seven-foot Lucifer. Wouldn't you love to see the debunker Punk'd?

On TV, Dawkins takes on soft targets, like creationists who reckon God created man in one day. This is hardly likely. Except in Jeremy Clarkson's case. He looks like a rush job.

But here's my question for the great man: if natural selection works, why are there so many dumb people in the world? Some of them Presidents ... Is being a congenital idiot an evolutionary asset?

Psychics

I've never met a psychic who wasn't a con artist, or watched a medium on TV who an intelligent 12-year-old couldn't have seen straight through like a pane of glass. The vast majority of these despicable creeps are fraudulent ghouls who prey on the bereaved, the confused, the lonely and the desperate. Nevertheless, the EU has recently decreed that fortune tellers, faith healers and astrologers must put up signs that say they are 'for entertainment only' and not 'experimentally proven'. And if they don't they'll see a tall dark stranger from Trading Standards who will drag them to court to face a hefty £5,000 fine. Why stop there? Can the teachings of the Catholic Church be proven? In the interests of consistency, the EU should insist that all religious figures from the Leytonstone Imam to Pope Benedict XVI can only appear in public if they are prepared to wear a sign saying: 'My beliefs cannot be experimentally proven and when embraced fanatically may cause the death of millions.'

Astrology

Astrologers believe our lives are governed by the constellations. Try saying that out loud in public, 'The stars in the sky decide my future', and not feeling like an idiot.

Once a cod-religion, astrology (and its fashionable spin-off astrotherapy), is now just another money-spinning scam designed to fleece the feeble-minded. It's based on the old, mistaken idea that the earth is the centre of the universe. Astrology originated before at least four of the planets on our solar system were known about; all the constellations have long since shifted, and astrologists completely ignore the inconvenient thirteenth star sign Ophiuchus...in other words, if you take Mystic Meg seriously you deserve to be taken for every penny you've got. But I would say that, I'm a Taurus.

Health and Safety

The modern dogma that seeks to eliminate every element of risk (and fun) from our lives. Left to their own devices, and with ready access to our money, these irritatingly obsessive busybodies would bubble-wrap the planet and encase every child in cotton wool. Newsflash: risk-taking made us what we are today. Without it, we would never have left Africa, let alone climbed mountains, split atoms or propelled ourselves into the air in metal craft. For the human race to progress, we have to be prepared to lose a few numb-nuts along the way. It's called natural selection. And it works.

Cosmic Ordering

This is a modern superstition/pseudo-religion popularised by the TV presenter Noel 'Crinkly Bottom' Edmonds. Noel maintains that if you write your secret desires on your hand, 'the Universe' will answer your prayers. Why? Because each of us is at one with the cosmos, you see, and once you realise that and tune in, your wishes will be granted. I'd suggest we put this to a test by all writing 'Edmonds RIP' on our hands and seeing what happens, but I've always had a soft spot for the gnome-like buffoon. Shall we do it with 'Gordon Brown resigns' instead?

Cosmic Ordering is a bit like going to Argos. You write down what you want, wait a while, and with any luck it turns up. It's the tooth fairy for grown-ups, an astral Father Christmas. It's huge swinging cobblers, of course, but people – programmed to be superstitious as we know – were taken in by it and bought the book *The Cosmic Ordering Service – A Guide to Realising Your Dreams* by Barbel Mohr in their tens of thousands. More than a million copies have been sold in Europe. It's an ideal belief system for our busy age: no need to waste your precious time going to church, reciting prayers or learning difficult mantras, you get unlimited benefits for zero commitment.

*   *   *

DEAL OR NO DEAL was what Edmonds ordered, a TV quiz show to make him a hit all over again. The show consists largely of people opening boxes that aren't theirs at random hoping to find money inside (Who thought this game up? A south-London postman?) Superstitious players often claim to have devised 'a system' to find the box with the most dosh. But as the show is entirely random, there can be no system. It's all guess work. Contestants attach meaning to something that has none. And as such, the show is a perfect metaphor for religious belief. Throughout the quiz, Noel has telephone conversations with an imaginary banker (or God) who tempts, frustrates and sometimes rewards the players according to His whims.

Freemasons

The conspiracy-minded, those on the left as well as the right, often insist that the world is secretly run by the Masons. Disappointingly, most lodges actually consist of accountants, shop-keepers, council officials, bored pensioners and retired policemen. See also, the Elks, Buffalos and Druids. I was once invited to a Druids' ladies night where the grand raffle prize was six rashers of bacon and a box of eggs. Run the world? They couldn't even put on a decent disco.

Porn

Most wives, like feminists, hate pornography. They say the

women in porn films don't look, dress, act or talk like real women. We know. That's precisely why we like them.

Airport Security

I got hauled up at Florida for having a rubber knife in my luggage from Disney's Pirates of the Caribbean ride. It's a child's toy, I said. 'You could use it as a cosh,' they replied. This is true, but it would be a lot easier to club the pilot to death with a rolled-up *Sunday Times*. Not much do with airport security makes sense, from the silly questions you have to answer (yeah, because a real terrorist would never dream of lying) to the things we can't take on planes any more: water, soap, shampoo, deodorants, shaving gear. To quote Bobby Slayton, everything terrorists don't use, we can't have. Airport security is nothing to do with stopping terrorism and everything to do with putting us in our place, making life difficult, reminding us we're peasants and showing us who is boss.

National Security

Gordon Brown wants to safeguard our civil liberties by locking up anyone he doesn't like the look of for six weeks without being charged. His mates at the soar-away *Sun* say that to vote against Brown's 42-day detention proposal is tantamount to voting for Al-Qaeda. Isn't the opposite true? If a few fanatical Islamic bombers panic us into giving the state draconian powers and weakening the rights of individual citizens, then those terrorists will have chalked up a substantial victory. They will have changed Britain, for the worse.

Banging people up to preserve our freedom? Priceless, Gordon. Orwell would have taken his hat off to you, son. But could there be other reasoning behind the idea? If Gordon could lock all of us up for six weeks either side of the next general election he might actually get back in.

Stress

Doesn't it strike you as odd that our ancestors who lived through world wars, mass unemployment, terrible poverty, plagues and epidemics didn't suffer from stress? You know why? They didn't have time! Instead of obsessing about themselves, they gritted their teeth, wiped their mouths and got on with things. Symptoms of stress are said to include impulse buying, smoking too much, over-eating and driving too fast. Or as my mother-in-law would call it, a perfect day out.

Man Pillows

Lonely Japanese women are lapping up the new Boyfriend's Arm Pillow. Kameo's man-shaped pillow is a headless torso with a stuffed arm that curls around the sleeper. It costs about £40 and gives a woman the illusion that she is snuggling up in bed with a loved one. Although surely for the full fake boyfriend effect, they'd also need a broom handle sticking in the small of their back.

New Age

New-Age beliefs are plain old-age mumbo-jumbo reinvented for the post-Christian age. Astral projection, crystals, aura therapy, holistic medicine, it's all voodoo and sorcery repackaged for the gullible. Special mention must go to Deepak Chopra who tailors his teaching to suit the wealthy and successful. According to Deepak, society's high-flyers are 'inherently very spiritual' (try and take that seriously while watching *Dragon's Den*; does anything about Deborah Meaden say 'spiritual' to you?). For the rich, he says, 'affluence is simply our natural state.' No wonder so many billionaires, politicians and stars take Deepak seriously. They're not filthy rich bastards screwing the rest of us underfoot any more. They are noble achievers, the chosen few, the deserving elite who rise because of the purity of their souls. All that money is just God's way of saying, gee thanks guys, thank you for being you. Now go screw a peasant.

Superheroes

TV superheroes are the modern equivalent of the ancient world's gods and heroes. Unfortunately, not much about them makes sense. Take David Banner who was exposed to gamma rays. That wouldn't have turned him into the Hulk, he would have got leukaemia.

Batman never impressed me much either, a millionaire with a taste for fancy dress living in a swanky mansion with his younger male ward ... isn't that Elton John and David Furnish?

The Flash can run around the Earth and back without you even knowing he's gone. So why doesn't he sweat? Why doesn't he wear out his trainers? And where does he get all his energy from? To run as far and as fast as he does, you'd have to eat like Heather Trot with worms.

Aquaman can breathe under water and talk to fish. Whoopedoo. What a thrilling conversation that must be. It'd be like An Audience with Dean Gaffney. He was cruel, that Aquaman. He dated a mermaid once and took her to a fish restaurant. Lovely girl: 36-24 and 86p a pound.

Peter Parker was bitten by a radioactive spider and turned in to Spiderman with an exciting range of arachnid attributes (although strangely not an exoskeleton). To date, not one villain has had the sense to trap him in a giant bath. Let's see ya get out of that, spidey baby.

I was always big fan of Superman, even though the explanations of his powers (Earth's gravity and our yellow sun) are as scientific as a black mass. But what really defies credibility is the idea that Superman and Lois Lane could ever make love. The bloke has got super-speed. What woman wants that? The Man of Steel must have a rod of iron. Imagine the friction burns. He's got super-strength too. If he banged her head against the headboard in the heat of passion, it'd go right through the wall. If he blew in her ear her head could end up in the Fortress of Solitude. And what about his seed? Everything else about him is super, so why wouldn't he have super-sperm? Think of all those perky little chaps poking around inside you, girls. And you think cystitis stings. (And if the sperm hurt, imagine how she'd feel when the baby starts kicking.)

There are other potential problems with their super-coupling. Picture the scene: Superman jumps on Lois only to find that the Invisible Man has got there first. Course it would be more of a problem for the Invisible Man.

UFOs

Sightings of Unidentified Flying Objects have gone through the roof over the last few decades, precisely mirroring the use of illicit drugs among the population. Since the sixties, kids and layabouts have been consuming acid, grass, skunk, mushrooms, Es and whiz by the bucket load. They're taking mind-bending, hallucinogenic substances and they're seeing alien space ships. Coincidence? I think not.

Eons ago, unexplained lights in the sky were put down to the Gods. Now, because science fiction is part of our popular culture, our first thought is that any unidentified object must be the work of those pesky aliens. UFOlogy is just the religion of the space age, a new set of superstitions in tune with today's hopes and wishes, with David Icke as its most demented prophet. Yet none of the religion's icons bear examination. The Roswell Myth is no more real than the folk belief in a Loch Ness monster – those blurry pictures of UFOs are very much an echo of the ones we used to see of Nessie.

Mathematically, it's probable that other intelligent life forms exist somewhere – the scariest thought in world history is that mankind might represent the pinnacle of nature's achievements. But the chances of us ever coming in to contact with another advanced species in this vast, expanding universe are so minute as to be pointless fretting about.

Most of today's sky-watchers are anoraks, the modern equivalent of train-spotters. Except there is no train to spot. MI5 recently released their files on UFO sightings. Some are intriguing, but the vast majority are easily explained: meteors, spy-planes, weather balloons, cloud formation, flocks of birds, satellites, experimental military craft, the aurora borealis. More recent UFO sightings have included a cruise ship in the Med and, in Wales, the moon. More interesting, however, is that MI5's files clearly show that sightings dropped with the introduction of colour TV, nearly doubled after *Close Encounters of the Third Kind* went on general release, and fell away steeply after the advent of the internet. It's an Undulating Fad, OK? A Useless Fading Obsession. And I cleaned that up ...

23

An English Revolution

So what is left of Britain? The Union is falling apart... we are over-taxed, under-represented and constantly deceived, and our politicians are self-serving creeps without an ounce of integrity. They're happier telling us how to live our lives than taking care of matters of State – for the very good reason that, in real terms, their political power is an illusion.

The White House runs our foreign policy, and Brussels dictates everything else.

Overseas, our brave, frontline troops are fighting a war that can't be won, while the Government starves them of funds for vital kit. Indeed, Brown's first decision as PM was to appoint our first part-time Defence Secretary. What an insult... what a farce.

The English are particularly screwed. Our country has been unconquered for nearly 1,000 years, yet we have rolled over and accepted a series of gross indignities. We've allowed free speech to be gagged; we've let successive

Governments chip away at our traditional liberties; we've given in to Political Correctness at every turn until we are too terrified of offending anyone to speak out about anything. We have sacrificed our birthright and for what?

The streets of Brown's Brave New Britain aren't exactly paved with gold. Home repossessions are set to rise by 50 per cent in 2008, and personal bankruptcies are running at more than 100,000 per annum; millions of children leave school illiterate; hospitals are closing; six million live on State hand-outs, and married couples are brutally punished by the tax and benefits system. Our topsy-turvy set-up rewards the idle and persecutes the hard working. The system is crazy, the country is a mess, and Britain, as we know it, is dying.

But it is not yet dead.

Can it be saved? Yes, but it's not going to be easy. First and foremost, for Britain to live, we must have freedom and independence. We have to be able to make our own laws, control our own borders and decide our own economic policy. To do that, we must leave the European Union.

For Britain to live, England must get a fair crack of the whip, so it's essential to create an English Parliament. It won't cost a penny more – it can occupy the Commons, with an elected second chamber for the UK replacing the House of Lords.

Free speech is the benchmark of a civilised society. At the moment, it isn't free enough. The laws of libel, slander and those banning incitement to violence are all we need. Scrap all the others, and scrap Ofcom, too. Voltaire had it right – you might not agree with what someone else says, but you should defend to the death their right to say it.

An English Revolution

Our schools and universities need to be liberated from the dead hand of Marxist thinking; let's do away with fashionable mumbo-jumbo and self-loathing. Learning and self-improvement aren't dirty words and neither is enterprise, initiative, courage or patriotism. Grammar schools worked, so let's restore them where they are wanted, along with discipline in the classroom.

The tax system is a nightmare that needs simplifying. Let's have a flat rate income tax; let people spend more of their own money. They can't do a worse job of it than Gormless Gordon.

Big Government is a menace; the Government's tentacles need to be hacked back so personal freedom and responsibility can blossom again.

Multinational companies, like supranational institutions, should be treated with suspicion. They don't have this country's best interests at heart. Small is beautiful; small businesses, pubs, restaurants and retailers are the backbone of local communities and should be encouraged, not penalised by red tape, taxes and busybody laws.

Too many MPs have sold us out; they need to be kept in check. MPs' expenses need to be reined in and their salaries should match the average wage – that would keep them on their toes, as would Proportional Representation and fixed-term parliaments of four years. The more genuine power that can be devolved to local communities, the better.

The old Parties have let us down, but the newer ones aren't up to the job in hand. There are genuine politicians in all three main Parties who care about our country and our people, who should be encouraged to work together in the new cause of national and individual freedom. The only alternative is armed resistance with the aim of secession from the EU and a declaration of independence. Pray it doesn't come to that.

Our ruling class is in the grip of the new European ideology; an ideology can only be defeated by a stronger one, and none is stronger than love of country. The only genuine alternative to globalisation and Europe's crypto-Marxism is radical liberalism tempered with benign nationalism – free of cranks and racists. I suspect this will arise in England first and inspire others throughout the UK.

We can be a free again, but we have to want it; all of us – the English, Welsh, Scots, and Northern Irish – have been through a lot together. Our forefathers made this country with their blood, their sweat and their sacrifice. And what a beautiful country it is. Was it all for nothing?

Our people have achieved so much in the past; we can achieve much again.